The Irish Parading Tradition

Ethnic and Intercommunity Conflict Series

General Editors: **Seamus Dunn**, Professor of Conflict Studies and Director, Centre for the Study of Conflict, and **Valerie Morgan**, Professor of History and Research Associate, Centre for the Study of Conflict, University of Ulster, Northern Ireland

With the end of the Cold War, the hitherto concealed existence of a great many other conflicts, relatively small in scale, long-lived, ethnic in character and intra- rather than inter-state has been revealed. The dramatic changes in the distribution of world power, along with the removal of some previously resolute forms of centralised restraint, have resulted in the re-emergence of older, historical ethnic quarrels, many of which either became violent and warlike or teetered, and continue to teeter, on the brink of violence. For these reasons, ethnic conflicts and consequent violence are likely to have the greatest impact on world affairs during the next period of history.

This new series examines a range of issues related to ethnic and inter-community conflict. Each book concentrates on a well-defined aspect of ethnic and inter-community conflict and approaches it from a comparative and international standpoint.

Rather than focus on the macrolevel, that is, on the grand and substantive matters of states and empires, this series argues that the fundamental causes of ethnic conflict are often to be found in the hidden roots and tangled social infrastructures of the opposing separated groups. It is the understanding of these foundations and the working out of their implications for policy and practical activity that may lead to ameliorative processes and the construction of transforming social mechanisms and programmes calculated to produce long-term peace.

The Irish Parading Tradition
Following the Drum

Edited by

T. G. Fraser
Professor of History
University of Ulster
Northern Ireland

First published in Great Britain 2000 by
MACMILLAN PRESS LTD
Houndmills, Basingstoke, Hampshire RG21 6XS and London
Companies and representatives throughout the world

A catalogue record for this book is available from the British Library.

ISBN 0–333–71838–0 hardcover
ISBN 0–333–91836–3 paperback

First published in the United States of America 2000 by
ST. MARTIN'S PRESS, INC.,
Scholarly and Reference Division,
175 Fifth Avenue, New York, N.Y. 10010

ISBN 0–312–23145–8

Library of Congress Cataloging-in-Publication Data
The Irish parading tradition : following the drum / edited by T. G. Fraser.
p.   cm. — (Ethnic and intercommunity conflict series)
Includes index.
ISBN 0–312–23145–8
1. Parades—Northern Ireland—History. 2. Parades—Ireland—History. 3. Irish–
–England—Social life and customs. 4. Irish—Scotland—Social life and customs.
5. Northern Ireland—Politics and government. 6. Ireland—Politics and
government. I. Fraser, T. G. II. Series.

GT4046.A2 I75   2000
394'.5 — dc21
                                                                99–089350

This book is printed on paper suitable for recycling and made from fully managed and sustained
forest sources.

10   9   8   7   6   5   4   3   2   1
09   08   07   06   05   04   03   02   01   00

Printed and bound in Great Britain by
Antony Rowe Ltd, Chippenham, Wiltshire

Contents

Series Editors' Preface

The range of matters dealt with in the Good Friday Agreement of 10 April 1998, upon which the new political process in Northern Ireland is based, represents – when examined closely – very clear evidence that the conflict had many dimensions and facets. This preface is being written in January 2000, when the new Executive and Assembly are both in place and beginning to try to deal, not just with the normal political matters facing any government, but also with the aftermath and emotional residues of a 30-year period of internal violence and conflict.

It has always been clear that, in the end, the beginnings of a solution lay in the creation of agreed political structures. But it has also been evident that such political change was closely related to – if not contingent upon – progress in relation to social and cultural matters such as equity, policing and human rights. All of these and more are dealt with in the Good Friday document, and institutions and structures are now in place that are setting about the complex and long-term process of planning and implementation in respect of these wider aspirations.

However, many of these cultural practices and behaviours are deeply imbedded within one or other of the two major communities and represent the sense of separation and difference that has been at the root of the conflict. This new book of essays deals with one of the most difficult and still unresolved matters – that is, parades and parading – a problem that has appeared on a number of occasions to have the potential to bring the whole carefully built peace process tumbling down. Its subject is therefore of great importance since it is crucial that we know and understand the historical, emotional and cultural significance of the need many communities feel to join together in public demonstrations of this sort.

The book looks in particular at the influence of the parading tradition within the wider Irish diaspora, and this provides a broad geographical perspective on the practice, and manages to demonstrate that parading, as a cultural and political expression of identity and commitment, is a widespread if not universal ritual used by groups in all sorts of contexts to ensure that their existence is both remembered and taken into account.

The book is therefore a valuable and original contribution to thinking about the role, purpose and importance of parading (and of public displays generally) in relation to group identity.

We would like to express our gratitude to Faber and Faber for their permission to use the quotation from Seamus Heaney on page 139.

The book is one of a series on ethnic and inter-community conflict; the series concentrates on international and comparative aspects of conflict, and on the underlying social and political patterns of behaviour that lie at the roots of intergroup conflict and division.

SEAMUS DUNN and VALERIE MORGAN

Acknowledgements

As will, I hope, be clear, this book is the result of a great deal of effort on the part of a large number of people. Its origins lie in a project based in the University of Ulster's Centre for the Study of Conflict, directed by Seamus Dunn and myself. This research was supported by the research sub-committee of the university's Faculty of Humanities and by the Central Community Relations Unit. None are responsible for the opinions expressed in this book, but thanks must go to Terry O'Keeffe, Felix Agnew, John Gillespie and Dennis McCoy. As part of this project, I attended parades, of all persuasions, across Northern Ireland for some four years. Key insights were provided by our research officers, Dominic Bryan and Neil Jarman, who between them have built up an unrivalled knowledge of parades, acquired through a unique combination of academic study and field experience. I cannot thank them enough. Dominic Bryan also commented on the individual chapters in the book, easing my task as editor. My wife, Grace Fraser, also a research officer at the Centre for the Study of Conflict, regularly accompanied me to parades, observing and assisting with interviews. Much of this is our shared experience. I am also grateful to my colleagues, Seamus Dunn and Valerie Morgan, for their continuing interest as series editors. Joanne Taggart coordinated the preparation of the final text with her customary skill and equanimity. Crown Copyright material in this book is reproduced by permission of the Controller of Her Majesty's Stationery Office and the Deputy Keeper of the Records, Public Record Office of Northern Ireland. The extract from Seamus Heaney's *Field Work* is reproduced with the permission of the poet. Events since 1995 have shown all too clearly the importance of parading issues to the people of Northern Ireland. It is the editor's hope that the essays which follow will contribute to an understanding of events whose essence lies deep in Irish history and society.

Notes on the Contributors

Joseph M. Bradley teaches at the University of Stirling. He is the author of *Sport, Culture, Politics and Scottish Society: Irish Immigrants and the Gaelic Athletic Association*.

Dominic Bryan is a Lecturer in the Institute of Irish Studies, the Queen's University of Belfast and is a former Research Officer in the Centre for the Study of Conflict at the University of Ulster. He is the author of *Orange Parades: Ritual, Tradition and Control*, as well as four research reports on parading.

Seamus Dunn is Professor of Conflict Studies and formerly Director of the Centre for the Study of Conflict at the University of Ulster. He has written and edited several books, including *Facets of the Conflict in Northern Ireland*.

Grace Fraser is a former Research Officer in the Centre for the Study of Conflict at the University of Ulster. She is the author of a number of articles on women and the Northern Ireland conflict.

T.G. Fraser is Professor of History and formerly Head of the School of History, Philosophy and Politics at the University of Ulster. He is the author and editor of a number of books, including *Ireland in Conflict, 1922–1998*.

Neil Jarman is a Development Officer and is a former Research Officer at the Centre for the Study of Conflict at the University of Ulster. He is the author of *Material Conflicts. Parades and Visual Displays in Northern Ireland*, as well as four research reports on parading.

Keith Jeffery is Professor of Modern History at the University of Ulster. He is author and editor of several books, including *A Military History of Ireland*, with Tom Bartlett.

James Kelly teaches at St Patrick's College Drumcondra. He has published several books on eighteenth-century Ireland, including *Prelude to Union: Anglo-Irish Politics in the 1780s*.

James Loughlin teaches at the University of Ulster. He is the author of several books, including *Ulster Unionism and British National Identity*.

Elaine McFarland teaches at Glasgow Caledonian University. She is the author of *Protestants First. Orangeism in 19th-Century Scotland*.

Donald M. MacRaild teaches at the University of Sunderland. He is the author of *Culture, Conflict and Migration: the Irish in Victorian Cumbria*.

Valerie Morgan is Professor in the School of History, Philosophy and Politics at the University of Ulster and is former Research Director of the Initiative on Conflict Resolution and Ethnicity. She is currently engaged in a study of women in nineteenth-century Ireland.

Introduction

T.G. Fraser

On 10 April 1998, Northern Ireland appeared to enter a new phase in its political evolution with the signing of the Good Friday Agreement. This Agreement, later endorsed in a referendum by 71.2 per cent of voters, was the culmination of a complex sequence of events which had their origins some ten years earlier. The climate for the political negotiations leading to the Agreement had been created by the declaration of a ceasefire by the Irish Republican Army (IRA) on 31 August 1994, followed by a similar move on the part of the Combined Loyalist Military Command, representing the main loyalist paramilitary groups, on 13 October. While progress was being made on the political front, the streets of Northern Ireland presented the very different spectacle of civil unrest. The thirty years of conflict had left a society which was probably more at odds with itself than it had been in generations. As had happened so often in Ireland's past, these tensions and frustrations found their outlet in bitter disputes over commemorative parading. While outsider observers found the images of street violence and confrontation perplexing, students of Irish history recognised a familiar pattern, albeit with some new themes. Using a combination of historical and anthropological techniques, this book charts the nature and evolution of the parading traditions in Ireland, and of the Irish in Great Britain, which are so important to an understanding of the dynamics of politics and society in Northern Ireland.

In July 1995, the attention of the world was caught by the word 'Drumcree'. The Church of the Ascension at Drumcree had hitherto been little noticed beyond the circle of its Church of Ireland congregation and the members of Portadown District Loyal Orange Lodge (LOL) No. 1, who by custom paraded to and from it for their annual service on the Sunday morning before the annual Twelfth of July celebrations.

Yet 'Drumcree' was to become the shorthand for a series of seemingly intractable confrontations over the rights and wrongs of parading which were to convulse areas of Northern Ireland over the next four years. That this should have happened ought to have come as no surprise to anyone acquainted with Irish history, since parading had long been a barometer of the political situation. Between the spring of 1985 and the autumn of 1986, Portadown had witnessed six serious riots, all of them triggered by the parading issue.[1] The latter year had been a time of particular loyalist frustration and alienation in the wake of the Anglo-Irish Agreement, which had been signed in November 1985. Portadown was not unique. In the course of 1995, tensions built over parades in a number of locations across Northern Ireland: at Dunloy in County Antrim, Bellaghy in County Londonderry, Castlederg in County Tyrone, on the Lower Ormeau Road in Belfast, and in the city whose very name expresses the divisions in Northern Irish society, Derry to its nationalist majority and Londonderry to its unionist minority.[2] Over the next year these disputes became even more intractable, so that the events of 1996 left community relations in tatters, while in July 1997 the prospect opened of a possible descent into civil strife. No observer of Irish affairs can afford to underestimate the seriousness of what was happening.

The parading tradition is an old one in Europe, with its origins in the church processions and trade guild processions of the middle ages. These rituals were used to display the power, wealth and prestige of the institutions concerned. They were also expressions of solidarity, ways in which the participants could feel a sense of identity and common purpose. With the rise of the nation-state in early modern Europe, parades also came to have a relationship with the state, something which is an essential theme of this book. Parades still perform this function throughout the world. The annual Bastille Day parades in France are an essential element in the mythology of the Republic. The mechanised military parade in Paris displays the country's pride in its long military tradition, small local parades of ex-servicemen enable veterans to recapture something of their past, while the events combine to bind everyone to a republican tradition which was not always common to French men and women. Only in a few villages in the Catholic and monarchist Vendée does an occasional note of dissent appear.

In the United States, Independence Day parades led by high school bands allow the various groups in society, whatever their ethnic origins, to unite in expressing their loyalty to the founding myths of the

Republic. The massive state parades held on May Day in Moscow and in the capitals of eastern Europe, when increasingly geriatric rulers basked in the apparent adulation of their people, were of a different order. Even less benign were the parades held in National Socialist Germany. As the new German state evolved its rituals, elaborate parades celebrated key dates in the history of the National Socialist party: Adolf Hitler's birthday, the anniversary of his coming to power or the 1923 Munich *putsch*, and the annual Nuremberg party congress. These choreographed events were designed to impress participants and spectators with the power and unity of the party and the state it dominated.

Parades have also been the voice of protest. Spontaneous parades in Leipzig and Dresden in the autumn of 1989 heralded the demise of the German Democratic Republic and, arguably, of communism itself. Such events challenge governments to respond. These parades would have had a very different, and tragic, outcome had Mikhail Gorbachev not counselled his east German allies against outright repression.[3] Equally, parades have acted as 'coat trailing' exercises. In the early 1930s, the National Socialists, then a small minority in the city's population, marched through working class districts to provoke street battles with Communists in Berlin. Sir Oswald Mosley's British Union of Fascists marched through heavily Jewish areas of east London with the same objective. Significantly, it was the so-called 'Battle of Cable Street' in 1936, when a major blackshirt parade was blocked, which produced the first modern British legislation on marching, the Public Order Act. This banned the use of political uniforms, and gave the police the power to re-route a march or to ban it altogether if a serious threat to public order was feared. In 1951, its main provisions were extended to Northern Ireland in the Public Order Act (Northern Ireland).[4] Finally, parades have been powerful expressions of cultural identity, especially when that culture has seemed to be under threat. One small, but telling, example may suffice to illustrate the point. In March 1939, the author John Lehmann observed one such parade in a Slovenian town of mixed Slovene and German population, Kocevje to the Slovenes but Gottschee to the Germans. The marchers belonged to the pan-Slav organisation, the Sokol, or 'Falcon'. Only twenty years away from the rule of the Austrian Habsburgs, as a result of Hitler's annexation of Austria, the Slovenes now had on their border the menacing power of the Third Reich. Lehmann noted the 'brave showing' of the Sokol parade, the men marching in traditional uniforms to the cheers of the crowd, while the local Germans pointedly went off on family expeditions elsewhere, or retired to the cafés to read the papers from Vienna and Berlin.[5] Students of Northern Ireland will have no trouble in recognising what was happening.

The critical question of the relationship between parades and the state runs through the chapters in this book. In this respect, it is necessary to identify at the start the main parading groups and the evolving nature of the state. The 'loyal orders', as they have become loosely termed, inevitably dominate much of the discussion, since their parades are the most numerous and conspicuous in contemporary Northern Ireland. Of the 2792 parades recorded by the Royal Ulster Constabulary (RUC) in 1994, 2520 were identified as 'loyalist'.[6] Chief amongst these organisations is the Loyal Orange Institution of Ireland, with an estimated membership of over 40 000. Outside Ireland, Orangeism's main strength lies in industrial Scotland, but there is still a substantial membership in Canada and Merseyside, as well as lodges in Australia, New Zealand, the United States, Ghana and Togo. Members from these other jurisdictions are welcome visitors in Orange parades in Northern Ireland. Members of the Orange Institution can become members of the Royal Black Institution, which is smaller and more conservative in tone. The Apprentice Boys of Derry is a completely separate Association devoted to commemorating the Siege of Derry in 1688–89. It has its headquarters in the Apprentice Boys Memorial Hall, and is governed by a General Committee in which the members of the eight Parent Clubs, all based in the city, have a majority, even though the bulk of the membership lives elsewhere.

The Orange Order, as it is generally known, was founded in 1795 after the Battle of the Diamond at Loughgall, near Portadown. It takes its name from King William III, Prince of Orange, whose victory over the Jacobites at the Battle of the Boyne in 1690 confirmed the Protestant Ascendancy in Ireland. Despite government disapproval of secret societies, in 1796 small-scale Orange parades were held, while the following year substantial demonstrations took place at Lurgan, Portadown, Lisburn and Belfast. In 1798, the new body proved its worth to the authorities when Orangemen were to the fore in suppressing the United Irishmen. Relations between the authorities and the Orangemen were problematic for much of the nineteenth century. In the 1830s, the prospect of a plot by Orangemen and 'Ultra' Tories to put the Duke of Cumberland on the throne led to the order's formal dissolution, though it survived at the popular level in the Ulster countryside. Sectarian tensions reached a peak with the affray at Dolly's Brae in 1849, followed by legislation banning parades. Similar tensions accompanied Orange parades in Scotland and England. But by the late nineteenth century, Orangeism had transcended its anti-Catholic origins to become the inspiration behind the emergence of Ulster Unionism and opposition to Home Rule, just as in industrial Scotland and parts of the north of England it had come to be associated with popular Conservatism.

It was only really with the creation of Northern Ireland as a separate entity in 1921 that the Orange Order became part of the establishment. Orangeism, which had long aspired to respectability, now became part of the fabric of the state. Its principal celebration, the Twelfth of July, was made a public holiday and its parades were an affirmation of the Protestant values and unionist creed which underpinned Northern Ireland. The 1950s and early 1960s probably saw the order's influence and self-confidence at their peak, with the members of well-filled lodges marching to hear speeches by Unionist cabinet ministers and visiting Conservative MPs. All of this changed dramatically in 1972 when Edward Heath's government abolished the Stormont parliament. From then on, Orange parades became essentially oppositional. Their character changed, too, as the nature of their accompanying bands evolved. While certain old-established flute bands remained, fewer pipe and military bands paraded, disappearing entirely from the Belfast parade. Instead, young working-class Protestant males formed the backbone of the 'Blood and Thunder' loyalist bands, sometimes signalling their sympathy with the loyalist paramilitary groups. These bands, which also held their independent band parades, increasingly set the tone of loyalist parades. As it had done the previous century, Orangeism was showing its capacity to adapt in the face of changing circumstances.

Not all parading was, or is, loyalist. Throughout the history of Northern Ireland, there had been nationalist parades drawing on well-established traditions, though these had always enjoyed a somewhat marginal existence. Even so, it was the civil rights marches in Derry on 5 October and 16 November 1968 which articulated nationalists' sense of grievance and alienation, changing for ever the face of Northern Ireland politics. The civil rights march of 30 January 1972 in the city resulted in the tragedy of 'Bloody Sunday' when fourteen men were killed by members of the Parachute Regiment. The large-scale parades held every year to commemorate this event were eloquent testimony to the scale of hurt felt in the nationalist community. The persistent appeal of the parading tradition can also be seen in the scale of the Shankill peace march of August 1976. This was an unprecedented example of how a public march in support of peace, embracing elements of both communities, could take place in an area of Belfast considered by many to be the preserve of one community. It was a test which the peace movement passed, even if the movement itself could not sustain the momentum generated by this extraordinary event.

Tensions over parading, especially loyalist parading, have come to rest on five key issues: territory, tradition, cultural identity, civil rights and politics. Foremost of these is territory. Even in nineteenth-century Scotland, this lay at the heart of disputes over Orange parades, and the issue was inevitably even more acute in Ireland. For Portadown's Orangemen, their right to parade back along the Garvaghy Road goes back to a tradition dating to the early nineteenth century. To the Apprentice Boys of Derry, the walls and the city contained within them are territory indelibly marked by the history and traditions of the siege. But territory changes hands over time. When Orangemen paraded from Drumcree church in the nineteenth century, the nationalist estates on the Garvaghy Road lay far in the future. The violence of the past thirty years had produced massive shifts in population by the mid-1990s. Whole areas of Belfast had changed, while the movement of Protestants from west of the Foyle had transformed the demography of Derry. This is what brought traditional parading routes into conflict with the wishes of residents. Tradition itself is not a constant. All traditions have been created at some time, while new ones are constantly being made. Loyalist bands have been in the business of establishing new 'traditions' over the past two decades. Hence, the often expressed distinction between a 'traditional' and a 'non-traditional' parade is not always easy to sustain.

While the Orange Order has always emphasised that it is a religious organisation, most Orangemen have accepted that there is a political dimension to the Institution's activities. Increasingly, too, the loyal orders have defended their parades as expressions of cultural identity, similar to the Bastille Day celebrations in France. They have also looked to the dimension of civil rights, turning to Article 11 of the European Convention on Human Rights which endorses the principle that 'Everyone has the right to peaceful assembly'. There has been an acceptance that this cannot be denied to unionists, just as Republican parades have been able to enter Belfast city centre. The point at issue has been the constraints implied by the word 'peaceful'. Finally, there is the critical connection between parading and politics. No one disputes that Orangeism has been an integral part of the unionist tradition in Ireland. Loyalist parades commemorate the events in the late seventeenth century, the Battle of the Boyne and the Siege of Derry, which were part of the Protestant Ascendancy. When nationalists claimed that these parades were 'triumphalist' that is what they meant. Nationalist and republican resentment became focused around the work of residents' groups, the Bogside Residents' Group in Derry, the Lower Ormeau Concerned Community in Belfast, and the Garvaghy Road Residents' Coalition in Portadown. Central to their agenda were the principles of 'consent' and 'parity of esteem'. The loyal orders found it difficult to accept that 'consent' was needed for their 'traditional' parades.

The British government's response to the crises of 1996 was to appoint an Independent Review of Parades and Marches under the Vice-Chancellor of Oxford University, Dr Peter North. When North's committee reported on 30 January 1997, its main recommendation was for the establishment of a Parades Commission which would be empowered to adjudicate on contentious parades. But reporting as it did in the dying months of a Conservative government in London, its recommendations were not in place by the following summer. The third Drumcree crisis was the first serious challenge facing the new Labour Secretary of State, Dr Marjorie Mowlam. On 6 July 1997, the decision was taken that the Portadown parade would be allowed down the Garvaghy Road. This was only done after a bitter confrontation between the security forces and the residents. Such was the furious reaction in nationalist areas of Northern Ireland, that a major breakdown in civil order seemed a possibility. Twelfth of July Orange demonstrations were due to take place on the following Saturday in four disputed areas, Armagh, the Ormeau Road, Newry and Derry city. Each of these held the possibility of bitter confrontation. Predictions of serious violence were made. On the evening of 10 July, the potential crisis was resolved when the Orange Order announced that these particular parades would not be held. The Parades Commission was in place by 1998. It was inevitable that attention would focus on its decision over the Drumcree parade. When the Commission ruled that the parade had to be re-routed away from the Garvaghy Road, the Orangemen stayed at Drumcree Church, beginning a confrontation which remained stubbornly in place throughout the following winter. If Northern Ireland was going through a peace process, it was a society which was still not at peace with itself. The parading issue was where these tensions found their focus and expression.

Notes

1. For analysis of this see Dominic Bryan, T.G. Fraser and Seamus Dunn, *Political Rituals: Loyalist Parades in Portadown* (Coleraine, 1995).
2. Neil Jarman and Dominic Bryan, *Parade and Protest: a Discussion of Parading Disputes in Northern Ireland* (Coleraine, 1996).
3. Raymond Pearson, *The Rise and Fall of the Soviet Empire* (London, 1998), p. 129.
4. *Independent Review of Parades and Marches 1997* (Belfast, 1997), pp. 89–90.
5. John Lehmann, 'Outside the Fold II: the Road to the Adriatic', *The Geographical Magazine*, vol. VIII, no. 5, pp. 363–70.
6. See Jarman and Bryan, *Parade and Protest*, p. 36.

1
The Emergence of Political Parading, 1660–1800

James Kelly

The origins of political parading in modern Ireland are to be found in the seventeenth and eighteenth centuries. The first noteworthy political parade was held in 1660, but though key dates on the commemorative calendar of Irish Protestants, which provided the occasion as well as the *raison d'être* for parading, were inaugurated shortly afterwards, parading did not become an established part of the Irish historical landscape until the eighteenth century. Like the commemorations of which they were a feature, parades helped to sustain the Protestant interest by providing it with communal opportunities both to recall its distinctive historical experience and to affirm its attachment, in the form of a shared monarchy, to the British connection. They thus contributed to the maintenance of the distinctively 'Protestant' and 'British' aspects of the Irish Protestant interest's identity at a time when commercial and constitutional grievances might have encouraged it to move in another direction.

Both the evolution of the commemorative calendar of 'Protestant Ireland' and the ideological import of the sermons delivered on such state 'holydays' as 23 October, 29 January, 29 May and 5 November have been the subject of important recent studies.[1] However, comparatively little attention has been accorded to the evolution of commemorative parading, and its concomitant, the participation of the Protestant public on such occasions.[2] Part of the reason for this may be that most state-sponsored commemorations did not lend themselves to popular public display; of equal significance, however, was the disinclination of Dublin Castle to foster the demonstrations of emotion and ideology such events encouraged. However, the Protestant public felt too passionately about its condition and history to accede passively to exclusive state arrangements, and they were enabled both to influence the pattern of commemoration and to carve out a participatory role by parading on those anniversaries they deemed most important.

Parading was a feature of Irish society before commemoration was established as a constituent of the leaven of Protestant identity in the 1660s. The most venerable and the most spectacular was the triennial 'riding the franchises' in Dublin when the lord mayor, civic officials and guilds perambulated the city boundaries in a ritualised affirmation of their authority and jurisdiction. Equivalent events, on a smaller scale, were held in other urban centres, while parades were also a feature of the commencement of quarter sessions and midsummer-day in some localities.[3] These ritualised displays were not without ideological or political implication. At the same time, they did not equate with the assertive affirmations made in England each 5 November when the discovery of the 'Gunpowder Plot' was celebrated.[4] Irish Protestants sought to inaugurate their own commemoration of Gunpowder Treason Day in 1614, but this did not receive statutory approval, and the first recorded 5 November commemoration in Ireland only took place forty years later. The fact that, like its English counterpart, it featured prayers, bonfires and artillery volleys, indicates just how much Irish commemorative practice owed to that already in place in its sister kingdom. It also attests to the awareness of the communal benefits of such events. This was confirmed when, as well as a tocsin, bonfires, fireworks and the distribution of hogsheads of wine to the crowd, the proclamation of the restoration of the monarchy on 14 May 1660 was marked by the parading and ceremonial incineration of the commonwealth in effigy and a celebratory procession by members of the Irish Convention and Dublin corporation, nobility and gentlemen.[5] Given their obvious enthusiasm for commemoration, it is not surprising that Irish Protestants set about inaugurating a ritual year thereafter, but instead of building on the 14 May 1660 precedent and making parading a central feature of each commemorative occasion, they opted for the official English Gunpowder Treason Day model. As a result, the ceremonies authorised by the Irish parliament to honour the anniversaries of the execution of Charles I (30 January), the outbreak of the 1641 Rebellion (23 October), the restoration of the monarchy and Charles II's birthday (29 May) were first and foremost 'holy-days' on which attendance at church was deemed more appropriate than public parading. This clearly did not satisfy all, as the Corporation of Waterford illustrated when it determined in 1663 that the mayor and council should process 'in theire solempest habit' from the guildhall to church each 30 January.[6]

Obviously, celebratory occasions, like 29 May and 23 April (the anniversary of Charles II's coronation), provided greater opportunity for displays of public joy than essentially doleful commemorations such as 23 October, and Waterford Corporation was to the fore once again in indicating what could be done. For instance, it chose to honour coronation day in 1663 by proceeding in a parade with the town's guilds and musicians, 'if any fitt cann bee gott', from the guild-hall to church where they met up with the 'youth of the free scoole' bearing 'garlands of flowers'.[7] In Youghal, meanwhile, the mayor, bailiffs and corporation combined the traditional and the new by making the 'riding the franchises' the central feature of its annual cele-bration of the restoration of Charles II. This practice was not imitated elsewhere, but reports of bonfires, *feux de joie* and the distribution of alcohol for communal toasting indicate that it was possible for the populace to celebrate occasions such as 29 May without parading.[8]

Given the high profile of public celebrations honouring Charles II, it is not surprising that the accession of James II to the throne witnessed an intensification of the public celebration of the monarchy. The eager burghers of Youghal, for example, honoured his coronation with a parade to church by the mayor, recorder and members of the corpora-tion 'in their gowns &c., with the sword, mace and the constables before them', following which they marched 'solemnly ... about the town'. Reports of what happened elsewhere are less complete, but it can be inferred that there was a military parade at Lisburn, and it is not unlikely that other celebrations also featured parades as well as the cus-tomary *feux de joie*, bonfires and toasts. Despite this and the celebration of James's birthday in 1686 at Youghal with a parade by municipal officials, attitudes to James II were sufficiently ambivalent for com-memorative occasions to become moments of contention between the King's Catholic supporters and his Protestant critics. This did not cause the disruption of any commemorative parades, but intrinsically Protestant occasions like 23 October and 5 November did attract hostile attention from resentful Catholics.[9]

This was the pattern throughout James II's brief reign. Indeed, had he remained on the throne for longer and had he inaugurated the Catholic dynasty he aspired to, both commemorative practice and political parading would have undergone fundamental change. Some hint of what might have emerged is provided by the heightened cele-bration of James II in 1688 and 1689 and by the attempt by the Jacobite parliament to repeal the 1661 legislation providing for the annual recollection of 23 October 1641. However, because William of

Orange successfully 'deliver[ed them] ... from popery and slavery' in 1690–91, Irish Protestants were able to ensure that the commemorative calendar mirrored their experiences and attachments, and the collection of relics of William of Orange during these years suggested that, as well as inaugurating appropriate commemorations of his deeds, they would be less acquiescent than their forebears if Dublin Castle attempted to sustain the efforts the Duke of Ormonde had made during the 1660s and 1670s to keep commemorative passions under control.[10]

The first indication that William of Orange would have a permanent impact on commemorative practice in Ireland was provided by Cork Corporation which determined on 1 October 1690, a mere two days after the event, that the entry of the Williamite army into their city should 'be kept as an anniversary [of] thanksgiving'.[11] Officials in Dublin were equally determined to demonstrate their gratitude to William because three weeks later, on the anniversary of the outbreak of the 1641 Rebellion, the Lords Justice, 'attended by all the lords spiritual and temporal, judges, officers of the army and others of the gentry in and about Dublin went from Clancarty House to St Patrick's Cathedral with the King at Arms, Herald at Arms and other officers in their formalities'. Neither this, the subsequent dinner at which 'the King and Herald at arms, with the maces before them, ... proclaimed their majesties titles', nor the tocsin and bonfires that broke the night sky were new of themselves, but the heightened emotion of the occasion made it, one contemporary mused, 'a day never to be forgotten'.[12] Certainly, the profile of commemoration and parading was enhanced by the event, as was demonstrated a fortnight later when William of Orange's birthday (4 November) and Gunpowder Treason Day were honoured with equivalent fervour. On the latter occasion, the fact that, as well as the King and Herald at Arms, the Lords Justices' procession to St Patrick's was accompanied 'by the nobility, judges and other persons of quality in town' suggested that parading seemed destined to become both more inclusive and participatory than previously.[13] However, though William's birthday (and other royal occasions) were prominent commemorative events during the 1690s, he was not accorded the compliment of an annual parade.[14]

In the eyes of government, it was preferable that the reverence Irish Protestants accorded William of Orange should be accommodated within existing commemorative arrangements. However, the fact that the anniversary of the Battle of the Boyne was celebrated unofficially and that the Corporation of Dublin erected a monument in his 'praise and honour' at the Tholsel in 1696 indicates that this did not satisfy all.[15] Dublin Corporation was the citadel of Williamite devotion in the 1690s, and it was appropriate, for this reason, that the equestrian statue of the king which it commissioned and which was unveiled on College Green on 1 July 1701 should be the signal for the inauguration of an annual commemorative parade. The 1 July 1701 was certainly a red-letter day in the history of Dublin as well as of commemoration since the day's proceedings commenced with a ceremonial procession from the Tholsel to the statue by 'the Lord Mayor, aldermen, sheriffs, wardens and common councilmen of the city … preceded by the city musicians and by the grenadier company of the Dublin militia'. The Corporation's eagerness to ensure that parading became an integral feature of Williamite commemoration thereafter was underlined by the manner in which they involved the lords justice and 'numbers of … noblemen and gentry' by prevailing on them to join with municipal officials in marching 'uncovered … three times' round the statue.[16]

Despite the undoubted impact of the parade that marked the ceremonial unveiling of Grinling Gibbons's statue of William of Orange, Dublin Castle officials were not at one with Dublin Corporation on the merit of an annual public commemoration of the Battle of the Boyne. The Corporation continued to honour the 1 July thereafter, but Dublin Castle reserved its salute to William for his birthday though the occasion was given greater weight by the addition of a parade led by the lord lieutenant (or, in his absence, the lords justice) round the statue. Following an early morning military gun salute, proceedings commenced with the assembly from noon of leading state and municipal officeholders and other dignitaries at Dublin Castle. At approximately three o'clock, the assembled notables exited the Castle in formation, and proceeded along streets lined with soldiers, via Dame Street and College Green, to Stephen's Green. Once they had completed their procession round the Green, the parade returned to College Green where it paid due homage to William of Orange by marching 'thrice around the statue, over which, after the procession had retired, three volleys of musketry were discharged'.[17] This was an impressive display. Moreover, since Dublin Corporation continued to celebrate the 1 July, the Battle of the Boyne did not go unacknowledged. Compared with 4 November, the 1 July ceremony was less impressive, but the fact that it was held at all attested to the fact that the 'glorious memory' of William of Orange did not need state support to be upheld. In this context, it is not insignificant that when, on 4 November 1713, Lord Chancellor Phipps sought to put a halt to the usual ceremonial parade by declining to lead it, the then High Sheriff took his place and lead the nobility and gentry along the usual route.[18]

By 1713, when Phipps took his controversial stand, the 4 November parade around King William's statue was firmly established as the most impressive commemorative event in the Irish calendar. It certainly eclipsed the processions to Christchurch by the lord lieutenant or lords justice attended by nobility and gentry which were the main public features of both the 23 October and 5 November commemorations, and the many monarchial occasions which also featured big gun salutes, *feux de joie*, tocsins, 'public fireworks', bonfires and other illuminations.[19] The fact that disgruntled Jacobites and Tories routinely targeted William's statue for vandalisation merely served to enhance its appeal.[20]

Things did not remain thus, however, since a deliberate, sustained and successful effort was made to elevate the profile of the monarchy in general and the new dynasty in particular on the accession of George I in 1714. In the main, these monarchial occasions were celebrated according to traditional norms, albeit on a more expansive scale,[21] but there were signs, too, that the authorities recognised the appeal and impact of parading because on the first anniversary of George I's accession, 28 May 1715, the nobles and gentry that gathered at Dublin Castle 'proceed[ed] in cavalcade to the Tholsel' where 'they were sumptuously entertained'. Athlone corporation staged a comparable event, on a smaller scale, by marching with the local garrison and musicians from the tholsel to the church.[22] Thereafter, it became commonplace in Dublin, on 'redletter days' for the monarchy, for officials and notables to march in state from Dublin Castle to Christchurch. In this context, it was appropriate that the Corporation of Dublin should march in ceremony to Essex Bridge on the eighth anniversary of George I's accession (1 August 1722) to join the large crowd that gathered for the unveiling of a statue of the king.[23]

Inevitably, the cultivation of monarchial occasions had a negative impact upon the observance of 'the glorious memory'. Indeed, the fact the public celebration of George II's accession and coronation in Dublin from 1727 featured a parade around Stephen's Green by the lord lieutenant or lords justice accompanied by two squadrons of horse soldiers suggests that the authorities now sought deliberately to elevate the Hanoverian succession at William's expense. Comparable events were not held throughout the country. But it is noteworthy that the anniversary of George II's accession was honoured in Lisburn in 1730 with a 'display' by the local garrison and that George II's birthday was honoured in Mountmellick in 1739 with a parade to the town square by 100 men in arms behind a drum chorus where they fired twelve rounds and performed military exercises.[24]

Such events attest to the successful manner in which attachment to the Hanoverian monarchy was cultivated. At the same time, there was unease in some quarters in the mid-1720s at the decline in the honorification of William of Orange. This was highlighted by Dublin Corporation's decision to 'la[y] aside his anniversary dinner at the *Tholsel'* in 1727 and 1728, and by the apparent lukewarmness of the Castle towards 4 November in the early 1730s.[25] However, the tide of sentiment shifted in William's favour from the mid-1730s onwards, and the inauguration of a popular parade on 1 July in 1740 attested to its rising public appeal.[26]

The decision of Robert Baillie, the designer of the House of Lords' tapestries depicting the Battle of the Boyne and the Siege of Londonderry, to march with forty veterans of both engagements through the city of Dublin wearing blue and orange cockades in June 1734 helped revitalise contemporary interest in the events of 1688–91. This took concrete form with the founding in Dublin of the Boyne Society. The membership of the Society came primarily from the Liberties of Dublin where the wearing of orange lilies and orange cockades on 1 July was already common practice, but though the Society was sufficiently well-established for its commemoration of 1 July to receive press notice in 1739, it did not achieve national eminence until the 50th anniversary celebrations of the Battle of the Boyne put it and popular parading firmly on the commemorative map.[27]

The high point of the golden jubilee celebrations of the Battle of the Boyne were the commemorative parades by the Boyne and Protestant societies. Each incorporated a march to church 'to hear a sermon' into its commemorative programme, to enormous popular acclaim. The respectable Protestant Society attracted a 'great crowd' of onlookers, but it was eclipsed by the more popular Boyne Society whose parade, 'with orange cockades in their hats, ... under arms, preceded by drums [and] trumpets', was greeted 'at almost every house by discharges of guns, pistols, etc'. This was only to be expected since the Earl of Meath's liberty, from where the marchers largely originated, was festooned with orange lilies. The inaugural commemoration of Battle of Aughrim eleven days later excited only slightly less passion.[28]

Despite these manifestations of popular Williamite fervour, Dublin Castle displayed no unease at the emergence of a public rival to its own commemorative events. The lords justice and nobility celebrated

William of Orange's birthday in the traditional way in 1740 by parading round the king's statue in their coaches and six, but the fact that they now had to compete if they aspired to retain their dominance of the commemorative calendar was underlined in 1741 when the Hanover Club marched in 'grand cavalcade' along the Castle's traditional route on 4 November.[29] No less saliently, the anniversary of the Battle of the Boyne was 'observed' in Dublin in 1741 'with the greatest demonstrations of joy ever known':

> the Boyne and Hanover societies or clubs met and joined and made an exceeding fine appearance, all in new cloaths with orange cockades and sword strings on their silver handled swords, and orange lillies stuck in the muzzels of their fuzees, and in that order they marched through the principal streets of this city and round that immortal Prince's effigies on horseback in College Green and back again, with great decorum and regularity and were saluted by the inhabitants and shopkeepers of all the streets they passed by a continual firing of guns and pistols over their heads and huzzaing.[30]

The Aughrim Society met with a similar response, on a smaller scale, on 12 July, following which parading became a central feature of the popular commemorations that were held on both days.[31]

Compared with the excitement popular parading generated, the fare put before the public by Dublin Castle increasingly appeared stale and unexciting. This was as true of the processions 'in state' by peers and officeholders to Christchurch on 23 October as it was of Castle-based royal occasions, despite the addition of visits to the theatre and balls for the elite.[32] Moreover, the gulf between official and popular commemorations was not closed in the years that followed, for though the apprehension of a Jacobite descent in 1744–45 did enhance the profile of monarchial commemorations, it also led to the foundation of new clubs which strengthened popular commemorative practice. By no means all of these clubs sponsored parades, but 'the very extraordinary manner' in which the Boyne Society celebrated the 1 July in 1747, and the march by 'the associated gentlemen of the law' the same evening vividly attests to the improved profile of popular parading over the previous decade. As Mrs Delany and others noted, 'King William's ... memory is *idolized* here almost to superstition', and this idolisation was put on public display every July.[33]

As well as the increased readiness to parade manifest in Dublin, the impact of the Boyne Society and of the appeal of popular commemoration is manifest in reports of parading outside the capital. As had long been the case, the commemorative devices resorted to outside Dublin consisted in the main of tocsins, *feux de joie*, bonfires, the drinking of toasts and other such familiar practices.[34] However, influenced by the example of the Boyne Society of Dublin, in Londonderry on 1 July 1759, 'gentlemen, clergy and merchants assembled … in the square of the Linen Hall and, preceded by a band of musick, the laiety with orange cockades, walked in regular order to the Guild hall'. In Clonmel, corporation officials 'perambulate[d] the Liberties and Franchises according to antient custom' on the same day eight years later, while processions were also organised in the strongly Protestant town of Bandon in County Cork.[35]

The pattern of commemoration that emerged during the mid-eighteenth century flourished with little change for nearly thirty years. Parading was but one, albeit important, aspect of this, and it continued to take its traditional two forms. The longest established were the processions of notables headed by the lord lieutenant or lords justice from Dublin Castle to Christchurch or from the mayoralty house to the same location for a religious service that took place on royal anniversaries or on state occasions such as the anniversary of the outbreak of the 1641 rebellion. These were familiar and, in the main, routine events, though the parade down College Green every 4 November provided the Castle with greater opportunity to impress the public.[36] If, as was alleged in the early 1760s, the Castle harboured doubts that it was appropriate to continue the 4 November procession, they were disabused by a short-lived controversy arising from the perception that King William's birthday was not being honoured with the passion it deserved, and few found reason to fault the Castle's engagement from 1765.[37] The 5 November celebrations, by contrast, offered the public little, as the annual procession to church of the lord mayor, aldermen, sheriffs and commons of Dublin Corporation was followed by a private entertainment at the mayoralty house. When parliament was sitting, peers and MPs also processed to church on this day, but since they went to different venues and did not engage in further festivities this too registered little impact with the population.[38] Even the corporation's practice each 23 October of marching in procession to Christchurch and marching back to the mayoralty house for an 'elegant entertainment' attended by 'a great number of the nobility, gentry and eminent citizens' could not mask the fact that this was an occasion for the elite.[39]

Certainly, by comparison, the parades driven by public commemorative enthusiasm were identifiably more dynamic and passionate. The

1 July was firmly established as the Protestant population's primary commemorative occasion,[40] and the foundation of Boyne Societies in Cork and Waterford bears witness to their attachment to parading since, like their older Dublin equivalent, they, too, honoured the anniversary of the Battle of the Boyne by marching in procession along a preordained route.[41] Elsewhere – in Kilkenny and Clonmel in the early 1770s, for example – 1 July commemorations existed independently of Boyne Societies.[42]

It is not clear how prominently, if at all, public parading featured in Kilkenny's 1 July commemoration, because commemorative societies were the primary custodians of popular parading during the third quarter of the eighteenth century. For example, the Aughrim Society of Dublin continued to ensure that the 12 July did not pass by in the capital without a parade by its members 'under arms, with green boughs and orange cockades in their hats' in the early 1770s,[43] while the Ancient and Loyal Society of Enniskilleners' sustained an annual procession each 28 July through the 1760s and early 1770s in honour of those who had defended Enniskillen against the Jacobites.[44] The Friendly Brothers of St Patrick, meanwhile, sustained an annual parade to St Patrick's Cathedral on 17 March,[45] while less well-known bodies like the Amicable Club, which participated in the celebration of William of Orange's birthday in Dublin in 1764, also helped to sustain the parading tradition.[46] In addition, as in Belfast in 1764, *ad hoc* bodies of gentlemen organised small parades by men sporting orange cockades on 4 November, while parades were also held in honour of George III's birthday in towns such as like Kinsale and Kilkenny.[47]

Though the pattern of commemorative practice seemed bound fast by the 1760s and early 1770s, the intrusion of patriot and other non-traditional slogans into the toasts that were called during some commemorative occasions in the early 1770s indicated that the prevailing consensus within the Protestant elite as to the place and purpose of commemoration was less complete than it appeared.[48] The outbreak of the American War of Independence certainly put this consensus to the test, but the early indications were that the crown would find dependable allies in the commemorative societies. Indeed, in Cork and elsewhere, members of the Boyne, Culloden and Aughrim Societies formed themselves into volunteer corps to help with the defence and policing of the kingdom.[49] Subsequently, local volunteer corps, as at Mountrath on 16 April (the anniversary of the Battle of Culloden) 1776, Bandon on 1 July 1777 and Belfast on 1 July 1779, paraded wearing orange cockades.[50] However, traditional political convictions dissolved in the

heady atmosphere of the late 1770s, as the Cork Boyne Society demonstrated when it participated in the local St Patrick's Day celebrations in
1779.[51]

Despite these indications that the existing commemorative mould
was less durable than it appeared, both the public and politicians were
taken by surprise on 4 November 1779 when a thousand armed Dublin
Volunteers marched in formation to King William's statue on College
Green bearing placards demanding concessions on the major political
issue of the moment – free trade:

> At 10 o'clock in the forenoon the different bodies of Volunteers of
> Dublin City and County. ... assembled at St Stephen's-green, and,
> having made a proper disposition, with drums beating and colours
> flying, they marched in files through York-street, Aungier-street,
> Bishop-street, Bride-street, Werburgh-street, Castle-street, Cork-hill,
> and Dame-street, till they arrived at College-green, where they
> arranged themselves around the statue of King William. ... At the
> discharge of a rocket, and taking the word of command from the
> Duke of Leinster, they fired three grand discharges ... After this,
> there was a discharge of small cannon. ... The statue and pedestal of
> King William were painted, and to the shields of the four sides were
> hung the following labels, in large capital letters: 1. 'Relief to
> Ireland'. 2. 'The Volunteers of Ireland; motto – Quinquaginta mille
> juncti, parati pro patria mori'. 3. 'A short Money Bill, – a free trade –
> or else!!!' 4 'The Glorious Revolution'.[52]

This was an awesome display by the Volunteers of their latent political
might, and patriots, understandably, were enraptured by what they
regarded as a 'glorious' demonstration of support for 'liberty and ...
country'.[53] Had they considered the matter longer, they might have
arrived at a less unambiguous verdict, because the Volunteers had virtually subverted one of the major commemorative occasions of the
Protestant interest by transforming it from a celebration of a *status quo*
into a demonstration in favour of change. This was all very well when,
as in 1779, the bulk of Protestant opinion supported the changes that
were being agitated, but this could not be assumed since the
Volunteers were not at one as to how they saw the future. In 1780, for
example, some corps did parade with shamrocks (as well as orange
cockades) during the St Patrick's Day celebrations, but most were
clearly more at ease participating in traditional commemorations such
as the king's birthday or 1 and 12 July.[54] Inevitably, when the

Volunteers attempted to register the same impact they had made in 1779 in 1781, 1782 and 1783, when more divisive constitutional issues were at issue, they created palpably less impact.[55] Following this, their commander-in-chief, Lord Charlemont, convinced most Volunteers to confine their activities to more traditional celebrative parading. The fact that by 1787 a modest 250 Volunteers marched their traditional route demonstrates the strength of the Protestant public's wish to revert to more familiar commemorative practice, as well as to the decline in volunteering.[56]

It was impossible to turn back the clock, however. The 4 November survived as a major commemorative occasion, but the 1780s witnessed the eclipse of several of the military commemorations that had been initiated in the 1740s and the emergence of St Patrick's Day as a respected public festival.[57] More consequently, rival liberal and conservative interests within the Protestant elite now treated commemorative events as potentially effective means to advance their political agenda, and the approaching centenary of William of Orange's deliverance provided conservatives with an ideal opportunity to press home the initiative they had regained during the mid-1780s.

Centenary commemorations commenced in Belfast in February 1788 with a parade by the army and Volunteers, *feux de joie* and 'expressions of veneration for the principles of liberty' brought into being by the Glorious Revolution. Ten months later, on 7 December 1788, the centenary commemoration of the siege of Londonderry was inaugurated by a large parade of dignitaries, volunteers, military, citizens and apprentices to a church service. After this, there was a further parade, a ceremonial re-enactment of the shutting of the city gates, the trooping of King James's colours (captured during the siege), and the parading and burning of an effigy of Robert Lundy. The following August, Derry's streets again echoed to footsteps as the raising of the siege was honoured with only slightly less enthusiasm than its commencement.[58]

Given these preliminaries, it comes as no surprise that the main event, the centenary of the Battle of the Boyne, featured an even more spectacular parade. Thousands travelled to Drogheda from all parts of the country for a week-long celebration which climaxed, appropriately, on 1 July. The day began with a parade by the Corporation and guilds of Drogheda to St Peter's Church, following which a large crowd proceeded to William of Orange's crossing place on the Boyne, where they were treated to a big gun salute and *feux de joie*.[59]

The presence of the Roman Catholic bishop and several of his clergy in the parade held in Derry on 1 August 1789 could be seen as indicating that the less denominationally exclusive attitude to parading that was in evidence in the early 1780s remained as strong as ever at the end of the decade. But, as the attempt to revive the 23 October commemoration in 1790 attests, sectarian passions remained vibrant.[60] Equally significantly, the refusal of some Volunteers to celebrate King William's birthday in 1792, following on the decision of the Belfast Whig Club in 1791 to devote more attention to celebrating the fall of the Bastille than the Battle of the Boyne, indicated that political liberals no longer identified 'the glorious memory' with what Jacqueline Hill has termed embracive 'ideas of civil liberty and religious toleration'. Subsequently, following a disappointing 1 July commemoration in Dublin in 1795, it was argued in liberal circles that in order to draw 'a veil over the distractions and hatreds of our ancestors' the battles of the Boyne and Aughrim should no longer be honoured.[61] Disturbed by such conclusions, and encouraged by the security they discovered in familiar practices, conservatives gravitated in increasing numbers in the late 1790s to the comfort and security of the traditional commemorative calendar. Indeed, like their forebears who had paraded with the Boyne or Culloden Society, they used these events as 'rallying points', and such was the appeal of the Protestant 'ascendant' message they advanced, that the foundation in Armagh of a society (the Orange Society, renamed Orange Order) committed to its retention, enabled them to bring thousands onto the streets for 12 July commemorations in Belfast, Lurgan and Portadown in 1796 and 1797.[62] Inevitably, because of the intensifying sectarianism that gripped Irish society in the late 1790s, such occasions produced confrontation and violence.[63]

The vigorous advocacy by the Orange Order in the late 1790s of a sectarian vision of the 'Glorious Memory' reanimated the 1 July, 4 November and a number of monarchial commemorations that had seemed in danger of falling into desuetude.[64] As had been the case for decades, these were occasions in which the Protestants of Ireland displayed their devotion to William of Orange by wearing orange cockades and lilies. The difference now was that the commemorative initiative rested firmly in the possession of ideological conservatives, rather than with Dublin Castle where it had long lain. More saliently for the future, as the end of the eighteenth century approached commemorative parading was more avowedly about asserting Protestant precedence over a resurgent Catholic population.[65]

Until the 1790s, more people died from the misuse of fireworks during the nightly illuminations that were a feature of commemorative occasions than from intra-communal violence. This did not reflect popular unanimity on the virtue of such events. Rather, the ideological opponents of celebrative parading, who were usually Jacobites or Tories, were powerless to do more than cause those who wished to parade minor inconvenience. The result was that the pattern of commemoration and celebration that Irish Protestants evolved developed free of such pressures.

During the Restoration era, much of the parading that took place was by Castle officials and the local nobility, and the concessions that were made to popular tastes largely took the form of the provision of alcohol for a popular toast. However, the experience of James II's reign gave the Protestant population a more direct stake in the commemorative process. During the first quarter of the eighteenth century, Dublin Corporation and Dublin Castle sustained the memory of William of Orange on their behalf with an impressive display each 4 November, but this was overshadowed by the cultivation of the monarchy from 1714, and it was not until the 1740s that the Protestant population finally carved out a role for themselves by making the commemorative parade in 1 July 'their' occasion. Jacqueline Hill has claimed that the identification of William of Orange 'with ideas of civil liberty and religious toleration' allowed Protestants of a conservative and a liberal political hue to come together on these occasions but this became increasingly difficult once the Volunteers introduced contemporary political issues. Their orderly and well-conducted displays of latent martial power lifted people's spirits rather than posing a challenge to traditional commemorative ways. However, once the question of recasting the political system to accommodate Catholics and others emerged, liberals and conservatives sought to use commemorative parading to advance their own particular political agenda. The United Irishmen briefly disrupted the control that upholders of the *status quo* had of commemorative parading, but with the emergence of the Orange Order the instinctive wish of most Protestants to preserve their ascendancy enabled them to regain that control. Like their forebears, the Boyne Society, the Orange Order recognised the communal value of parading but since, unlike the societies that had emerged during the mid-eighteenth century, they were a national organisation, they could organise more imposing events. However, because they operated in a more confrontational political climate, parading was less a carnival with a political message than an assertion of political ascendancy, and this, inevitably, invited an aggressive response.

Notes

1. T.C. Barnard, 'The Uses of 23 October and Irish Protestant Celebrations' in *English Historical Review*, 106 (1991), pp. 889–921; R. Eccleshall, 'Anglican Political Thought in the Century after the Revolution of 1688' in R. Eccleshall, D.G. Boyce, V. Geoghegan (eds), *Political Thought in Ireland since the Seventeenth Century* (London, 1993), pp. 36–72; James Kelly, 'The Glorious and immortal memory': commemoration and Protestant Identity in Ireland 1660–1800', *Royal Irish Academy Proceedings*, 94C (1994), pp. 25–52; J. Hill, 'National Festivals, the State and "Protestant ascendancy" in Ireland, 1790–1829' in *Irish Historical Studies*, xxiv (1984–8), pp. 30–51.

2. Barnard, 'The Uses of 23 October', pp. 913–14; Sean Connolly, *Religion, Law and power: the making of Protestant Ireland 1660–1760* (Oxford, 1992), pp. 133–4.

3. Lennox Barrow, 'Riding the Franchises' in *Dublin Historical Record*, 33 (1979–80), pp. 135–8; idem, 'The Franchises of Dublin', in *Dublin Historical Record*, 36 (1982–3), pp. 68–80; [J.R. Walsh], *Sketches of Ireland Sixty Years Ago* (Dublin, 1847), pp. 50–7; J. Hill, *From Patriots to Unionists: Dublin Civic Politics and Irish Protestant Patriotism* (Oxford, 1997), p. 44; John Swift, *History of the Dublin Bakers and Others* (Dublin, 1948), pp. 134–42; John Gilbert, *A History of Dublin* (3 vols, Dublin, 1854–5), i, 169; Jim Kemmey (ed.), *A Limerick Anthology* (Dublin, 1996), pp. 33, 242–3.

4. Ronald Hutton, *The Rise and Fall of Merry England: the Ritual Year 1400–1700* (Oxford, 1994), p. 182.

5. Hutton, *The Ritual Year*, pp. 82–6; Connolly, *Religion, Law and Power*, p. 10.

6. Kelly, 'The Glorious ... memory', pp. 6–7; Barnard, 'The Uses of 23 October', p. 890; Thomas Gogarty (ed.), *The Council Book of the Corporation of Drogheda ... 1649 to 1734* (Drogheda, 1915), p. 127; Seamus Pender (ed.), *Council Books of the Corporation of Waterford 1662–1700* (Dublin, 1964), p. 23. It is also noteworthy that Waterford Corporation ordained that shops and taverns should close and the playing of games be prohibited on 30 January.

7. Gogarty (ed.), *Corporation Book of Drogheda* (Drogheda, 1915), p. 127; Pender (ed.), *Council Books of ... Waterford*, pp. 23, 42.

8. Richard Caulfeild (ed.), *The Council Book of the Corporation of Youghal* (Guildford, 1878), pp. 326 333–4, 338–9, 346; Gogarty, *Corporation Book of ... Drogheda*, p. 127.

9. Caulfeild, *Corporation of Youghal*, pp. 366–7, 373, 378–9; Gogarty (ed.), *Corporation Book of Drogheda*, p. 209; Stanhope to Rawdon, 21 February 1785 in H.M.C. *Hastings* (London, 1930), iii, 395; Connolly, *Religion, Law and Power*, p. 36.

10. Barnard, 'The Uses of 23 October', pp. 893–4; John Gilbert (ed.), *Calendar of Ancient Records of Dublin* (Dublin, 1895), v, 5, pp. 475, 482–3, 489, 501–2, 504; 'Extracts from the Private Memorandum Book of Captain George Gafney of Kilkenny' in *Proceedings and Transactions of Kilkenny and South-East of Ireland Archaeological Society*, 3 (1854–5), p. 165; 'Diary of Elizabeth Freke', *Journal of the Cork Historical and Archaeological Society*, 17 (1911), p. 5; 'Two unpublished diaries of the Battle of the Boyne', *Ulster Journal of*

Archaeology, 4 (1856), pp. 87, 88, 93; J.G. Simms, 'Remembering 1690' in *Studies* (1974), pp. 238–9.

11. Richard Caulfeild, *Council Book of the Corporation of Cork* (Guilford, 1876), p. 208.
12. *Dublin Intelligence*, 28 October 1690; Gilbert, *History of Dublin*, iii, 21.
13. Gilbert, *History of Dublin*, iii, 21–2.
14. John Gilbert (ed.), *Calendar of Ancient Records of Dublin* (Dublin, 1896), vi, 38–9, 46–7, 88, 89–90, 136–9; Pender (ed.), *Council Books of Waterford*, pp. 300, 318–9, 329; Caulfeild, *Corporation Book of Youghal*, p. 382; *Dublin Intelligence*, 17 February 1691, 11 May 1693.
15. David Hayton, 'Anglo-Irish Attitudes: Changing Perceptions of National Identity among the protestant ascendancy in Ireland ca 1690–1750' in *Studies in Eighteenth-Century Culture*, 17 (1987), p. 147; Gilbert (ed.), *Ancient Records of Dublin*, vi, 161.
16. Gilbert (ed.), *Ancient Records of Dublin*, vi, ix–xi, 232, 235, 237, 239, 248–9; Gilbert, *History of Dublin*, iii, 40.
17. *Dublin Intelligence*, 14 July 1712; Gilbert, *History of Dublin*, iii, 42; Hill, 'National festivals', pp. 32–3.
18. *Dublin Intelligence*, 14 July 1712; Hill, *From Patriots to Unionists*, p. 157.
19. John Ainsworth (ed.), *Inchiquin Manuscripts* (Dublin, 1961), p. 72; *Dublin Gazette*, 25 October 1707, 9 March, 24 April 1708, 8 November 1709; 24 October, 7 November 1710, 6 November 1711; *Dublin Intelligence*, 6 November 1711, 8 November 1712.
20. Kelly, 'The Glorious ... memory', pp. 32–3; Gilbert, *History of Dublin*, iii, 42–45; Simms, 'Remembering 1690', pp. 234–5; 'Elizabeth Freke's diary' in *Journal of the Cork Historical and Archaeological Society*, 17 (1911), p. 89.
21. *Pue's Occurrences*, 1 February 1718; Connolly, *Religion, Law and Power*, p. 1; Caulfeild, *Corporation Book of Cork*, pp. 368–70, 374; Ainsworth (ed.), *Inchiquin manuscripts*, p. 125; Caulfeild, *Corporation Book of Youghal*, p. 409.
22. *Dublin Intelligence*, 31 May, 7 June 1715.
23. *Dublin Intelligence*, 20 October 1716; Hume's *Dublin Courant*, 4 August 1722.
24. *Dublin Gazette*, 14 June 1729, 15 June 1730, 17 June, 17 October 1732; *Pue's Occurrences*, 13 October 1733, 6 November 1739; Kelly, 'The glorious ... memory', pp. 36–7.
25. Jonathan Swift and Thomas Sheridan, *The Intelligencer* (ed. James Woolley) (Oxford, 1992), pp. 106, 112, 200. Dublin Castle did not parade to King William's statue in 1732 (*Dublin Gazette*, 7 November 1732).
26. Kelly, 'The Glorious ... Memory', pp. 37–8.
27. *Pue's Occurrences*, 15 June 1734, 6 November 1739; *Dublin Gazette*, 7 July 1739.
28. *Dublin Gazette*, 1, 5, 8, 12, 15 July; *Dublin Newsletter*, 5 July; *Pue's Occurrences*, 15 July 1740; see also Gilbert, *History of Dublin*, iii, 42.
29. *Dublin Newsletter*, 2 August 1740; *Dublin Gazette*, 25 October, 8 November 1740.
30. *Dublin Gazette*, 4 July; see also *Pue's Occurrences*, 4 July; *Dublin Newsletter*, 4 July; *Faulkner's Dublin Journal*, 4 July 1741.
31. *Pue's Occurrences*, 3, 20 July 1742; *Dublin Courant*, 3, 13 July 1744; Gilbert, *History of Dublin*, iii, 42.
32. Compare the sources listed in note 31 and *Pue's Occurrences*, 3, 20 July 1742, *Dublin Courant*, 3, 13 July 1744 with *Dublin Newsletter*, 24, 31 October *1741; Dublin Courant*, 14 June, 14 October 1746, 17 October, 3 November 1747.

33. Kelly, 'The glorious ... memory', pp. 39–40; *Dublin Courant*, 18, 21, 25 January, 14, 21, 25 October, 8 November 1746, 4 July, 3 November 1747; Lady Llanover (ed.), *Autobiography and Correspondence of Mary Granville, Mrs Delany* (6 vols, London, 1861–2), iii, 54; James Kelly (ed.), *The letters of Lord Chief Baron Edward Willes to the Earl of Warwick 1757–62* (Aberystwyth, 1990), pp. 27–8.

34. See, for example, Caulfield, ed., *Corporation Book of Cork passim*; *Dublin Newsletter*, 14 October 1740; *Faulkner's Dublin Journal*, 8 July 1749, 17 July 1750.

35. *Faulkner's Dublin Journal*, 17 July 1759; *Freeman's Journal*, 7 July 1767; W.P. Burke, *History of Clonmel* (Waterford, 1907), p. 147; George Bennett, *The History of Bandon* (Cork, 1869), p. 299.

36. One is provided with an insight into the less than wholehearted enthusiasm for them by the fact that the Lord Mayor of Dublin deferred celebrating the anniversary of the Restoration in 1759 because he was 'having an entertainment that night' (*Universal Advertizer*, 22 May, 2 June 1759); see also *Universal Advertizer* 3 February 1759, *Public Gazeteer*, 30 May 1761.

37. Hill, *From Patriots to Unionists*, pp. 157–8; *Freeman's Journal*, 8 September, 30 October 1764; *Dublin Gazette*, 5, 9 November 1765.

38. *Freeman's Journal*, 8 November 1763; *Hibernian Journal*, 9 November 1772, 6 November 1775; *Finn's Leinster Journal*, 10 November 1773, 12 November 1774. When 4 November fell on a Sunday (as it did in 1770) the parade normally held on that day was held over until the fifth. Thus on 5 November 1770, Lord Townshend 'proceeded in state attended by a squadron of horse; the lord mayor with the city regalia, attended by the high sheriffs and aldermen; the lord high chancellor in his state coach, the judges etc. through Dame Street, College Green, and returned by the equestrian statue of King William on College Green to the Castle' (*Finn's Leinster Journal*, 10 November 1770).

39. *Hibernian Journal*, 27 October 1773. Cork Corporation conducted itself similarly each 29 September (F.H. Tuckey, *The County and City of Cork remembrancer* (Cork, 1837), p. 146).

40. See, for example, *Hibernian Journal*, 5 July 1773; *Finn's Leinster Journal*, 14 May 1774.

41. Tuckey, *Cork Remembrancer*, pp. 166, 167, 171; *Finn's Leinster Journal*, 7 July 1773, 6, 9 July 1774.

42. *Finn's Leinster Journal*, 3 July 1773, 6 July 1774.

43. *Finn's Leinster Journal*, 15 July 1769, 16 July 1774; *Hibernian Journal*, 15 July 1771, 14 July 1773, 13 July 1774.

44. *Public Gazetteer*, 31 July 1762; *Finn's Leinster Journal*, 4 August 1770, 3 August 1773; *Hibernian Journal*, 24 July 1772.

45. *Faulkner's Dublin Journal*, 21 March 1758; *Universal Advertizer*, 20 March 1759; *Finn's Leinster Journal*, 30 March 1771.

46. *Freeman's Journal*, 3 November 1764. It should be added that loyalist clubs (*Pue's Occurrences*, 10, 14, 17 August 1756) like the Cumberland Brotherhood (*Dublin Gazette*, 27 April 1765) and the Dettingen Society (*Dublin Gazette*, 18 June 1765, *Dublin Mercury*, 23 June 1767, *Hibernian Journal*, 20 June 1774) sustained commemorations that did not involve parading.

47. *Freeman's Journal*, 10 November 1764; Tuckey, *Cork Remembrancer*, p. 155; *Finn's Leinster Journal*, 8 June 1774.

48. Kelly, 'The Glorious ... memory', pp. 44–5.
49. Tuckey, *Cork Remembrancer*, p. 177; Brady, *Catholics in the Press*, pp. 189–90; P.O Snodaigh, 'Notes on the Volunteers ... of County Cavan' in *Breifne*, iii (1968), pp. 321, 331.
50. *Finn's Leinster Journal*, 24 April 1776; *Hibernian Journal*, 9 July 1777; Thomas MacNevin, *History of the Volunteers of 1782* (Dublin, [1882]), p. 77n.
51. Tuckey, *Cork Remembrancer*, p. 179.
52. Gilbert, *History of Dublin*, iii, 46–7; *The Freeman's Journal*, 6 November 1779; James Kelly, 'James Napper Tandy: Radical and Republican' in J. Kelly and U. MacGearailt (eds), *Dublin and Dubliners: Essays in the History and Literature of Dublin City* (Dublin, 1990), 4.
53. *The Triumph of Prudence over Passion* (4 vols, Dublin, 0000), i, 5; see also *Finn's Leinster Journal*, 10 November 1779; Hill, 'National festivals', 33–4.
54. *Cork Remembrancer*, 182; *Hibernian Journal*, 27 March, 12, 19, 30 June, 5, 10, 14, 19 July, 11 August, 3, 6 November 1780; Gilbert, *History of Dublin*, iii, 48.
55. Gilbert, *History of Dublin*, iii, 48–50; *Hibernian Journal*, 7 November 1781; *Dublin Evening Post*, 4 November 1783; Simms, 'Celebrating 1690', 239–40.
56. Burgoyne to Charlemont, 1 June 1782 in H.M.C., *Charlemont* (2 vols, London, 189), i, 403; *Hibernian Journal*, 5 June 1782. *Volunteer Evening Post*, 4 November 1784; *Dublin Chronicle*, 6 November 1787, 14 August 1788.
57. Hill, 'National festivals', p. 31; *Volunteer Evening Post*, 16 March 1784, 29 March 1785; *Dublin Chronicle*, 29 March 1788; Hill, *From Patriots to Unionists*, p. 242; Kelly, 'The glorious ... memory', p. 48.
58. Robert Simpson, *The Annals of Derry* (Limavady, 1987), pp. 183–6; *Dublin Chronicle*, 19 February, 6, 24 December 1788, 3 January 1789.
59. *Dublin Chronicle*, 1 June 1790; Simms, 'Celebrating 1690', 236. [check]
60. *Dublin Chronicle*, 21 October 1790.
61. Maurice Craig, *The Volunteer Earl* (London, 1948), p. 230; Marianne Elliott, *Wolfe Tone: Prophet of Irish Independence* (London, 1989), p. 186; Hill, 'National festivals', 36–7; *Dublin Evening Post*, 2 July 1795. Certain events, like the siege of Enniskillen, were no longer commemorated (*Freeman's Journal*, 30 July 1796).
62. Simms, 'Celebrating 1690', p. 240; K. Whelan, 'The Origins of the Orange Order' in *Bullán*, 2 (1996), pp. 19–20; J. Smyth, 'The Men of No Popery: the Origins of the Orange Order', *History Ireland* 3(1995), p. 52; Nancy Curtin, 'The Origins of Irish Republicanism: the United Irishmen in Dublin and Ulster 1791–98' (PhD., University of Wisconsin – Madison, 1988), p. 677.
63. Brendan MacEvoy, 'Peep of Day Boys and Defenders in the County Armagh', *Seanchas Ardmhacha*, 12 (1987), p. 76; P. de Brún, 'A Song Relative to a Fight between the Kerry Militia and some Yeomen at Stewartstown, County Tyrone, July 1797', *Journal of the Kerry Archaeological and Historical Society*, 6 (1973), pp. 106–7.
64. Curtin, 'The origins of Irish republicanism', pp. 677, 728.
65. Simms, 'Commemorating 1690', p. 241; *Freeman's Journal*, 2 July, 5 November 1799, 28 October, 1, 6 November 1800; *Cork Remembrancer*, pp. 214–15.

2
Parades and Politics: Liberal Governments and the Orange Order, 1880–86

James Loughlin

The development of the Orange Order as a factor in the Ulster problem was coeval with the latter's emergence as a specifically political issue in the early 1880s. As the Order grew in strength its relationship with the Liberal governments of this period (1880–85 and January–July 1886) became, and remained, problematical. As they have today, Orange processions and demonstrations then had the capacity to occasion civil disorder and to impact dramatically on politics. Despite the considerable differences in the political contexts of the 1880s and our own time, the problems raised for impartial government in the North have a close correspondence. Accordingly, an examination of the parades issue in the 1880s can enhance our understanding of a central and enduring dimension of the Ulster problem.

At no point in time from the establishment of the Orange Order, following a sectarian riot in County Armagh in 1795, was the relationship between it and British administrations congenial. Even during the 1798 Rebellion an alliance with Orangeism was only accepted out of necessity. When the threat posed by the United Irishmen was eliminated the alliance was quickly ended. The government's approach to Orangeism was then repeated during subsequent crisis periods in the nineteenth century when Irish nationalism threatened the Union: reluctant alliance followed by rapid disengagement. Reliable supporters of the Union in a crisis Orangemen may have been, but the organisation was otherwise an embarrassment; especially so as the state, having incorporated Catholic Ireland within its borders in 1801, moved gradually and with difficulty – via Catholic emancipation in 1829 and Anglican disestablishment in 1869 – from a position of close identification with the Protestant interest to one of equidistance between Ireland's religious communities as the century unfolded.

27

Indeed, in 1836 the Order's dissolution and reorganisation was compelled following widespread rumours that it planned to replace King William IV with his brother, the Duke of Cumberland, the titular head of the Orange organisation. Yet reorganisation did little to reduce the disorder associated with Orangeism. On 12 July 1849, a particularly vicious riot between Orangemen and Catholics at Dolly's Brae, near Magheramayo, County Down, resulted in the deaths of 30 Catholics. This incident naturally caused great alarm, and especially as the Earl of Roden, one of the most influential Conservative landlords in Ulster, was associated with Orange demonstrations that were held before the conflict erupted. The violence at Dolly's Brae provoked anti-procession legislation in 1850, in the form of the Party Processions Act. Orangemen led by William Johnston of Ballykilbeg, County Down, succeeded in forcing the repeal of the legislation in 1872, but its repeal did not signal a rapprochement between the state and the Order.[1] By this time, there was little to be gained in the wider British context for any government through a close association with Orangeism. By the last decades of the nineteenth century, analogous celebrations in Britain to those of the Orange Order – such as 5 November when an effigy of Guy Fawkes was burned – were losing their anti-Catholic dimensions, while public processions and meetings in general were becoming more controlled, disciplined and free from disorder.[2] In this context, the frequent association between Orange processions and disorder in Ulster came to be viewed with increasing distaste.

Of course, it was not the case that violence attended all, or the majority, of Orange processions, or political processions in general. A parliamentary inquiry into the connection between parades and violence over the period 1872–80 identified an association in only a minority of cases. Of 976 Orange and Orange-related processions, only 40 suffered 'molestation'. The same was generally true of nationalist and Catholic processions. But what was significant as a pointer to developments in the 1880s was that while 703 nationalist/Catholic processions took place, significantly fewer than the Orange-related number (86) over twice as many experienced 'molestation'.[3]

The 1880s were very different politically from the 1870s. These were years of acute political crisis, with the land war of 1879–82 providing the basis for the development of a mass nationalist movement under the leadership of Charles Stewart Parnell seeming to threaten the Union; and as the movement sought to make headway in Ulster it stimulated a sectarian response that greatly complicated the role of government in its attempts to act impartially between the nationalist and loyalist communities.

For the Liberal government of William Ewart Gladstone, which assumed office following the general election of 1880, Ireland, then about to experience the worst phase of the land war, came as an unwelcome surprise. Given the coercive tactics employed by the Land League to implement its writ during the agrarian struggle, Gladstone and his cabinet were loath to accept that it truly represented Irish public opinion. The period of his second ministry (1880–85) would be a learning one on Irish affairs for Gladstone, culminating in his acceptance of Parnell as the authentic leader of nationalist Ireland, and in his readiness to give effect to this acceptance through the conferring of home rule. But for much of this period and certainly in its early stages, Gladstone believed it was both possible to win Ireland away from Parnellism through a policy of stern application of the law to root out crime and reformist legislation to atone for the English misgovernment of the past that, he believed, was chiefly responsible for the disorganised state of Irish society. There is evidence that Gladstone recognised Ireland as a distinct national entity within the United Kingdom from the late 1860s, but his view was that it had yet to be shown that Ireland really wanted national independence. If, after the most enlightened efforts on Westminster's behalf to resolve Ireland's problems, that case could be proved, then home rule might have to be accepted. But not until then.[4]

The most important speech Gladstone made on Ireland during this ministry was at Leeds on 7 October 1881. It followed in the wake of a series of militant speeches by Parnell and his suspicious reaction to the highly important Land Act of 1881, which conceded the 'three Fs' to Irish tenant farmers – fixity of tenure, fair rent and free sale of the tenant's interest in his holding. The act was a great concession, amounting to dual ownership of Irish land, and Gladstone read Parnell's advice to the farmers that they should test the act in the courts before rushing to embrace it, as an attempt to undermine it. Accordingly in his Leeds speech Gladstone railed against Parnell, warning him that 'the resources of civilisation were not yet exhausted'. But he also railed against the feebleness of the loyal classes in Ireland for their failure adequately to support the forces of law and order and urged them to come forward now.[5]

Gladstone's condemnation of Parnell was a signal for the pre-planned arrest and imprisonment of nationalist leaders in a desperate and ill-judged attempt to destroy the power of the Land League.[6]

Moreover, his call for the loyal classes to rouse themselves was insufficiently attuned to the complexities of the Irish political environ- ment and had a quite unintended consequence: it was taken as the green light for autonomous action to combat nationalism by the Orange Order. Indeed the Order was offended that Gladstone appeared to be ignorant of, and had not acknowledged, the efforts it had already made to support beleaguered landlords through its Emergency Committee.[7] In reply to the Secretary of the Committee, Bro. Athol J. Dudgeon, who had written to repair the gap in Gladstone's knowledge, his Private Secretary, Edward Hamilton, conveyed Gladstone's view that what he said at Leeds was not meant to apply to 'the Association' and that he 'was well aware and he gladly confesses that in particular issues great courage and manful energy were exhibited in support of law and public order, as well as of private rights'.[8]

There the correspondence ended, but it is significant that Gladstone's reply acknowledged the Emergency Committee's activities only in the most general way. In fact, Gladstone was most disinclined to applaud the activities of an organisation like the Orange Order, with a long- established reputation for bigotry and violence. The fact that the Emergency Committee 'was a purely Orange association ... made it very difficult for him to pat it on the back'.[9] The celebrated episode in November 1880 when the Emergency Committee despatched a body of armed Orangemen to assist Captain Boycott at Lough Mask, County Mayo, was viewed by the Chief Secretary, W.E. Forster, as carrying the danger of civil war and he took steps to have its size reduced. Loyalist opinion in the South, including Boycott, had similar fears.[10] In fact, much as Gladstone disliked extreme nationalism in Ireland, he could still compare it favourably with Orangeism. Of the violence associated with nationalist and Orange demonstrations in 1872, following the repeal of the Party Processions Act, he observed that while both were reprehensible he was reluctant to include the green flag among their 'ugly features': 'after all it is the national flag of Ireland and has there- fore a footing distinct from and higher than the orange one'.[11] Gladstone may have abhorred Parnellism, but he saw it as a product of the dysfunctional state of Irish society that had been created by English misgovernment. The Orange Order, however, was a manifesta- tion of how that misgovernment had been effected. As such, the Order could not have an instrumental role in the resolution of the Irish ques- tion. If, after the Land Act of 1881 had time to take effect, Ireland was still 'divided between Orangemen and law-haters', he observed, 'then our task is hopeless'.[12] At the time Gladstone expressed this opinion he included Parnell among the 'law-haters', but over the period of his second ministry that view would gradually change, unlike his opinion of Orangeism.

Nevertheless, it is worth noting in this context that despite Gladstone's personal distaste for Orangeism, those such as Earls Spencer and Cowper, charged with the actual government of Ireland, and defining their ultimate purpose as the defence of the union, realised that they could not afford to alienate Orangeism completely. Spencer, one of the very few great Whig landowners to support Gladstone on the home rule issue in 1886, observed in 1881, shortly after Gladstone's Leeds speech: 'The active support of Orangemen and Protestants is the ultimate resource of English rule in Ireland, but ought to be kept until every other card has been played.' At that time special constables might be raised, but to do so before then would be to put the government in the embarrassing position of having to refuse the Orange offers of assistance.[13] Spencer's attitude to Orangeism was characteristic of British administrations generally in nineteenth-century Ireland, but the relations between Liberal administrations – inclined to reform and the conciliation of Catholics – and Orangeism carried difficulties that did not apply to the same extent to Tory administrations.[14] In the early 1880s the government found itself having to pursue a problematical course, attempting to establish the legitimacy of British rule in the eyes of Irish Catholics so as to undermine Parnellism, yet having to bear in mind that it might ultimately have to embrace Orangeism if the severity of the Irish problem demanded it. And the government's position was made immensely more difficult by the autonomous action taken by the Orange Order to counter the Parnellite movement.

Historically, the strength of the Orange Order had waxed and waned with the rise and fall of nationalist movements.[15] That the revival Orangeism experienced in the 1880s has not been reversed since then is indicative of the seriousness of the threat to their membership of the United Kingdom the unionist community has perceived. Reliable statistics on the growth of the Order in the 1880s, however, are difficult to establish. The newspaper closest to the organisation, the *Belfast News-Letter*, estimated the strength of its 'active' membership at this time as between 50 000 and 60 000, together with 'many thousands' of sympathisers.[16] Perhaps a more indicative guide to the Order's growth is the number of Orange Halls established in Ulster in the period 1881–90, 1881 being a year in which the organisation was already experiencing increased growth (Table 2.1).

Table 2.1   Number of Orange Halls in Ulster 1881–90[17]

Year	No.
1881	134
1887	167
1890	218

In organising to meet the nationalist threat, which in 1880 included attempts by the Land League – which had some success – to attract Protestant tenant farmers to its ranks, the Orange Order constructed a plan of action: every Land League meeting would be met with a counter-meeting; those Protestants – in some cases whole lodges – who had joined the Land League would be expelled from the Order: firearms would be acquired and drilling organised.[18] In so doing the pattern of Orange opposition to Irish nationalism up to 1886 and beyond was laid. Counter-meetings became the most controversial means by which nationalism was opposed, but in themselves they were less a source of conflict than the act of processing to and from the location of meetings. Thus, while Orange processions and demonstrations on traditional anniversary occasions could, as in the past, provide the occasion for conflict, it tended to be processions occasioned by the dynamics of the loyalist-nationalist conflict that were more productive of violence and disorder in this period; and consequently of problems of law enforcement for the Irish administration, some of which have changed little since the 1880s.

In this context it is worth noting that, just as plastic baton rounds were introduced to Northern Ireland in the 1970s as a less lethal means of riot control than bullets, so in 1880 was buckshot introduced for the same reason.[19] But its use to quell a riot associated with an Orange demonstration in Dungannon demonstrated that, just as with plastic baton rounds, buckshot proved much more lethal than the administration had forseen, and just as fruitful of controversy.[20] The controversy over the Dungannon riot raised a number of concerns for nationalists about the impartiality of the police and magistracy,[21] but perhaps its most surprising aspect was the evidence it revealed of how little W.E. Forster and the Irish administration understood the importance of marching to the Orange tradition.[22]

Disputes over processions at this time were mainly a function of the developing land struggle in the North. Nationalists, as we have noted, did have some success in attracting Protestant support, but this was done largely by the tactic of disengaging the agrarian question from nationalist arguments and concentrating only on the former. It was a tactic that Ulster landlords were not slow to expose in their efforts to thwart the League's objectives.[23] Their support and involvement was instrumental in the revival of Orangeism, but the nationalists assisted also. In deciding to run a Nationalist candidate at the Tyrone by-election of September 1881, they forced a split in the Presbyterian–Roman Catholic alliance on which Ulster Liberalism was based. And although the Liberal candidate, Thomas Dickson, was elected, a situation had been created which Orangeism could exploit. Thereafter, the fortunes of the Land League in Ulster suffered, while the Orange Order grew in strength.[24] But while the tactics employed by the Orange Order to oppose the League in the North may have been effective, they allowed nationalists an opportunity to open another line of attack in pursuit of the larger objective of exposing the iniquities of British rule in Ireland.

Despite the employment of a rhetoric extolling obedience to the law, the fact that Orange leaders openly armed their followers was a clear indication that they intended to oppose the Land League with something stronger than the power of speech. Many examples of Orange lawlessness emerged, but one that nationalists exploited effectively was that of Captain Mervyn Archdale, a Fermanagh Justice of the Peace, who having acquired arms and organised drilling, deliberately led a procession of Orangemen into a violent attack on Land Leaguers in December 1880. But despite urging from both Liberal and Nationalist MPs, the Chief Secretary, Forster, refused to remove Archdale from the local magistracy,[25] while a promise to amend the law relating to the carrying of arms had little practical effect.[26] The action of Orangemen who were also magistrates encouraging violent activities which, nationalists plausibly argued, deliberately subverted the right to free speech, focused attention initially on the source of the controversy – most often an Orange procession – but attention soon spread to a range of contentious issues in the social environment of Ulster that sanctioned such behaviour, especially the overwhelmingly Protestant membership of the local magistracy and their apparent abuse of their powers.[27] Given that the role of magistrates would be central factors in the disputes involving party processions in succeeding years an examination of them as an agency of government is instructive.

It is important to distinguish between the unpaid local magistracy, of whom Archdale was a typical example in the Ulster context – charged with the maintenance of the peace, but far too often reflecting local community prejudices and letting them dictate their actions – and the paid, and more powerful, Resident Magistrates. For many landlord-magistrates such as Archdale the price of establishing, or maintaining, their roles as loyalist leaders was to indulge Orange passions by organis-ing popular opposition to nationalist demonstrations. This activity often placed them in an ambiguous relationship with the law – threat-ening defiance of it, while at the same time offering their followers a degree of immunity from the consequences of so doing by virtue of their position; while again, their organising and leading role gave them a measure of control over Orange activities, thereby inhibiting the Irish administration from taking action against them.[28] The Resident Magistrates, in contrast, had a closer, more integrated relationship with the state authorities in Dublin. They had been established in 1836 with the purpose of functioning as the eyes and ears of the Chief Secretary in each locality, and to whom they had to submit regular reports on the state of their districts. At the same time no specific guidelines gov-erning their actions were, or, it was believed, could be, given: 'They were simply to make their services as magistrates as useful as possible, especially by attending petty sessions and fairs', though they were given instructions on how to gather information for inclusion in the diary that had to be submitted to the Chief Secretary each month.[29] Earl Cowper, the first Irish Viceroy of Gladstone's second administra-tion, came to regard them as uncomplicated and reliable instruments of the Irish administration at local level.[30] In fact, as a body, they were much less uniformly effective than Cowper suggests, having a history of inefficiency, laziness, partisanship and unreliability of judgement.[31] As we shall see, not all should be so described, but as a law-enforcement body with considerable freedom of action, the Resident Magistracy, could be a very uncertain instrument of government.[32]

The reassurance that the Orange Order drew from the reverses the Land League received in Ulster was short-lived. Always uncomfortable with a Liberal administration,[33] the 'Kilmainham Treaty' of 1882 looked to the Orangemen very much like an informal alliance of gov-ernment and revolutionists, while the Phoenix Park murders which fol-lowed shortly afterwards, together with a Fenian bombing campaign in London, convinced Ulster loyalists of the need for vigilance.[34] Accordingly, when Timothy Healy caused one of the great political shocks of the period by winning the County Monaghan seat at a by-election in 1883 – 'the seemingly impossible had come to pass'[35] – and signalled the nationalist 'invasion of Ulster' the following autumn, the Orange Order organised to meet the challenge. The world-view of Orangeism during the campaign can be garnered from the resolutions passed at Orange meetings and slogans displayed on placards. Briefly summarised, the Parnellite movement was a 'Fenian murder league', desiring to foment rebellion in Ulster – 'the Imperial province' – with the purpose of establishing a Romanist and communist government. The presence in the North of this 'treasonable conspiracy' was an affront to the constitutional rights and liberties of loyalists, and since the Irish administration was apathetic to the danger Parnellism posed to the Union it was incumbent on the loyalists of Ulster to oppose it 'by any means in our power'. In so doing they were merely responding to the call Gladstone had made at Leeds in 1881 for the loyal classes to come forward and oppose revolutionary nationalism.[36]

What concerned the Order, in particular, was that the nationalist campaign was intended to encourage nationalists to register to vote. It was known that a major extension of the franchise was planned in the near future, and that the political power of loyalism in Ulster would be diminished as a result.[37] The Orange campaign employed the well-tried strategy of holding counter-meetings at the same locations as those chosen by nationalists, with the purpose of denying the nationalists a hearing by forcing the government to ban both meetings on peace-preservation grounds. To make the campaign effective the threat of violence had to be made explicit. Thus, as they had during the land war, so now Orange leaders openly armed their followers and employed a violent rhetoric. It was a dangerous strategy, excusing its very dubious legality on the ground that Orangemen were only compensating for the failures of the state.

Running from late September 1883 through to early 1884, a conflict between nationalists and Orangeism occurred, taking the form of oppositional processions and public meetings, and ranging across counties Fermanagh, Cavan, Down, Londonderry, Armagh and Tyrone. But nationalists, with the experience of the land struggle behind them had a better appreciation of the opposition they could expect and before the campaign started had been pressing the government in parliament on the deficiencies of law-enforcement in the North, especially associations between police, magistrates and the Orange Order.[38]

The counter-meeting strategy pursued by the Orange Order was fairly effective in its purpose from late September through to early November. At this point, however, the government began to ban only the counter-meetings to reduce the potential for violence; and gradually a government policy on processions and meetings emerged. Aimed, effectively, at the Orange Order, it forbade counter-meetings called merely for the purpose of confrontation or with the purpose of having an opposition meeting banned.[39] The policy, in fact, was occasioned by a major controversy which erupted on 16 October 1883, at Rosslea, County Fermanagh. A local magistrate, Lord Rossmore, rejected the request of a (Roman Catholic) Resident Magistrate, Hugh M'Ternan, to re-route a procession of belligerent Orangemen he was leading away from a nationalist meeting, so as to avoid the risk of a violent conflict. M'Ternan, with the support of police statements, reported Rossmore's conduct to the Undersecretary at Dublin Castle. The resulting inquiry elicited from Rossmore a defence of his actions which justified the Orange campaign to stamp out revolutionary nationalism in the North, in accordance with the call made by Gladstone in his Leeds speech of 1881. Rossmore did not plead ignorance of the danger of violence inherent in the situation at Rosslea, something which, he was informed, could have excused his actions; while his claim that M'Ternan actually gave him permission to proceed was strenuously denied by M'Ternan, and not believed by the Dublin authorities. He was, accordingly, dismissed from the magistracy.[40]

The controversy surrounding the Rossmore incident fed off a volatile political atmosphere in the North, already heightened by a political tour of Ulster made in early October by Sir Stafford Northcote, parliamentary leader of the Tory Party; and which, to Northcote's chagrin, was associated with political extremism when followers of an Orange demonstration attacked a convent in which the Mother Superior lay dying.[41] At the end of the month another serious incident involving political processions occurred. The decision of a sub-committee of Londonderry Corporation to let the Corporation Hall for a nationalist meeting on 1 November, to be addressed by the Lord Mayor of Dublin on the franchise question, was strenuously opposed by local loyalists. To prevent the meeting, a group of Apprentice Boys invaded the Hall and when a nationalist procession escorting the Lord Mayor arrived on the scene, shots were fired from the Hall, wounding two people in the procession.[42] The political crisis occasioned by the nationalist 'invasion of Ulster' climaxed at Dromore, County Tyrone. Here an Orange counter-meeting, ostensibly organised in support of Rossmore but in reality intended to have a nationalist meeting banned, led to the death by bayonetting of Samuel Giffen, a 'flax dresser' from Portadown, as the Orange processionists attempted to attack the nationalist meeting.[43] But while the issues raised during this controversy were essentially the same as during the land war, and the government response similar, the fact that an avalanche of declarations of support for Rossmore from the Irish magistracy emerged[44] helped to give them a much higher profile, and, accordingly, made more difficult the administration's task of undermining, through impartial government, Irish support for the Parnellite movement.

In fact, the government's ability to arbitrate fairly between national-ists and loyalists was hampered by a tension inherent in its pursuit, in different contexts and time-frames, of two separate objectives. On the one hand, in the immediate context of violent party processions, there was a non-political public interest to be upheld and which often neces-sitated striking a balance between the right to march and measures necessary to maintain the peace; one the other hand, and in the longer term, there was the maintenance of union, in pursuit of which the Parnellites were defined as the main adversary and which inhibited the administration from taking measures that would seriously alienate the 'loyal classes'. Of the two objectives, it was the second that was more important at this time for the Irish administration; and this view was especially strong among the local agents of the state, the magis-tracy, drawn overwhelmingly from the non-Catholic population. Indeed, it is worth noting in this context that the guidelines supplied to Resident Magistrates – ostensibly more direct agents of state policy than the unpaid local magistracy – for the purpose of compiling their monthly reports to Dublin Castle, did not prioritise peace preservation *per se*, but the threat to the state posed by the Parnellite movement.[45] The magistrates' public declarations of support for Rossmore, then, were wholly consistent with the political objective of the government; however, they actually worked to retard its realisation.

If it was right to dismiss Rossmore for his conduct at Rosslea, nation-alists argued, surely all those magistrates who enthusiastically endorsed his conduct should also be dismissed? Their action had 'utterly destroyed all confidence in the administration of the law ... until the magisterial bench be re-modelled and popularised the people of Ireland must remain convinced that they need not seek for justice'.[46] The Chief Secretary's reason for not taking action, namely, that Rossmore was dismissed for dangerous conduct , a much more serious affair than the mere expression of opinion,[47] sounded weak and unconvincing. In truth a mass dismissal of magistrates was neither practicable or politi-cally feasible; and given its fundamental interests, the administration was keen not to provoke a major crisis with the union's problematical supporters in the North. As we have noted,[48] in Dublin Castle's corre-spondence with Rossmore it was indicated to him that had he claimed ignorance of the dangers inherent in the situation at Rosslea he could have escaped dismissal. In this context it is also worth noting that another troublesome agent of the Irish administration at this time, the Fisheries Inspector and Orange leader, William 'Ballykilbeg' Johnston, was dismissed from his post, for contravening the rule banning civil servants engaging in party politics, only reluctantly and after sustained pressure from nationalists.[49]

Gladstone's hope in the early 1880s that the Catholic Irish could be weaned away from Parnellism by reform and impartial administration was never likely to be realised. But the task was made much more difficult by the issue of party processions and demonstrations. Much as Ulster loyalism was distasteful to the administration it might have to reply on it, as previous administrations had done, if a violent nationalist upheaval occurred. But on the ground, its agents were so closely enmeshed with the loyalist community that it was impossible for the administration – in the interests of fair government – completely to dissociate itself from Orangeism. The abuses this situation gave rise to could only have been effectively dealt with had an independent Court of Appeal existed before which cases of the maladministration of justice in Ireland could be brought – a point Parnell was to make and which the Home Secretary, Sir William Harcourt, no friend of Irish nationalism, agreed with. But as none existed all he could do was assure Parnell that the Irish administration was doing the best it could 'in the circumstances'.[50] In the circumstances, some initiatives were taken, such as the formulation of a policy on party processions and meetings, and assurances given that the serious religious imbalance in membership of the magistracy would be tackled.[51] Nevertheless, party processions and the violence associated with them continued to fuel political animosities as the Ulster problem came to take definite shape in the run-up to the home rule crisis of 1886. Nationalist concern was expressed in 1885 at a decision to try Belfast Orangemen who had fired on nationalist processionists in Newry in June 1884, with the result that an 'Orange' jury promptly acquitted them; and of the likelihood of a similar case in Keady, County Armagh, being treated in the same way.[52] The role of the magistracy in the parades issue remained a serious concern; as did political parades generally. As the emergence of the Ulster problem as one of the most formidable obstacles to home rule was registered, in the carnage and destruction of the Belfast riots of 1886,[53] party processions came to be identified as one of the central mechanisms responsible for sustaining their longevity:

> It was made manifest to us, upon the testimony of the most respectable witnesses of all classes and creeds, that the processions,

erections of arches and bonfires are a fruitful cause of rioting and disturbance ... even an excursion through the town of schoolchildren ... if accompanied by a band, appears effectively to lead to an attack either by the processionists or by the mobs who collect on hearing the band.[54]

When the smoke of the riots cleared, however, it was evident to the loyalist community that the political environment was now much more congenial than it had been since 1880. The home rule question had effected an earthquake in British politics, dividing and weakening the Liberal Party and producing a powerful unionist movement committed to the rejection of home rule for Ireland; a movement, moreover, that would increasingly appreciate the importance of Ulster unionism to its cause. A sign of that appreciation was evident almost immediately, when the Tory administration that succeeded the Liberal government at the general election of July 1886 appointed Lord Londonderry Viceroy of Ireland. That a new and more congenial order was now in place was evident also in the preparation of coercion meas ures to deal with the nationalist threat, but especially in the restoration of Lord Rossmore to the Commission of the Peace in 1887, shortly after he had publicly denounced Gladstone as a mad dog that ought to be destroyed.[55]

Looking back over the early 1880s from September 1886, Ulster loyalists could congratulate themselves on having thwarted the nationalist campaign to win the North for the home rule cause. Theirs was a campaign fought mainly through Orange processions and demonstrations; however, the violence of language and deed attending these processions impaired the quality of that success. In the long run political extremism would contribute much to keeping north-east Ulster within the United Kingdom, but at the cost of alienation from mainland British opinion.[56] That state of affairs has persisted to the present day, while much else has changed since the 1880s, the British interest in Ireland especially.

Orange extremism in the late nineteenth century was accepted politically as part of the price of maintaining the union, but the union of Great Britain and Northern Ireland now only remains intact so long as a majority of people in Northern Ireland desire it. The unionist community is no longer regarded as central to the integrity of the British state, which itself has changed radically, constitutionally and imaginatively, since the 1880s. Yet it is still the case, that because of the vehement Britishness of Ulster unionism and the close relationship between the unionist community and the agencies of law and order, British administrations have found it difficult to manage Orange parades without, at the same time, leaving themselves vulnerable to charges of complicity in their more controversial and morally contentious aspects.

Notes

1. For a useful survey of state–Orange relations up to 1870, see Hereward Senior, 'The Early Orange Order 1795–1870' in T.D. Williams (ed.), *Secret Societies in Ireland* (Dublin and New York, 1973), pp. 36–45. On the Dolly's Brae incident, in particular, see Kevin B. Nowlan, *The Politics of Repeal: a Study in the Relations between Great Britain and Ireland 1841–1850* (London and Toronto, 1965), p. 228; D.J. Hickey and J.E. Doherty, *A Dictionary of Irish History 1800–1980* (Dublin, 1987), pp. 133–4.

2. See, for example, R.D. Storch, '"Please to Remember the Fifth of November": Conflict, Solidarity and Public Order in Southern England 1815–1900' in R.D. Storch (ed.), *Popular Culture and Custom in Nineteenth Century England* (London, 1982), pp. 71–99.

3. *Return, as far as Practicable, of all Party Processions whether Orange, Nationalist, Amnesty, 'Martyr', or Other, Specifying Those which did not Suffer Molestation which have taken Place in Ireland since the Repeal of the Party Processions Act in 1872* , H.C. 1880 (380 – Session 2), lx, 395–432 ; *Return in Continuation ... up to 30 Day of August 1880*, H.C. 1880 (389 – Session 2), lx, 435–47.

4. For a nuanced assessment of Gladstone's attitude to Ireland and home rule at this time, see J.L. Hammond, *Gladstone and the Irish Nation* (London, 1938), Chs 8 and 11.

5. *The Times*, 8 October 1881.

6. The arrest merely provoked a great increase in agrarian crime. See Paul Bew, *Land and the National Question in Ireland 1858–82* (Dublin, 1979).

7. The Emergency Committee was established by the Grand Orange Lodge of Ireland on 3 November 1880 to help the victims of Land League persecution. During the spring and summer of 1881 it had upwards of 300 labourers, chiefly from counties Armagh, Monaghan and Cavan working on boycotted estates and farms in 19 Irish counties. From 1880–85 it spent almost £22,000, of which £3,000 was spent on arms and ammunition (Aiken McClelland, 'Johnston of Ballykilbeg', MPhil, New University of Ulster, 1977, pp. 87–8).

8. See Dudgeon to Gladstone, 1 November 1881; Hamilton to Dudgeon, 5 November 1881 in *1881–1890: Index to the Principal Resolutions, Addresses and Co., Passed by the Grand Orange Lodge of Ireland Commencing June 1881 and Ending December 1890, Usefully and Alphabetically Arranged by Bro. William E. Hill* (Dublin, 1891), p. 65 (hereafter *1880–1890: Index to Principal Resolutions*, etc).

9. W.E. Forster to anonymous correspondent, 14 December 1881 in T. Wemyss Reid, *The Life of W.E. Forster* (2 vols, London, 1888), ii, 376.

10. See Joyce Marlow, *Captain Boycott and the Irish* (London, 1973), pp. 158–73.
11. Gladstone to Earl Spencer, 27 August 1872 in H.C.G. Matthew (ed.), *The Gladstone Diaries, with Cabinet Minutes and Prime Ministerial Correspondence*: Vol. VIII, July 1871–December 1874 (Oxford, 1982), pp. 101–2.
12. Gladstone to Forster, 31 October 1881 in *Hammond*, p. 246.
13. Spencer to Cowper, 19 October 1881, in *Earl Cowper*, a *Memoir by His Wife* (London, 1913), p. 535. In May 1882 Spencer would succeed Cowper as Viceroy, and – following the murders of Lord Frederick Cavendish and T.H. Burke by the extremist group, the Invincibles, in the Phoenix Park – G.O. Trevelyan succeed Forster as Chief Secretary.
14. Virginia Crossman, *Politics, Law and Order in Nineteenth Century Ireland* (Dublin, 1996), pp. 100–1.
15. Senior, pp. 40–5.
16. See *Belfast News-Letter* (BNL), 14 July 1879; 3 January 1884.
17. Adapted from statistics contained in *1881–1890: Index to Principal Resolutions*, etc.
18. R.W. Kirkpatrick, 'The Origins and Development of the Land War in Mid-Ulster 1881–1890' in F.S.L. Lyons and Richard Hawkins (eds), *Ireland Under the Union: Varieties of Tension: Essays in Honour of T.W. Moody* (Oxford, 1980), pp. 228–9.
19. It was introduced following an inquiry into a fatality which occurred when police acted to quell a riot associated with a nationalist parade in Lurgan. See *Lurgan Riots Commission: Report dated 31 Day of October 1879 made by Lurgan Riots Inquiry Commissioners to His Grace, the Lord Lieutenant of Ireland*, H.C. 1880 (130), lx, 389–93.
20. See Forster's defense of it, *Hansard, Third Series* (hereafter *Hansard 3*), vol. cclv (23 August 1880), col. 1848.
21. Speeches of J.L. Finnigan, cols 1849–50; Parnell, cols 1854–6; R O'Shaugnessy, cols 1856–7; T.D. Sullivan, cols 1857–9.
22. Ibid. (17 August 1880), col. 1376.
23. For extensive quotations from nationalist speeches exposing this 'duplicity', see Col. Edward Saunderson, *Two Irelands: or Loyalty Versus Treason* (Dublin, 1884).
24. Kirkpatrick, pp. 228–33. See also the late Frank Wright's impressive *Two Lands on One Soil: Ulster Politics Before Home Rule* (Dublin, 1996), Ch. 13.
25. Kirkpatrick, p. 230.
26. *Hansard 3*, vol. cclvii (11 January 1881), cols 440–41.
27. See Kirkpatrick, p. 230; Healy, Forster, *Hansard 3*, vol. cclviii (17 February 1881), cols 1089–90.
28. Wright, pp. 476–80, 503–7.
29. R.B. McDowell, *The Irish Administration 1801–1914* (London, 1964), pp. 114–15.
30. Cowper to the editor, *The Times*, 5 January 1886.
31. See K.T. Hoppen, *Elections, Politics and Society in Ireland 1832–1885* (Oxford, 1985), pp. 408–9.
32. *Earl Cowper*, p. 491. RMs had the freedom to direct troops – a function of the 'constitutional ambiguity' that existed between the army and the police. Thus the 'army's role in Ireland turned on the quality of the per formance of the Irish police'. See Elizabeth A. Muenger, *The British*

Military Dilemma in Ireland: Occupation Politics 1886–1914 (Lawrence, Kansas and Dublin, 1991), p. 81.

33. Crossman, pp. 124–9, 100–1.
34. The 'treaty' was an understanding arrived at in April 1882 between Gladstone and Parnell in which, in return for the release of nationalist leaders from jail, Parnell agreed to actively dissuade agrarian violence.
35. On the political impact of the win, see *Annual Register 1883* (London, 1884), chronicle, pp. 302–4; John Magee, 'The Monaghan Election and the "Invasion of Ulster"', *Clogher Record*, vol. III, no. 2 (1974), pp. 147–66.
36. The most extensive contemporary coverage of the loyalist reaction to the nationalist 'invasion' of the North is provided by J. Wallace Taylor, *The Rossmore Incident: an Account of the Various Nationalist and Anti-Nationalist Meetings held in Ulster in the Autumn of 1883* (Dublin, 1884). See also the following issues of the *BNL*: 24–9 September; 5, 10 October 1883; 1–20 January 1884.
37. At the general election of November 1885 Parnellites won a majority of the seats in Ulster (17–16).
38. See, for example, questions by T.M. Healy, and J. Small (22, 25 August 1883) to the Chief Secretary (Irish National Archives (INA), Chief Secretary's Office, Registered Papers (CSORP/1883/642); Healy, Justin McCarthy (*Hansard 3*, vol. cclxxxiii (13 August 1883), cols 254–5). All questions asked in the Commons were investigated by the Chief Secretary's office, though there are many gaps in the INA files.
39. *List of proclaimed meetings in Ulster; Copy of Correspondence Between the Irish Government and Lord Arthur Hill on the Subject of the Prohibition of Counter-Demonstrations* [C. – 4065] (INA, CSORP/1884/28200).
40. The complete correspondence between Rossmore and Dublin Castle is contained in J. Wallace Taylor, 1884, appendix 1.
41. See A.B. Cooke, 'A Conservative Party Leader in Ulster: Sir Stafford Northcote's Diary of a Visit to the Province, October 1883', *Proceedings of the Royal Irish Academy*, vol. 75, section C, no. 4, pp. 69–71; Andrew Lang, *Sir Stafford Northcote: First Earl of Iddesleigh* (2 vols, Edinburgh and London, 1890), ii, 252. Nationalist opinion would come to view Northcote's visit as an originating cause of the Belfast riots of 1886 (Anon. 'The Riots in Belfast'. *Fortnightly Review* xl (September 1886) p. 279).
42. The parliamentary inquiry into the events at Derry found that while the Apprentice Boys were responsible for the violence, the source of the disorder lay with the decision to allow nationalists to use the Hall. See *Londonderry Sentinel (LS)*, 12 February 1884. On legalities which constrained police action, see Spencer to Gladstone, 28 February 1884 in Charles Townshend, *Political Violence in Ireland: Government and Resistance Since 1848* (Oxford, 1983), p. 184.
43. See the military report on the Dromore incident by Col. R. Bennett, commander of troops, 1 January 1884 (INA, CSORP/1884/28200).
44. A complete list of the magistrates supporting Rossmore is included in Taylor.
45. See, for example, Hugh M'Ternan's report for September 1884 (INA, CSORP/1884/169515).

46. E. McNally, Town Clerk, Ballymacross, County Monaghan to Chief Secretary, 10 March 1884, enclosing resolutions of Town Commissioners on the Irish magistracy (INA, CSORP/1884/6846). McNally's communication expressed the opinion of nationalists generally on the Irish magistracy.
47. See Trevelyan's reply to Sexton on this point (*Hansard 3*, vol. cclxxxiv (8 February 1884), col. 303.
48. See above, p. 11.
49. See McClelland, pp. 88–92.
50. See Parnell, Harcourt, *Hansard 3*, vol. cccxxxviii (6 May 1884), cols 632–5.
51. Parliamentary debate on the Irish magistracy, reported in *LS*, 8 April 1884.
52. T. Sexton, newspaper clipping of parliamentary question, 6 March 1885 (INA, CSORP/1885/14205); J. Deasy to Chief Secretary, 10 March 1885 (INA, CSORP/1885/14205, 14223, 14221).
53. Following in the wake of the defeat of the first home rule bill, the riots, which started with a sectarian squabble in the shipyards, ran through June to September, causing 32 deaths and many thousands of pounds worth of damage. They consisted mainly of violent conflict between loyalists and the police.
54. *Report of the Commissioners of Inquiry 1886, Respecting the Origins and Circumstances of the Riots in Belfast in June, July August and September 1886, etc.*, H.C. 1887 [C. – 5029], xviii, 16.
55. T.D. Sullivan, *Troubled Times in Irish Politics* (Dublin, 1905), pp. 305–6.
56. For example, see the condemnation of Orange violence in Belfast in *Annual Register 1886* (London, 1887), pp. 308–9; *Illustrated London News*, 11 June, 14, 21 August 1886.

3

'The Bunkum of Ulsteria': the Orange Marching Tradition in Late Victorian Cumbria

Donald M. MacRaild

The Orange march in late Victorian Cumbria might appear, at first sight, to have been an isolated, anachronistic and largely harmless expression of devotion to a dead king.[1] After all, the region was far from the main theatre of British politics, and lacked the massive early-century Irish immigrations that so influenced the Orange traditions of Liverpool and Glasgow. Yet from the mid-Victorian years, Cumbria, too, developed a large Orange movement that was noted for displays of strength that often occasioned communal unrest. It was the public belligerence of Orangemen, and their sometimes violent defence of the union, which led one Barrow nationalist, F.J. Devlin, to dismiss the movement as 'the bunkum of Ulsteria' and 'a banditti of marauders, committing massacre in the name of God, exercising despotic powers in the name of liberty'.[2]

Even outside Irish nationalist circles, Orangeism was often perceived in such terms. The local press regularly harangued both Orange and Green traditions for their uniquely brutal forms of street theatre, and, by so doing, echoed the views of many non-Irish readers. An 'English Protestant', for example, complained to the *Barrow Herald* that the Order was simply a 'mischievous, turbulent, and disreputable combination of factious Irishmen', who, 'whatever may be the claim or rights of Orangemen in Ireland, ... have no locus standi here'.[3] The northern Orange Order was certainly disputatious, but it continued to thrive in the face of such opposition, and in fact drew strength from the enmity of others.

The main forum for expressing the collective identity of Orangeism was the annual 'Glorious Twelfth' parade, when lodges came from all parts of Cumbria to celebrate the victories of King Billy. Throughout this period Orangemen utilised the parading tradition – the Orange 'march', or 'walk' – to express their commitment to the historic Protestant Ascendancy in Britain and Ireland. At these marches, a strident reverence of the Williamite settlement was employed to challenge any group which might threaten the *status quo*. Catholics, socialists, secularists and home rule nationalists were at various times subjected to public condemnation by the Cumbrian Orangemen. The movement professed a simple but cohesive religious and political identity which gave shape to vague notions of patriotic duty; and it was this identity that, during the home rule crises, northern Tories mobilised for their own ends. The Orange Order thus constituted a crucial component of working-class Toryism in the north-west of England.

As in other areas such as western Scotland, the grass roots of Cumbrian Orangeism had an especially Irish character. However, its laudation of Church and State, monarchy and Empire, ensured a considerable sprinkling of non-Irish leaders, members and sympathisers. It was certainly a cross-national mix of people who came together to celebrate the 'Glorious Twelfth' each year. As a measure of their strength, and as a public display of this peculiar form of group loyalty, this important annual jamboree assumed a far greater social and political relevance than might ordinarily be expected from a simple parade. The march in fact became an important part of the social fabric in towns where Irish settlement reached notable proportions.

This chapter examines some of the most important features of Orange parading culture in one such area, Cumbria, in the later Victorian years. It seeks to explain why Orange marches were important in this period by considering the content, rituals and meaning of the parading tradition in the region. First, however, the chapter offers a brief consideration of the emergence of the Orange marching tradition in Britain and in Cumbria.

Early Cumbrian Orangeism did not compare well with neighbouring movements in Lancashire and Scotland. Although there had been lodges in the region from early in the nineteenth century, these were small and inward-looking groups that demonstrated none of the vigour and public noisiness that became their hallmark in the 1870s. Meetings were held in taverns, and William of Orange was celebrated with toasts and dinners, but nothing more elaborate or resplendent occurred. These early instances of Orangeism lacked the popular appeal of the later period, attracting lower middle-class support, rather than that of the labouring class.

The first Orange parade occurred in Ireland on 12 July 1796, although the tradition passed to England within a decade. Very early in their history, Orange marches gained a reputation for violence. There was a large and bloody riot associated with the Manchester celebrations of the 'Glorious Twelfth' in 1807, but it was not until 1819 and 1820 that Liverpool witnessed similar occurrences. Although the authorities remained generally sceptical and marches were often banned, violence continued to light up the 'Glorious Twelfth' throughout the 1820s and 30s.[4] The problems associated with these public demonstrations were added to by the clandestine, pseudo-Masonic ritualism of Orangeism, which further alienated outsiders. This was especially true in the restive years after 1815, when the professed loyalism of the Orange tradition did not prevent it being criticised. At the same time, the quest for respectability went on. In the 1820s, when Tory Ultras were roused in opposition to O'Connell's quest for Catholic Emancipation and moves to extend the franchise, the Order temporarily fell in with a dubious collection of well-heeled reactionaries, including the Dukes of Cumberland and York. As far as northern Orangeism was concerned, this association was ill-advised, short-lived and fruitless. When it was suggested that Orange muscle was to be exerted in support of the dukes' plot to establish a regency, a hostile Royal Commission was appointed and the Order was liquidated. The movement returned to its provincial roots – in Lancashire particularly – and it was here, from this point in the mid-1830s, that the modern English Order began to grow.[5]

The Cumbria Order seems distant from this talk of regencies and risings. In 1830, when there were 230 lodges in Britain (with 77 in Lancashire, 39 in Scotland and 36 in Yorkshire) there were only ten in the North of England: five in Cumbria, comprising two each in Carlisle and Whitehaven and one in Kendal; and five in the North East, with two in Newcastle, and one each in Sunderland, Wallsend and Morpeth.[6] Little was heard of Cumbrian Orangeism until the 1860s, by which time Fenianism and developing iron-mining and metal-manufacturing centres in the west of the region were creating a favourable climate for Orangeism to prosper.[7] Fenianism aroused latent anti-Catholic sentiments, while industrialisation attracted a host of migrants from nearby Ulster. Yet even in the 1860s the 'Glorious Twelfth' attracted only a few dozen men for the usual hearty meal and loyal toasts. The Orange marching tradition of western Scotland and Cumbria only became a major social force after 1870, following the repeal of the Party Processions Act. Although the Scottish lodges were growing before this date, the explosion from this point is quite remarkable. In 1872, for example, Glasgow's 32 lodges mustered a march of only 1500 strong; in the following year, the figure was perhaps ten times that figure. Even in Liverpool, where the movement was already strong, membership was increased so greatly in the same decade that in 1876 the largest crowd in English Orange history – between 60 000 and 80 000 – flocked to cheer on more than 7000 processors.[8] In Cumbria, the emergence of a large Orange movement is all the more remarkable given the Order's tiny proportions and reclusive tendencies in the previous generations.

Cumbrian Orangeism, as well as being fuelled by deeply-felt antagonisms towards Fenianism and Catholicism, also received in 1871 a boost from the visit of William Murphy, the infamous no-popery lecturer.[9] Murphy's rabble-rousing and incendiary style caused great upheavals across the Midlands and Lancashire. His visit to the Orangemen of Whitehaven was ended prematurely by a brutal attack by 200 to 300 Irish Catholic miners from nearby Cleator Moor, the region's 'Little Ireland'. Murphy was left desperately ill, and the town remained in a state of near-riot for months afterwards. Less than a year later, he died from his injuries and local Orangemen, incensed by the turn of events, began publicly to muster in a way that was new to the region. Within four months of Murphy's death, Cumbria Orangemen had taken to the streets for the first time. The Whitehaven brethren, who had then increased to two lodges, were joined in their march by lodges from Egremont, Workington and Cleator Moor.[10] Dressed in their orange and purple regalia, and supported by their traditionally noisy music, this was a bold and provocative remembrance of Murphy. The early 1870s also witnessed albeit less fraught Orange awakenings in the south of the region, around the rapidly-growing shipbuilding town of Barrow-in-Furness.

For the rest of the decade, Cumbrian Orangeism continued to grow. By the 1880s the Order was represented by sometimes five or six lodges in the larger towns of Carlisle, Maryport, Workington, Whitehaven and Barrow, while even smaller mining colonies such as Moor Row (near Cleator), Scalegill and Frizington contained a single lodge. Small towns or larger villages such as Egremont and Askam usually had two or three lodges. The July parades tended to muster around 20 lodges, though there were occasions when many more were present, such as in Barrow in 1882 when 50 turned out from as far afield as Carlisle and Burnley.[11] Although the size of the Orange parade varied considerably, turnouts were generally impressive for what was an isolated and semi-rural area. While the first Orange parade in Cumbrian history saw only 400 to 500 marchers descend on

Whitehaven in 1872, the average for the region in the 1870s and 1880s was between 1500 and 2000, with usually a similar number of onlookers, lining the route to wave and cheer. Sometimes the crowds were much larger, as in July 1874 when sixteen lodges and 1500 Orangemen, who had gathered in Whitehaven to celebrate Orange Day, were supported by a crowd of 4000 to 5000.[12] No parade in Cumbrian history was larger that in Askam on 12 July 1877 where some 5000 to 6000 joined forces from all over Cumbria.[13] This figure would certainly have matched many of the marches that occurred in Glasgow or Liverpool at about the same time.

The startling progress of Cumbrian Orangeism in the 1870s suggests that the movement quickly reached out beyond its traditional Irish Protestant supporters. The lodgemen were able to attract support from some quite influential sympathisers, especially members of the local Anglican clerics, and these men played an important part in Cumbria's Orange marching tradition. The Rev G.B. Armes of Cleator Moor, for example, was one of the most prominent clerical members of the Cumbrian Order. He was Grand Master of the Moor Row lodge, and was present at most annual gatherings for thirty years after the 1870s. Usually, though, these clerics were willing to speak on the platform about religious matters but refrained from joining a lodge. The leadership of the lodges was undoubtedly provided by middle-class members, many of them well-to-do industrialists and politicians. All of these principal players seemed willing to march proudly at the head of their lodges; while few eschewed the chance to pronounce at great length on religious and political matters, soaking up the adulation of the applauding masses who gathered round. Prominent examples of the Cumbrian Orange leadership included William Gradwell, a Barrow builder and one-time mayor, and James Kennedy, a prominent Furness iron-master. Both men were worshipful masters and had lodges named in their honour. Similar recognition was bestowed upon notable Cumbrian families such as the Senhouses, the Wyndhams (Earls of Leconfield) and the Cavendish-Bentincks.

These clerics, industrialists and minor aristocracy were important to the Order because they invested a certain moral and civic authority. More important, however, were the ordinary foot soldiers whose attention to pseudo-military attire, music and the rhythms of the marching tradition made the movement what it was: loud, uncompromising and, above all, public. The lieutenants of the movement are almost as little-known to us as the faceless members of the rank and file. John Bawden, the Cleator Moor iron-mines foreman, who became Grand

Master at Cleator in the 1880s, is an exception simply because he enjoyed a brief episode of infamy when he was accused of murdering an Irish nationalist, Henry Tumelty, during the locally-infamous Orange Day riot at Cleator Moor of 1884. Bawden was acquitted and fell back into relative obscurity before dying two years later.[14] At the bottom of the pile were the thousands of ordinary members, without whose enthusiasm Cumbrian Orangeism would have remained a club for middle-class members to enjoy good food and a toast or two.[15] Beyond them were the women and children who often added the most to the colour and occasion of Orange parades, and who had their own female and juvenile lodges.

With such a strong base of working-class support, it is perhaps understandable that pageantry and ceremony came to be viewed as an important part of the parading tradition. For ordinary members the parade itself offered a brief chance to dress up and to feel important and strong. Members expended considerable sums on banners which were displayed on the 'Glorious Twelfth'; these were large, bright and highly decorated; carrying images in paint, and words in silk or braid, many of them carried the portrait of a local grandee on one side and of William of Orange himself on the other. Others were more creative. The Whitehaven Temperance Lodge (195), for example, caused quite a stir when in 1875 members unveiled a new banner which bore a likeness of William Murphy, sat on a chair with a bible in his hand. Underneath his portrait was this inscription: 'Whitehaven's memorial to the martyr for Protestantism and liberty – William Murphy'.[16]

Shows of colour were not restricted to banners and flags. Although members uniformly wore rather sombre bowler hats and Sunday best suits, these were set off with colourful sashes, Orange lilies, ribbons and medals. This made for a striking display, as one newspaper in 1885 commented: 'The Orangemen looked wonderfully well as they promenaded the principal streets of the town. With their yellow scarves, glittering medals and silver lace they make a goodly show.'[17] And another witness remarked: 'To say nothing of orange, there was black, purple, scarlet and green scarves and aprons in profusion, with cabalistic signs by the dozen – crossbones, hearts, hands, &c.'[18] Just why the lodges acquired such a military and carnival atmosphere was generally lost on the local press, though one writer managed an explanation of the colourful pageantry of Orange parades: 'One of two of the more demonstrative females were clothed from head to foot in orange garments, and had done as much for their children, on the same principle, we presume, that led Mr. Vincent Crummles's first tragedy man to black himself all over when he played Othello – he felt the part so strongly that he went into it as if he meant it.'[19]

The territorialism associated with Ulster Orangeism in the late 20th century was much less apparent in 19th-century Cumbria. This is mainly because the Irish Catholics of the region did not live in sharply segregated communities: there was no Garvaghy Road in Barrow, and no Bogside in Whitehaven. Yet Victorian lodgemen were creatures of habit, and each year they began by gathering at the station to greet travelling brethren before setting off to march around the streets of the host town. There were often as many bands as there were lodges. Marches took place in the morning, with the half-way point being marked by a mass gathering in some large field or other, where leaders and invited guests (often Ulster clerics) regaled the throng with tales of the strength and fortitude of the Order. Sometimes picnics were eaten at this point, and refreshments, though not always alcohol, were provided. The processors then usually marched round the streets one more time before visiting lodges headed for the station and local lodges gathered for an evening of entertainment, with more speeches and further refreshments. The marchers of Cumbria may have lacked the spatial focus that was offered by the social geography of Liverpool or Belfast, but they still delighted in the opportunity to march past local Catholic churches and chapels, sometimes circling them like Indians round a wagon train, even if such antagonistic behaviour was often discouraged by the authorities. Although rogue bandsmen, usually full of drink, would sometimes stagger around the town late at night, bashing their drums in the hope of eliciting a response from irate Catholics, the question of territory only really became a serious issue on once occasion in Cumbria's Orange history. This was in Barrow in 1882, during the heated debates which followed the Phoenix Park Murders. Lord Frederick Cavendish was well-known in Barrow as the son of the Duke of Devonshire upon whose land the town was built. Local Irish Catholics were subject to great verbal pressure, and relations deteriorated further when the Land League was banned from using the Town Hall by the Orange Mayor, William Gradwell, who admitted acting on a petition from 873 local Orangemen. Anger reached even greater pitch when, in July of that year, the local lodges were permitted to march past the Catholic church of St Mary's for the first time. As we know, the control of public space was (and is) important to Orangemen. It derives from the old Ulster belief that 'where you can parade you can control'.

The Orange parade was symbolic of such tradition and power; its noise and colour was like that of a courting bird, rousing suitors and rivals alike. Even the tunes played by bandsmen were loaded with historical meaning. As observer noted in his neat description of the 'Boyne Water' and 'Croppies Lie Down' as 'two well-known tunes that are used to revive the memory of bitter Irish feuds dating near two centuries back'.[20] Tunes such as these, more than any other aspect of Orangeism, often angered the Catholics who were forced to hear them. Cleator Moor's Catholic priests blamed the town's fatal riot of 1884 on the same musical provocation. The music may have incensed Catholics but it also had an incendiary effect on the marchers. As Fr Burchall explained: the Orangemen 'danced frantically past the church, playing the party tune "Boyne Water" ... with such a display of frantic feeling before such excitable people as ours are, a breach of the peace was only to be expected'.[21] Some of the bands accompanying the marchers were more musical than muscular, and often attracted positive comments. Perhaps understandably, then, the press was quick to criticise the more swaggering examples among the bandsmen. Such was the case with one band, at the Cleator march in 1884, which 'consisting of two fifers followed by two big drummers who belaboured their drums with a couple of sticks each, making the most deafening and intolerable din'.[22] A similarly dismissive observation was made at Barrow: 'in the centre of the procession were a couple of fife players who were aided in their musical efforts by a drummer, whose arms were in motion like the sails of a windmill, in the work of punishing both sides of his drum. He succeeded in making a noise, there is no doubt'.[23] Such combinations of enthusiasm and aggression were viewed warily by most outside the movement itself. On a hot July day in 1878, press criticism was levelled at two drummers who insisted on playing outside Trinity Church, Whitehaven, even though Canon Dalton was trying to deliver a sermon to their fellow Orangemen inside. This description of these two men illustrates both the exuberance of the musicians and the contempt in which they were often held:

> Two brethren, attached to as many drums, came to anchor near the Church, and, in their shirt sleeves, and with perspiration streaming down their faces, banged away manfully for nearly half an hour, with less regard to music and time than would have been needed for the gambols of a dancing bear. The object the performers seemed to have set themselves was to ascertain which of them could deliver the greatest number of strokes per minute on the drum. The din, added to by innumerable other big drums, the shrill squeaking of a legion of 'wry-necked fifes', and the blare of two or three brass

bands, each playing a separate 'tune', if one may so style it, made up a row that was indescribable. ... [24]

Apart from the threat posed by loud music, the greatest potential risk of violence came from indulgence in drink. Many Orangemen claimed to be totally abstemious; indeed, the word 'temperance' featured on the banners of many lodges. Yet the leadership still felt the need to exhort the rank and file not to be drunk. Despite these appeals, drinking remained popular, as was the case in 1887 when there were 'conspicuous and numerous instances of intemperance, in which females appeared to be no one whit behind the sterner sex'.[25] On the same occasion, the chairman of the Orange event, Joseph Stephenson, berated the disorderly element. 'All this cussing and swearing and the abuse of intoxicating drinks', he said, 'were forbidden by their rules'; thus, 'it was only by the neglect of these rules that their Order was disgraced'. The Worshipful Master of Distington area, Bro. Elliot, agreed with Stephenson, stating that 'It hurt ... when he saw men putting regalias on them, and staggering in and out of public-houses'.[26] There was, then, a clear tension between the imbibers and abstainers, though the former were more influential in many aspects of Cumbrian street culture.

Much of the violence of these parades was anticipated by members. Marchers often carried weapons which, though mostly for show, were found to be effective when skirmishes broke out. Swords, pikes, spears and firearms were common; and, though their pistols were usually charged with blanks, at least one death, and countless wounds, were caused by gun-fire in this period. Even the more passive members were usually prepared for a fist-fight. An interesting insight into the prevailing attitudes is provided by the account of a journalist who travelled to one march with a train-load of lodgemen and their wives. It was July 1885, and, with memories of the Cleator Moor debacle still fresh in their minds, the Orangemen were preparing themselves for any eventuality, talking at length about the 'prospect of a "go in"':

> One of the processionists (a fine looking specimen of the British workman) ... was of the opinion that the Orangemen should be armed with police batons, simply as weapons of defence, of course, and, in a way which was not altogether agreeable to his fellow passengers, he illustrated how a man might by this means be placed hors de combat with the minimum of exertion.

The same reporter told how one woman, with a child of six in her company, was 'probably more foolish than mischievous' when she 'hoped there would be a "jolly good row"'.[27]

In the 1870s, the Orange platform was dominated by clerics such as the Rev. G.B. Armes and the Rev F.W. Wickes, who saw Orangeism mainly in denominational terms. They spoke habitually on matters such as ritualism in the Church of England, or in denouncing the influence of Roman Catholicism. The Orangemen, for whom the rhetoric of open-air addresses was a highlight of the parade, cheered with great pride any attempt to expose Anglo-Catholic priests in the locality or any slur on the Catholic faith. However, a change can be discerned in Cumbrian Orangeism from the early 1880s as the movement became more overtly political. With Parnell's home rule movement gathering momentum, Orangeism assumed a new political relevance. While priests still pounded their bibles, the lay leadership began to blend anti-Catholic rhetoric into the patriotic unionism and empire loyalism which was beginning to dominate proceedings. Cumbrian Orange big-wigs were thus playing a much more prominent role by trying to politicise the Order. The Liberal press was appalled by this new political edge to Orangeism, but the movement's new meaning continued to grow, with Tory politicians increasingly willing to climb on to the Orange stump to recruit supporters.

At every public meeting held by Cumbrian Orangemen, countless speakers swore their undying opposition to the Catholic Church; this tradition was long-living and continued to thrive even when political issues laid a far greater claim to Orange support. In this sense, Orangemen must be viewed as part of a fearsome tradition of British anti-Catholicism, which, as Norman says, 'though it had obvious points of similarity with European expressions of ideological objections to Catholic beliefs and practices, was quite unique'.[28] The roots of anti-Catholicism may have lain deep in the sixteenth century, but the 19th was clearly marked by developments which either awakened or hardened traditional Protestant fears. Orange speakers, who expounded remorselessly on the historic threat from Catholicism, occasionally displayed a bizarre view of history, disregarding the ideal of truth so acclaimed by the Orangemen. While addressing one gathering in 1882 a local worthy, Mr Huddleston, defended the Orangeman's increasing tendency to fuse politics and religion. He asked: 'What was Romanism if not political? Did they (the Romanists) not plan the Franco-German war, so that if they conquered Germany they would come over here and conquer us [?]'[29] By comparison, one history lesson for South

Furness Orangemen was positively enlightened: 'The Chairman referred to the great conflagration in London 200 years ago, which he said was the result of Jesuitical priestcraft, but after the fire London prospered more gloriously than before, and the Church of Rome, baffled in its efforts, began to decline'.[30]

Thus it was that the Orange Day celebrations were viewed by members to be more than just a colourful procession or a day out for the family. Orangeism had meaning, 'a grand idea underlying' which was 'made manifest in the whole'; members were Protestants, 'linked together in one true Protestant faith'.[31] Defence of this Protestantism was the great connection for Orangemen, and the parades and the open-air public meetings were meant to affirm their commitment to this cause; while in the event sinister references to their potential for violent resistance often emerged. Thus Rev. Armes told the Orangemen in 1875 that they were not fighting men, 'unless their country called them to fight'. However, he added, 'should their services ever be required – and he prayed to God that they never might – he had no doubt that "Derry", "Aughrim", "Enniskillen", and "The Boyne" would be fought over again with the same result'.[32] The celebration of the Boyne, Aughrim, Enniskillen and the siege of Derry was at least justified by virtue of their existence in fact but whether those victories actually saved Ireland 'from Popery, slavery, knavery, brass money, and wooden shoes', as one Orange speaker claimed, is altogether a more contentious question.[33]

Within the Orangeman's hatred of Catholicism, anti-sacerdotalism was central.[34] On countless occasions when clerics ascended to the Orange platform they were at pains to denounce the priest's role as intermediary for Christ and his people. Orange Protestants instead emphasised a direct link with Christ; a relationship mediated only by the true word of God.[35] Rev. Wickes of Whitehaven even went so far as to ascribe the existence of the British empire to an open bible. 'Look around on the vast extent of the British dominions', he exhorted the processionists:

> what had raised Britain until it was the admiration of the world? Some people might be ready to exclaim its arts, and its commerce, its manufactures, its wealth, and its intelligence, its army, and its navy, but the Christian would rather say, "Because it is the land of Bibles, because each for himself, from the prince to the peasant, may possess a copy of the Word of God". ... [36]

Catholic priests were the subject of regular attack by Orange speakers; in particular, their participation in confession was vehemently denounced. The alleged immorality of unmarried men, using the status conferred by the holy office, to quiz young married women about their marital relations was relayed repeatedly to eager Orange audiences. In the mid-Victorian years, a legion of popular Protestant lecturers toured areas of Irish settlement whipping up their audiences, including Orangemen, with sensationalised tales of the carnality of Catholicism. Such was the case with William Murphy's most infamous lecture, 'The Confessional Unmasked'. This piece of pure theatre saw Murphy and his partner, George MacKay, dress up as a priest and a young woman, before the former led the other to the confessional box and began to ask probing questions about 'her' sexual conduct within marriage. The end result was nearly always the same: huge jocularity or horror from Protestants in the hall; uproar and often violent denial from Catholics.[37] Playing on such emotions also ensured adulation for the small-fry of the Orange movement – men such as the Rev. Haslem of Whitehaven, who, at the gathering in 1878, attacked ritualism, monasteries and nunneries, advertised the published version of 'The Confessional Unmasked', and offered his support for any attempt to license confessionals. His words were met with cheers.[38]

While anti-Catholicism clearly defined Orange views of religion, it also shaped their view of temporal political matters. At one Orange march in 1880, William Sykes, a Preston Orangemen of provincial standing, expressed anger that an apostate Protestant, the Marquis of Ripon, should be appointed Viceroy of India. The remark earned a stern rebuke from a member of the Liberal press who witnessed the speech: 'A Catholic and a Dissenter, as Englishmen, have as much right to a civil appointment as have Protestants of the Establishment. Religious bigotry, sooner or later, must depart this life; but now and then we are reminded that some people of seventeenth century ideas are still in the flesh'.[39] Yet the movement was not ready to 'depart this life'; Orangeism was an important outlet for working-class political views, providing a distillation into clearer terms of their often ethereal and irrelevant historical vision. Orangemen upheld the Protestantism of the constitution and ardently defended the union, which thus led to a uniting of Orangemen and Tories in the home-rule period.

This political link expressed a sharper agenda than was implied by prosaic utterances in favour of the Protestant Ascendancy. By the

1880s, the language of the marching tradition was being used to offer straightforward political support for the Conservatives, as well as to denigrate popery. Figures such as Salisbury and Hartington became venerated as potential saviours of empire; allies who showed the same 'zealous watchfulness' over sacred British institutions as did the Orangemen; fellow warriors in the battle against 'Atheism, Socialism and Radicalism combined'.[40] The Orange demonstration at Cockermouth in July 1885 expressed contentment with the Disraelian bequest of 'Tory democracy', a 'spirited foreign policy' and the 'defence of empire'. By contrast, Gladstone was portrayed as a bumbling fool, 'Grand Old Muddles', and when one of the crowd shouted 'down with Gladstone', the Worshipful Master of the Harrington area quipped that he was already down, 'hanging his lip like a motherless foal'.[41]

There is no doubt that the great furore over political issues such as the franchise, church reform, and, of course, home rule, exercised Orangemen. Certainly, the events of 1886 and 1893 had great significance for the Orangemen of Cumbria. The marches reflected this by continuing to attract outside attention. The Liberal press remained sceptical as to the point of Orangeism, and had difficulty understanding how so many Irish and like-minded English could expend such energy on these anachronistic memorials to past events. Much more, however, the Liberal press was appalled by what it viewed as the shameless political hijacking of the movement. This extract captures the general mood well:

> is reverence for the scriptures, loyalty to the throne, and obedience to the laws of our country, confined to the Tories? He could be dubbed a bigot and ignoramus who answered the question in the affirmative. ... The Orange organisations have no right to palm off upon the people – under the guise of rejoicing at the historic victory of the Boyne – a bitter, bigoted and ignorant hatred of the Liberal Government and the whole Liberal Party of today ... Orangeism exists – or ought to – as the enduring symbol of a victory which secured us an open Bible, freedom from Papal authority, and a sovereign and constitution in accordance with the national will. But the demonstration last Saturday in Barrow, from beginning to end ... was devoted exclusively to a tirade against the Liberal Government and a laudation of Toryism, as thoroughly out of place and unsuited as would have been an exposition of the arguments for and against the Channel Tunnel.[42]

There is little doubt that the mood of the Orange Order and of its marches changed over time. The greatest modification came during the years when home rule dominated British politics. It was then that the movement had acquired a new political currency. Thereafter, much of this impetus faded away. This was due to a number of factors: in part, there was a declining interest in religious questions; and it must be remembered that most workers were, as Alan Lee has pointed out, in part in the context of Orangeism, largely indifferent to the claims of the churches.[43] In addition, Victorian 'popular' movements were not subscribed to by a 'majority', and, with migration falling away to a fraction of its former levels, inter-war Orangeism suffered according. A shrinking support meant that by the 1920s only 500 or so members were turning out on the 'Glorious Twelfth'. After home rule reached the statute book, Orangeism in Cumbria returned to its former position as an anachronistic and unyielding voice of the Protestant faith. Although Orangemen had opposed socialism since the 1880s, its anti-left rhetoric carried much less weight in the early twentieth century than pro-unionism had done at the end of the nineteenth.[44] Moreover, Orange leaders were ambiguous about the labour movement: on one occasion, for example, it was argued Orangemen could vote Labour, but not for the creed professed by the local Labour MPs, Cape and Gavan Duffy, 'because that was "rank Socialism", and they could not vote for Socialism'.[45] Perhaps members followed this advice and voted Tory? Many had done so since 1885 when new electoral powers had been bestowed on the urban working class. In truth, after the Great War Orangeism in Cumbria was too weak to have real political clout, as was shown by the election of Cape, Gavan Duffy and others.

Even in the 1880s, however, the strength of the Cumbria movement lay with its pageantry. And in the twentieth century, Orangemen continued to follow the ceremonial customs which made their forebears so noteworthy. The same rhetorical devices were employed with the same power; only the audiences were smaller. In July 1925 the Provincial Grand Master, Bro. Donnan, perhaps encapsulated the movement's return to an earlier form of religious evangelicalism with his sharp denunciation of the parish magazine of a local Anglican minister, R.H. Hawkins of Maryport. In an attack that echoed the concerns of militant Protestants in the previous century, Donnan lambasted Hawkins for offering the confessional to members of the Church of England. Donnan thought it disgraceful 'to have people holding such views in the Protestant Church.' Donnan was incensed that 'they were receiving Protestant pay and doing the work of the Church of Rome.

If they were honest in their belief', he continued, 'they could leave the Protestant Church, and like Cardinal Newman, go over to the Church of Rome'.[46] Such elements of Orangeism, it seems, were timeless.

Notes

1. Frank Neal, *Sectarian Violence: the Liverpool Experience, 1819–1914* (Manchester, 1988) is the principal study of English Orange traditions. See also his 'Manchester origins of the Orange Order', *Manchester Region History Review*, 4, 2 (1990–1), pp. 12–24; W.J. Lowe, *The Irish in Mid-Victorian Lancashire: the Making of a Working-Class Community* (New York, 1990), Ch. 6; D.M. MacRaild, *Culture, Conflict and Migration: the Irish in Victorian Cumbria* (Liverpool, 1997), Chs 5 and 6. For Scotland, see Elaine McFarland's chapter in this volume.
2. F.J. Devlin, letter, *Barrow Herald*, 10 June 1893.
3. *Barrow Herald*, 19 July 1879.
4. Neal, *Sectarian Violence*, pp. 17, 21, 30–31.
5. *Select Committee Report on Orange Institutions in Great Britain and the Colonies* (1835).
6. *Report on Orange Institution*, Appendix 19; Neal, 'Manchester origins', table 2, p. 19.
7. For more on this, see D.M. MacRaild, 'Culture, Conflict and Labour Migration: Victorian Cumbria's Ulster connection', *Saothar*, 21 (1996).
8. McFarland, *Protestants First*, p. 71. Neal, *Sectarian Violence*, pp. 70–2, 184.
9. For Murphy's short but active career, see W.L. Arnstein, 'The Murphy Riots: a Victorian dilemma', *Victorian Studies*, 19, 1 (1975); Donald C. Richter, *Riotous Victorians* (Athens, Ohio, 1981), pp. 34–49. For his Cumbrian sojourn, see MacRaild, *Culture, Conflict and Migration*.
10. *Whitehaven Herald*, 13 July 1872; CRO Carlisle, CQ/PW/8 contains magistrates' correspondences concerning Murphy's visit.
11. *Barrow Herald*, 15 July 1882.
12. *Whitehaven Herald*, 16 July 1874.
13. Ibid., 14 July 1877.
14. See *Carlisle Express*, 26 July, 1884; MacRaild, *Culture, Conflict and Migration*. 'Cleator Moor Co-operative', Carlisle Library local history collection: 1B9 CLE339; see also CRO Carlisle, CQ/PW/9.
15. The best attempt to theorise Orangeism, in terms of membership and their aspirations, is McFarland, *Protestants First: Orangeism in 19th-Century Scotland* (Edinburgh, 1990), Chs 2 and 5.
16. *Whitehaven News*, 15 July 1875.
17. Ibid., 16 July 1885.
18. Ibid., 18 July 1878.
19. Ibid., 18 July 1878.
20. Ibid., 17 July 1887.
21. Ibid., 17 July 1884.
22. Ibid., 17 July 1884.

Donald M. MacRaild 59

23. *Barrow Herald*, 19 July 1880.
24. *Whitehaven News*, 18 July 1878.
25. Ibid., 14 July 1887.
26. Ibid., 14 July 1887.
27. Ibid., 16 July 1885.
28. E.R. Norman, *Anti-Catholicism in Victorian England* (London 1968), p. 20. The historiography of Victorian anti-Catholicism is too great to recount here. A good starting point is Paz, *Anti-Catholicism in Mid-Victorian England* (Stanford, Cal., 1992) which contains a rich bibliography.
29. *Barrow Herald*, 15 July 1882.
30. Rev. J.B. McKenzie, chairman of the Askam Orange Day celebrations in 1877. *Barrow Herald*, 12 July 1877. This mixing of anti-Catholicism and history was an age-old formula. See, for example, J.A. Sharpe *Early Modern England: a Social History, 1550–1760* (London, 1987), p. 1.
31. *Whitehaven News*, 18 July 1884.
32. Ibid., 15 July 1875.
33. Ibid., 14 July 1884.
34. This point is illustrated by G.F.A. Best, 'Popular Protestantism in Victorian Britain', in R. Robson (ed.), *Ideas and Institutions of Victorian Britain* (London, 1967), pp. 115–142.
35. *Barrow Herald*, 13 July 1883.
36. *Whitehaven News*, 15 July 1874.
37. Norman, *Anti-Catholicism*, p. 13; Arnstein, 'Murphy Riots'; MacRaild, *Culture Conflict and Migration*, Ch. 6.
38. *Whitehaven News*, 18 July 1878.
39. *Barrow Herald*, 13 July 1880. Ripon was received into Catholic communion in September 1874. See *Concise DNB*, III, p. 2556.
40. *Whitehaven News*, 16 July 1885.
41. Ibid., 16 July 1885.
42. *Barrow Herald*, 18 July 1884.
43. Alan Lee, 'Conservatism, traditionalism and the British working class, 1880–1918' in D.E. Martin and D. Rubinstein (eds), *Ideology and the Labour Movement: Essays Presented to John Saville* (London, 1979), pp. 90–1.
44. Anti-socialist language was especially prominent during the 1906 election campaign. See, for example, the words of Sir Charles Cayzer, Conservative MP for Barrow: *Barrow Herald*, 6 January 1906. He was defeated by the Labour Party's Charlie Duncan.
45. *Cumberland News*, 18 July 1925. The struggles of the Order were similar elsewhere in the 1920s. See, for example, an excellent study of the Scottish dimensions: Graham Walker, 'The Orange Order in Scotland Between the Wars', *International Journal of Social History*, 37, 2, 1992.
46. *Cumberland News*, 18 July 1925.

4

Marching from the Margins: Twelfth July Parades in Scotland, 1820–1914

Elaine McFarland

While struggling to map the 'post-modern condition', social theorists have increasingly discovered space, not as an innocent background, but as 'an active constituent component of hegemonic power – the medium and the message of domination and subordination'.[1] Social and cultural life is now shaped, it is argued, by the logic of spatial organisation rather than time and to the fluidity of spatial is contrasted identities entailed in this process is contrasted the fixity of 'pre-modern' identities, typically founded on religion.[2]

This conceptual framework may assist its exponents in grasping the variety of new social relations, but its apparent novelty should not obscure the reality that spatial consciousness has a much longer and less rarefied pedigree across a range of social groups and quite independent of academic discourse. Indeed, this chapter will analyse a particularly robust and populist 'pre-modern' example of *overlapping* spatial and religious identities: namely, the history of Orange parading in Scotland.

As Orangemen in Scotland were to become conscious during the course of the nineteenth century and beyond, claiming physical space entailed also claiming political and ideological space. This was at a premium for a struggling politico-religious organisation whose members were largely working class migrants from the counties of Ulster.[3] The primary mechanism which developed in order to assert their claims was that of public display. A range of options were available from celebrations of Orange anniversaries, such as the Battle of the Diamond and the relief of Derry, to Orange church and funeral processions, but, above all, it was the Twelfth of July Boyne commemoration parade which became the preferred mode of public ceremony. This was mainly due to the event's overwhelming symbolic value: for it was the Boyne victory, argued the Orangemen, which had guaranteed them the freedom of public meeting and by implication the very right to march. In Scotland, these parades underwent a significant evolution during the nineteenth century. They began in the early 1820s with sporadic, small-scale and poorly disciplined processions often attended by faction fighting. By the 1870s they had become carefully choreographed mass public rituals, winding through the main thoroughfares of the West of Scotland's towns and cities.

We can distinguish three levels on which these events operated. First, just as the lodges themselves served as a familiar rallying point for migrants at a time of social and economic dislocation, parades offered a public opportunity to reaffirm group solidarity and to celebrate the shared values and continuity of lodge membership. Thus Twelfth celebrations offered an alternative definition of place, as 'working class slums' became 'Orange bastions' ... at least for one day of the year.

Yet, the identity asserted on these occasions also had a second, more negative dimension, requiring the preservation of the rights and custom against outsiders and unwanted social change. In practice, this entailed the maintenance of territorial and political ascendancy in the face of the hereditary enemy: Roman Catholics. As the official historians of Orangeism illustrate, this entailed an acute spatial awareness:

> What mattered to the ordinary man was to be able to feel that his own position and those of his family were secure. ... Where you could walk you were dominant and the other things followed.[4]

While these traditional concerns continued to animate the rank and file Orangeman, Orange leaders grew increasingly anxious to use Twelfth parades to gain access to the mainstream of Scottish society and politics by a display of the Order's numerical power and respectability. American social historians have already illustrated the processes by which marginal groups have used similar 'public dramas' to comment on prevailing urban-industrial relations and to press for participation on their own terms.[5] The peculiar challenge for Orangemen in Scotland was that they did not wish to recognise their marginality. Instead, they considered themselves fully entitled to a share in the dominant culture and value system by reason of their common Protestantism and loyalty to the Crown Their response produced a unique mixture of resistance and triumphalism which could not conceal their continuing failure, despite mass mobilisation, to become 'a power in the land'.

Orangeism in Scotland had a quiet and inauspicious beginning as a spontaneous offshoot from its Irish parent body.[6] The first lodges were introduced by militia regiments returning from service in the 1798 United Irishmen's Rebellion, but it is likely that many of the original Orangemen were themselves Ulster migrants, notably weavers and small craftsmen whose independence had been eroded in the Province's north-eastern counties. This group were instrumental in establishing lodges in the early Scottish Orange centres of Ayrshire and the South West.

Initial growth between 1800 and 1820 was not prodigious, but a definite expansion of Orangeism took place as the lodges reached Glasgow and Lanarkshire, again with significant Ulster involvement.[7] Early lodges seem to have functioned as ex-servicemen's clubs and benefit societies, and it took until 1821 until their members felt sufficiently confident to introduce Scotland to their practice of 'Grand Orange Processions'. In practice, these were less than impressive. Only three lodges took part in the first ceremonial parade through the principal streets of Glasgow when they were roughly handled by Catholic Irish spectators and taken into protective custody.[8] The pattern of confrontation was repeated the following year with a turnout of 127 lodge members, supplemented by female supporters, but subsequent parades were cancelled and no public Orange processions seem to have been held in Glasgow until the 1840s.[9] Meanwhile, the focus shifted to other centres of Irish migration. In the later 1820s and early 1830s serious party disturbances around the Twelfth occurred at Newton Stewart, Dumfries and Dalkeith, Airdrie and Port Glasgow. Already the idea of combat was becoming routinised so that the cessation of actual parading did not mean the absence of violent outbreaks. The display of sashes from the windows of lodge rooms was now enough to provoke a large-scale riot.[10]

Although the purpose of the original parades was ostensibly, 'to collect money for the distressed Irish', these concealed a less charitable purpose. In holding public processions, the Orangemen were not only celebrating the shared traditions and mythologies of their own migrant community, they were also seeking to impose a familiar sense of 'order' on their new surroundings by regulating relations between Protestants and Catholics in the interests of the former. Marching became a symbolic instrument for asserting Protestant power at a local level, with the display of regalia, cockades, sashes and scarfs and the route of march itself expressing the Orangemen's determination to resist perceived threats. Music also played an important role. Before the relatively sanitised 'Sash My Father Wore' or 'Derry's Walls', the most popular and provocative party tunes were 'Boyne Water' and 'Croppies Lie Down', the strains of which were the catalyst for many a Twelfth fracas in Scotland, especially when played near Catholic chapels which represented the most visible symbols of their opponents' residential concentration.[11]

However, the Scottish context was to present the Orangemen with a complex set of problems in attempting to reassert their traditional 'rights'. No longer were their actions a matter of restating an unwritten *status quo* of Protestant ascendancy, but instead involved staking out *new* territory. For migration had entailed, as Hesse comments, 'a dynamic and uneven social process, carrying with it a sense of coming to terms with conditions and experiences, about settling what is contested and what is accepted: settling up and settling down'.[12]

In the first place, Protestant migrants had to grasp that they were only one part of a large-scale population movement from Ireland, outnumbered by as many as three or four to one by their Catholic countrymen.[13] In addition, the localities into which the Irish had settled were burgeoning industrial and urban centres which resembled frontier towns. In areas such as Coatbridge and Airdrie in Lanarkshire residential segregation along ethnic and religious lines was well underway from the 1820s, but the physical boundaries of the opposing communities were still fluid and contested. In these circumstances, the Orangemen's traditional opponents were far from a cowed minority and collisions along the districts encompassed by marching routes were almost inevitable. Indeed, as Campbell points out, the more the Irish became absorbed into the mining labour force in Lanarkshire by mid-century, the more the county gained a reputation for Orange and Green disputes.[14] On 12 July 1854, for example, an Orange procession was held at Airdrie, causing the Catholic Irish of the district to feel aggrieved and ' … determined to be avenged at the first opportunity.' This came the following morning with an attack on an Orange band playing 'party tunes', resulting in charges of rioting and murder.[15] Similarly, in July 1857, 300 Coatbridge Orangemen, returning from an Orange parade, were attacked and routed by a Catholic mob.[16] As a result, public Orange demonstrations were banned in the Lanarkshire for the next ten years. The Sheriffs of the industrial counties of Ayr and Renfrew where similar violent outbreaks swiftly followed suit.[17]

This decisive official response suggests that it was not simply at the level of the local community that Orangemen faced an unfavourable balance of power in their country of adoption. Magistrates, the judiciary and the police in Scotland generally maintained a stubbornly independent attitude towards sectarian disturbances: the Glasgow police, for example, were actually hailed by 'great Irish cheers' on their removal of a King Billy placard from a local tavern during the 1848 Twelfth celebrations.[18] This stance contrasted with the alleged handling of the Orangemen by the Dublin police, 'the whole of which, officers and men are composed of the Orange Party, and with the reputed partiality towards the lodges shown by the authorities in Liverpool, the Order's other major area of importation in Britain.[19]

To a large extent, this official neutrality stemmed from the widespread distrust the authorities felt towards *all* popular processions, which were universally suspected of concealing criminal purposes.[20] In order to regulate these Scotland had no blanket equivalent of the 1850 Party Processions Act. Instead, the Scottish legal system had bequeathed a haphazard set of controls, originating from the seventeenth century. The basic problem was one of maintaining public order, and when the criminal proceedings *post factum* which had been been employed in the 1820s and 1830s failed to contain the escalation of Party violence, legal prohibition and its energetic enforcement became the norm. Accordingly in July 1859 when the Sheriff of Lanarkshire issued his annual proclamation banning Twelfth processions, this was underlined by the deployment of 100 policemen, armed with cutlasses, at Coatbridge and Moodiesburn. They kept in constant contact with the Glasgow force who for their part similarly prevented a planned Orange steamer excursion to Ayr.[21]

The efficiency and zeal of magistrates and police officers in checking Orange demonstrations was also praised repeatedly in the Scottish press, who from the outset of parading in Scotland had proclaimed their own variation of contemptuous impartiality, 'deprecating all assemblies which tend to agitate the public mind and rouse Party feelings', and also highlighting the lowly social origins and 'alien' quality of the processionists.[22] As the *Glasgow Courier* commented in July 1849, 'these Party displays, which however well meant, were not for this latitude. They are importations as unwelcome as many of the Irish themselves'.[23]

In short, after more than thirty years, Orangeism in Scotland had gained a high, but hardly enviable, public profile. Essentially a clear gulf had opened up by mid-century between the Orangemen's self image as 'Faith Defenders' and the lowly status they held in literate Scottish opinion. The latter was in no doubt that Twelfth parades represented merely 'the rag-tag and bob-tail and all the haughty honours of rampant Orangeism'.[24]

The 1860s was a decade of mixed fortunes for the Orange Institution in Scotland. The organisation witnessed rapid numerical expansion, although its centres of growth remained firmly rooted in Glasgow and the West of Scotland.[25] As the Order itself realised, these developments reflected less the sudden recruitment of native Scots, but rather an accelerating labour migration from Ulster.[26]

In a recent reassessment of this migration drawing on late-nineteenth-century census material, Foster has suggested that the employment which these migrants found on Clydeside had a larger semi-skilled or unskilled basis than has commonly been supposed.[27] While wages for skilled work in Belfast were approximately the same as those on Clydeside, unskilled wages remained at less than 60 per cent of the Glasgow level up until the Great War.[28] Protestant skilled workers thus had little inclination to test Scottish labour markets where sectarian leverage was not automatic, but unskilled workers, both Protestant and Catholic, had sound financial incentives. Indeed, this would have been particularly the case for Catholics with shipyard experience.

This surprising confluence between the social and occupational fates of the Protestant and Catholic Irish may in turn indicate an instrumental undercurrent in the expansion of Orange membership. Irish Protestant workers, apparently indistinguishable to potential employers from their Catholic counterparts, struggled to maximise their position in local labour markets, using local systems of influence, such as lodge membership. As in Belfast, where the Order sought to defend particular localities and simultaneously control niche labour markets, these processes also had a significant geographical dimension. As Lobban suggests for the Greenock case, the residential concentration of both Protestants and Catholics mirrored their monopolies of local semi and unskilled employment.[29] From Foster's study this pattern may be of wider applicability with Protestants less likely to live in Dumbarton and Clydebank and more likely to live in Partick, Linthouse (Govan), Kinning Park and Plantation in Glasgow.[30] This strategy may indeed have trapped Irish Protestants into a pattern of enclave employment, presenting similar problems of wider social assimilation as those experienced by Irish Catholics.

There was not only a continuation in marginal status of lodge members in the 1860s, the Order as an organisation also suffered persistent official and popular disapproval in Scotland. Public Twelfth processions were annually proscribed, the Glasgow Police still regarding both these and rumoured St Patrick's Day demonstrations with an even-handed distaste.[31] Even during the period of the Fenian alarms in 1867, a proposed march in Glasgow to commemorate the Manchester Martyrs aroused anxiety, not only on the grounds that is was 'an insulting Fenian demonstration', but because it threatened to provoke 'a retributive display' by 4000 Orangemen, bringing 'the excitable elements of a faction fight, destructing to the peace of the city ... seething before the eyes of the authorities'.[32]

These circumstances presented the leadership of the Orange Institution in Scotland with a difficult dilemma. On the one hand, inactivity was a curse for the Order, as the Orange 'psyche' needed to be on the defensive against the physical and ideological threats of Popery. Indoor celebrations of the Twelfth did not compensate for the pageantry and pugnacity of parading, the result being a faltering of lodges even in areas of previous strength, such as Airdrie and Maybole.[33] Alternatively, the Greenock lodges responded by catching the Belfast Mail Steamer to enjoy the celebrations which were held in Ulster in defiance of the Party Processions and Party Emblems Acts.[34] Maintaining internal discipline was a further concern. The Orange leadership was legitimated by its ability to maintain a vigorous public profile for Orangeism in the face of legal restrictions. Failure in this regard was liable to lead to charges of 'lukewarm Protestantism' from a restive rank and file and an acceleration of the dissention and schism which were already characteristic of both Scottish Orangeism and the Irish nationalist movement in the 1860s.[35]

On the other hand, to encourage public parades contrary to the law, especially if these followed the combative form of the 1840s and 1850s, would carry severe penalties. Furthermore, such a strategy ran contrary to a much grander vision of the place of Orangeism in Scottish society which Grand Lodge leaders were coming to entertain. This vision had two main components, the balance between them shifting with successive Grand Masters. The first was to establish a rejuvenated Order as an agent of moral improvement and Protestant evangelism. The second was to win for Orangeism the social and political clout which its leaders felt its numerical strength and proven loyalty entitled it.

The tactics employed to realise this vision and resolve the broader dilemma revolved precisely around the formalising and ordering of Orange public activity. Twelfth processions were to be tightly controlled by the Order's leadership and internal boards of enquiry swiftly instituted to investigate possible allegations of 'Orange rowdyism'.[36] Far from being 'merely recruiting parties' as Grand Lodge leaders publicly claimed, the mass demonstrations which resulted were designed to impress old enemies and new allies alike by their display of growing Orange strength and above all by their 'respectability', an ethos which had a powerful resonance in Scottish society.[37] Ironically, these efforts were paralleled by the attempts of Catholic migrants in various locations to present to the host society a similar illustration of the power and influence of their church and community through the medium of St Patrick's Day parades and *Corpus Christi* processions.[38] In Glasgow, too, the Irish National Association, pledged to raising the standing of the Irish Catholic community in the city, embarked in 1865 on the first of series of processions and excursions, displaying to all their capacity for 'good humour and rational enjoyment'.[39]

Before this reinvented parading 'tradition' could be put into practice, the main task for the Orangemen was to win permission from the authorities to march. The Grand Lodge accomplished this during the course of the late 1860s by convincing magistrates that they were willing both to exercise responsibility and restraint over the issue of public processions. In July 1868, for example, no prohibition of Twelfth parades was necessary as the Grand Lodge gave the Glasgow magistrates their solemn assurance that no procession would take place, while the following year they, 'discouraged promenading and outward manifestations on the Twelfth, so that none of the brethren might come into collision with their hereditary enemies'.[40] The Order was also assisted here by a growing willingness on the part of the authorities to recognise public processions in general as legitimate forms of collective activity and expression, as the balance of legal and press opinion swung away from prohibition and back towards the *post factum* punishment in the event of a breach of the peace: for, as the *Glasgow News* argued, to act otherwise 'could be to throw doubt on the liberties of the British Constitution ... '[41]

Having displayed ability in policing its own members, the Order gained its reward on 12 July 1872 when a mass public parade was at last held in Glasgow:

> Arrangements made by the heads of the Orange party evidenced so strong a desire for order that the authorities deemed it inadvisable to interfere and they only stipulated that the place of assemblage and the route of march should be kept strictly private and no party tunes be played in the street.[42]

These stipulations on privacy and party tunes soon fell into abeyance and Glasgow was soon to prove itself as the ideal 'walking city', often featuring as the centrepiece for Orange celebrations. Its central core was compressed within a single square mile and offered a grid of open streets containing a mix of commercial and residential activity which could easily be filled and dominated by Orange symbols and music.[43] The disruption to the daily flow of urban life was maximised up until 1886 by the practice of holding Twelfth parades on the actual anniversary rather than the nearest Saturday.[44] Indeed, for some commentators their city was too well suited to such purposes, having 'long endured the windings of many demonstrations through her seats, Home Rule, Rome Rule, Trade Rule, Orange Rule and No Rule at all ....'[45]

Just as they combined festivity with a definite sense of purpose, the Orange demonstrations claimed both elements of carnival, an all-embracing public spectacle, and more formalised ritual procession, designed for observation rather than participation.[46] In this way, the parade of lodges led by their officers and accompanied by their banners, flags and regalia, was regularly accompanied by a throng of spectators and supporters whose unappealing aspect seldom failed to raise comment from a hostile press: in 1881, the *Glasgow Herald* noted that the parade in Glasgow was watched by, 'a large crowd of East Enders, principally mill girls, loafers desirous of a little mild excitement and [the] slatternly-looking who made the affair an excuse for neglecting their household duties'.[47]

These events required considerable logistical skill from their organisers. During the 1870s and 1880s, the Glasgow contingent of lodges alone mustered around 4000 members.[48] The format of the demonstrations was also fairly complex and made full use of developments of the transport infrastructure in the West of Scotland. A 'Grand Demonstration' would be held at a location specified by the Grand Lodge, originally at Glasgow Green, but later at various semi-rural locations outside the city. This arrangement, coupled with the fact that the Twelfth fell on or near Glasgow Fair Friday, contributed to the holiday atmosphere. All over the West of Scotland feeder demonstrations took place, numbering over a dozen in some years, with lodge members mustering and marching through the main streets of their respective towns to railway stations or, in the case of Clyde Coast towns, steamer embarkation points. Orange ranks also contained 'a large proportion of women', who 'were not behind their companions in their decorations. ... '[49] Arriving at their destination, they were addressed by a range of Grand Lodge speakers and their guests. The *Glasgow Herald* dismissed these platforms with pithy contempt:

Fervid orators extolled the memory of their pet prince, praised the Protestant Ascendancy, harped on the old story – ever welcome to the ears of the Orangemen – of 'the Boyne' and sang the 'the praises of the Boys of 'Derry', pitched mercilessly into Gladstone and the Pope, panegyrised the Conservative leadership of Salisbury and sound government'.[50]

After the initial novelty of being permitted to parade had passed in the early 1870s, Twelfth attendance was liable to fluctuate, albeit around an impressive baseline of 15–20 000. Not even the efficient arrangements of the Grand Lodge could escape the ravages of a Scottish July. Turnout also tended to reflect local economic downturns, hardly surprising given the Order's occupational profile.[51] In contrast, in periods of political tension the 'right to march' seems to have regained its symbolic power. In 1886, the year of the first Home Rule Bill, a markedly increased complement marched from Glasgow to Cowlairs and 57 lodges rallied at Motherwell.[52] The impetus again returned with the 1892 Home Rule Bill, the demonstration of that year being 'one of the most imposing ever to take place', with the procession to Govan over one mile long.[53] Turnout initially faltered in the new century, but in 1902, 25 000 celebrated the Twelfth in Edinburgh and as the third Home Rule crisis gathered momentum in 1912, a record 40 000 gathered at Coatbridge. Special trains brought in contingents from Glasgow, Paisley, Greenock, Port Glasgow, Dalry, Kilbirnie, Falkirk, Coatbridge and Prestonpans and the procession, including juvenile lodges for the first time, was accompanied by 74 bands and took two and a half hours to pass a given point.[54]

Clearly, by the beginning of the twentieth century, it would appear that the nature of Orange activity had shifted decisively from street fighting to mass public ritual. What is less certain is whether the sheer numbers on display in Twelfth parades would be sufficient to transcend the Order's marginal status in Scottish society. Capturing public thoroughfares, as John Berger has indicated, may confirm to participants a common purpose and opportunity, but also represents a 'temporary stage on which they dramatise the power they still lack'.[55]

In order to convince Scottish public opinion that Orangeism was 'pure Protestantism in action', the organisation's well-established reputation for collective lawlessness had still to be countered. Here the Grand Lodge met with qualified success. The closely marshalled parades of the late nineteenth century and beyond, using the 'neutral' civic space of major Scottish cities and towns, were generally of 'the most reputable and orderly character'.[56] The Order's reward was a modest, but growing representation from clerical visitors and Conservative luminaries, such as William Whitelaw MP, who granted the Order the use of their land for demonstrations and even spoke in support of resolutions prepared by the Grand Lodge.[57]

Yet, the day still retained its potential for violent confrontation. Rather than city centre thoroughfares, the flashpoints were residential areas along the line of feeder marches. While morning parades were usually conducted in a restrained and orthodox fashion, the danger came when lodges were returning homewards after the 'Grand Demonstration'. As in the 1840s and 1850s, Lanarkshire remained particularly tense around the Twelfth. A typically severe outbreak in Motherwell followed in 1886 when the Orangemen marching back to their lodge rooms were followed by a large crowd, largely female, with free fights and stone throwing breaking out.[58] These scenes were repeated the next year when the Motherwell Orangemen were assailed with shouts of 'Down with Billy' on passing the local chapel. The arrival of a Catholic contingent from Coatbridge increased the excitement when they tore down Orange lilies and trampled them underfoot. A riot was only prevented by means of a mounted police charge.[59]

In Glasgow confrontations tended to be on a smaller scale, but the areas of Ulster Protestant concentration, Govan, Kinning Park and Partick, were particularly sensitive.[60] Boundaries seem to have been fairly well defined by the end of the nineteenth century and a web of unspoken 'understandings' between neighbouring Protestant and Catholic communities on issues of territory and unacceptable provocation managed to keep trouble at bay for most of the year. These agreements were, however, delicately balanced and could be broken by attempts to assert local power by testing the right to march, especially if such attempts coincided with periods of political conflict on a national level, such as the home rule crises. Observers noted that tension began to mount as July approached as these areas became 'perfect Bedlams' or 'pocket versions of Hades', 'with the beating of the big drum and the screeching of flutes'.[61] Partick Cross, a Catholic enclave amongst an otherwise Orange stronghold, was often a battleground, given the Govan Orangemen insistence on crossing by ferry and marching to and from the city centre using this route.[62] Trouble on these occasions continued to be kept in check by prompt and impartial official action, although the legal situation regarding public processions still remained patchy and confused despite the Burgh

Police (Scotland) Act 1892 which gave magistrates in some areas the power to prohibit or regulate demonstrations.[63]

The persistence of sporadic physical violence suggests the relevance which the original functions of the Twelfth processions as expressions of solidarity and supremacy continued to hold for rank and file Orangeism. Less socially distanced from ordinary members than the Irish Grand Lodge and with a predominantly lower middle class and artisan component, the Scottish leadership may have grasped this, but this did not prevent them from using Twelfth platforms in an attempt to transform individual members' behaviour in line with their quest for respectable status.[64] Of special concern was the prospect of drunkenness among their membership, a popular stereotype in Scotland that 'the Orangeman anywhere is seldom a teetotaller and a tipsy Orangeman is nothing if not provocative'.[65] Accordingly, the brethren were counselled that 'they would not be worse Orangemen on account of total abstinence of intoxicating drinks' and that therefore they were bound to end the day in a peaceable and orderly manner and do nothing that would injure the Cause ... '[66]

As to the success of this reform programme, it is interesting to note that at the very Twelfth celebrations at which the latter exhortations were made, 'some black sheep were observed slipping away from the ranks and making tracks, early in the day as it was, for convenient public houses and a few others demonstrated by their conduct that they had been imbibing earlier'.[67] Indeed, it was to be a constant of Twelfth demonstrations for the next thirty years and beyond that only some two to three hundred stalwarts gathered around the platform for the 'speechifying' while the great majority preferred more conventional holiday pursuits. The extent to which drink continued to play a part in Twelfth festivities may also explain why trouble was most likely on the lodges' *return* journeys. Understandably perhaps, leaders such as Grand Master, George McLeod, were 'not particularly fond of such gatherings' and preferred their own alcohol-free Fifth of November soirées which were enthusiastically promoted during the 1870s and 1880s, but were less enthusiastically received by their members.

The Grand Lodge's concern to move with order and respectability was only one element in their strategy to nudge Orangeism into the centre of Scottish life. They were in no doubt that in this respect they were mainly claiming their historic due, growing increasingly frustrated when others failed to recognise the common ground between the anti-papal element in Scottish history and the events surrounding the Glorious Revolution and the Williamite campaign in Ireland on which their own movement was based. As William Johnston of Ballykilbeg sympathised with his Greenock audience:

> In Scotland you are misunderstood and misrepresented, you are spoken of as though you were a mere Irish faction, a foreign import brought to disturb the peace of the country. You are no such thing. If you were rightly understood and your principles looked into you would soon be found to be the true apostolic descendents of John Knox. If other people have forgot the contest waged in Scotland for an Open Bible, the Orangemen have not forgotten it.[68]

There existed various barriers to reducing the 'alien' quality of Orangemen in Scotland, not least the fact, acknowledged by Johnstone, that the Order *was* essentially an Irish movement in terms of history, membership and political identification. Successive Twelfth demonstrations, however impressive and well-organised, could do little to diminish this perception or indeed Orangeism's generally lowly public reputation.

Relationships with the Scottish press also remained difficult. As marches became more routinised in the late 1880s and 1890s so did newspaper coverage, with prospects for grouse on the other 'Glorious Twelfth' raising more journalistic excitement than the Orangemen's activities. These 'pageants of the proletariat' were now noted in a quizzical fashion which continued to stress the 'curiously Irish' and 'densely ignorant'.[69] Yet this dismissive tolerance lasted only as long as the Twelfth remained peaceable. When in 1898 disturbances flared in Glasgow for the first time in over a decade, as returning processionists deviated from the prescribed line of march and 'trespassed' into a Catholic residential pocket, the *Glasgow Herald* moved onto a furious attack which transcended its own anti-home rule sentiments:

> In this age of banished shibboleths and growing commonsense, it is remarkable how tenaciously certain bigots cling to outworn superstitions and idiotic prejudices. The cult of Orangeism may be truthfully said to have become the laughing stock of sensible Britons … In recent years the thing has become utterly effete and ridiculous, dwindling to a mere rabble of roughs and children with a fringe of women in the attire of faded Orange and Protestant heroes.[70]

When set beside this unfavourable public image, the growing numbers of churchmen and politicians willing to appear on Twelfth platforms may seem paradoxical. Yet, these new 'alliances' were in themselves evidence of the structural constraints which continued to operate on Orangeism in a Scottish setting. In the case of the churches, while the Order did have its clerical enthusiasts these formed a minority amongst their colleagues, and were often themselves Ulstermen and thus already familiar with Orangeism on its home ground. More commonly, those Scottish clergymen who wished contact with the Orangemen preferred the sedate November soirées to the rumbustious Twelfth, but saw in the massed ranks of the latter an opportunity for much-needed missionary activity. To some extent, this distance simply reflected clerical distaste at Orangeism's arrogant claims to be superior to mere competing denominational interests which sat uneasily with the unsavoury reputation of the lodges. However, it was also indicative of more complex disjunctures between the ecclesiastical situations of Ireland and Scotland which denied the Orangemen an automatic welcome in either the Episcopalian counterpart of the Church of Ireland or in the Presbyterian Church of Scotland.[71]

The public rapprochement with Conservative party figures was perhaps a more genuine phenomenon. From the 1860s, the Order's political relationships had been uneven and often tense. Orangemen did have a high public profile as Conservative 'footsoldiers' in key wards at election time, but this grassroots presence was not translated into meaningful representation on the party's directing bodies. By the 1890s, the new generation of Conservatives, impressed by the sheer numbers the Order could turn out on the Twelfth, were less squeamish about recognising Orange support, identifying less with the Order's pejorative associations in Scotland and more with its role in Ireland as an effective popular bulwark against home rule.[72] While the higher public visibility of such politicians was to some extent matched by increased Orange involvement on Conservative committees, these developments were still localised in the Order's traditional strongholds where, it was argued, they could best do their duty by turning out the working class vote. Essentially, the Orangemen were only one of a series of valuable interest groups amid the Conservative Party's general expansion and growth in confidence from the late nineteenth century. Crucially, this expansion was insufficient to reverse the pervasive hegemony of Liberalism in Scotland, so that the political force which the Order sought out as an ally was itself compromised in its quest for power.

To conclude, after almost a century of parading in Scotland the Orangemen were still struggling to claim a space for themselves in the social and political mainstream. Yet, arguably, mass demonstrations *were* successful on their own terms. Not only have they survived from the 1870s with their basic format intact, but the number of marches in Scotland has continued to expand, with over 1500 during the parading calendar in the Strathclyde area alone, increasingly raising problems of policing costs rather than public order.[73] Again, this may suggest that the traditional focus of the parades as a visual expression of contested terrain and community power have proved more robust than any grander ambitions which the Orange leadership sought to impose on them. As a current member of the Order expressed it: Orange walks represent, 'the mass anniversary of what we can do against Catholics'.[74] Indeed, such has been the strength of territory as a focus for Orange identity, that links with historic strongholds such as Bridgeton in Glasgow have survived sixty years of slum clearance and comprehensive redevelopment, with dispersed populations returning yearly to celebrate the Twelfth.[75] Yet, if public parades and community solidarity have helped keep Orangeism alive, continuity has also been evident in the perception of the Scottish press and wider public opinion that the parades are the sum total of Orangeism, and that these are vulgar curiosity pieces which 'encourage bigotry' and which have no place in modern Scotland.[76] It may be significant for the future of parading in Scotland, that today's Orangemen are likely to pay as little heed to 'the Scottish press and wider public opinion' as their nineteenth-century brethren.

Notes

1. D. Massey, 'Space, Place and Gender', *LSE Magazine*, Spring, 1992, 32–4.
2. *Place and the Politics of Identity*, M. Keith and S. Pile (eds), (London, 1993).
3. E.W. McFarland, *Protestants First: Orangeism in Nineteenth Century Scotland* (Edinburgh, 1990), pp. 70–91.
4   M.W. Dewar, *Orangeism: a New Historical Appreciation* (Belfast, 1973), p. 83.
5. S. A. Marston, 'Public Rituals and Community Power: St Patrick's Day Parades in Lowell, Massachusetts, 1841–74, *Political Geography Quarterly*, 8/3, July 1989, pp. 255–69; S.G. Dawes, *Parades and Power: Street Theatre in Nineteenth Century Philadelphia* (Phildelphia), 1986.
6. McFarland, *Protestants First*, pp. 49–51.
7. *First Report of the Parliamentary Commission for Enquiry into the Condition of the Poorer Classes in Ireland*, Appendix G, 'Report into the Irish Poor in Great Britain', 1827, p. 105.
8. *Glasgow Courier,* 14 July 1821.
9. *An Account of the Proceedings at the Orange Procession*, Wylie Street Literature, University of Glasgow, Special Collections, nd [1822]; *Glasgow Courier*, 13 July 1842.

10. *Glasgow Courier*, 14 July 1823; *Dumfries Weekly Journal*, 4 July 1826; *Glasgow Courier*, 14 July 1831; *Glasgow Herald*, 17 July 1829.
11. The lyrics, too, combined a powerful statement of combative sectarianism. The chorus of 'Croppies Lie Down', for example, was sometimes changed to 'Papists lie down': *Report from the Select Committee Appointed to Enquire into the Origin, Nature, Extent and Tendency of Orange Lodges in Great Britain and the Colonies*, House of Commons 1836[605], 116. Other provocative tunes were 'Prussian Drums' and 'More Holy Water'.
12. B. Hesse, 'Racialization through Contested Times and Spaces', in *Place and the Politics*, p. 161.
13. G. Walker, 'The Protestant Irish in Scotland', in *Irish Immigrants in Scottish Society*, ed. T. Devine (Edinburgh), 1990, p. 49.
14. A.B. Campbell, *The Lanarkshire Miners* (Edinburgh), 1974, p. 183.
15. *Glasgow Sentinel,* 5 August 1854.
16. *Glasgow Herald*, 17 July 1857.
17. Lord Advocate's Papers: AD 58/70, 'Disturbances between Orangemen and Catholics in Ayrshire', Scottish Records Office; *Glasgow Herald,* 17 July 1847.
18. *Glasgow Herald,* 14 July 1848.
19. *Glasgow Herald,* 22 December 1822. In Liverpool the Twelfth procession in 1851 resulted in 70 arrests, none of whom were Orangemen: F. Neal, *Sectarian Violence. The Liverpool Experience 1819–1914* (Manchester, 1988), 139.
20. J.L. Murdoch, 'Policing Public Processions in Scotland', *Journal of the Law Society*, March, 1983, 98. By no means were all processions of a sectarian composition. July 1841, for example, saw a teetotal demonstration 'held alike by Protestant and Roman Catholic', *Glasgow Herald,* 17 July 1841.
21. *Glasgow Herald*, 14 July 1859. For further examples of policing see, *Glasgow Herald,* 14 July 1831; *Glasgow Argus*, 18 July 1836; *Glasgow Herald*, 14 July 1858.
22. *Glasgow Courier,* 14 July 1821.
23. *Glasgow Courier,* 17 July 1849.
24. *Glasgow Sentinel*, 16 July 1853.
25. McFarland, *Protestants First*, pp. 73–4.
26. J. Cloughley, 'The History of Orangeism in Scotland', *Belfast Weekly News* 23 November 1929.
27. J. Foster and C. Madigan, 'The Missing Irish Protestants: a New Approach to Immigration and Ethnicity in Victorian Britain', unpublished paper.
28. Ibid, pp. 8–9.
29. R.D. Lobban, 'The Irish Community in Greenock in the Nineteenth Century', *Irish Geography*, VI, 1972, pp. 270–81.
30. Foster, 'The Missing Irish Protestants', p. 5.
31. Strathclyde Regional Archives, E4/2/7, Chief Constable's Letterbook, 16 March 1867.
32. *Glasgow Herald,* 13 December 1867.
33. *North British Daily Mail*, 14 July 1870.
34. *Glasgow Herald*, 12 July 1868.
35. McFarland, *Protestants First*, 39–42, 65–6. Two parallel Orange organisations were operating in Scotland from 1859 : 'The Orange Association of Scotland' and 'The Orange Institution of Great Britain'. They re-united in 1877 under the title 'The Loyal Orange Institution of Scotland.

36. *Glasgow News,* 12 August 1876.
37. *Glasgow Herald,* 13 July 1883; *Glasgow News,* 13 July 1877.
38. Marston, 'Public Rituals'; S. Fielding, *Class and Ethnicity: Irish Catholics in England, 1880–1939,* pp. 72–8.
39. *Glasgow Free Press,* 22 July 1865.
40. Strathclyde Regional Archives, E4/2/7, Chief Constable's Letterbook, 9 July 1868; *North British Daily Mail* 13 July 1869.
41. *Glasgow News,* 27 July 1878. This stood in contrast to its previous editorial on 30 July 1874 which argued, 'the true remedy is prevention'.
42. *Glasgow News,* 13 July 1872.
43. See Marston 'Public Rituals …' for the case of Lowell, Mass.
44. *Glasgow News,* 13 July 1886.
45. *Glasgow News,* 30 July 1874.
46. See S. Smith, 'Bounding the Borders: Claiming Space and Making Place in Rural Scotland', *Transactions of the Institute of British Geographers,* 18, 3, 1993, pp. 292.
47. *Glasgow Herald,* 13 July 1881.
48. McFarland, *Protestants First,* pp. 70–1.
49. *Glasgow Herald,* 13 July 1874; see 13 July 1886 and 1887 for further examples of women's continued participation.
50. *Glasgow Herald,* 13 July 1874.
51. 'Dull trade' regularly influenced turnout in Greenock and Govan, both with large casual labour markets: *Glasgow Herald,* 16 July 1873; 13 July 1878.
52. *Glasgow Herald,* 13 July 1886.
53. *Glasgow Herald,* 13 July 1892.
54. *Glasgow Herald,* 8 July 1912.
55. J. Berger, quoted in Marston, 'Public Rituals', p. 266.
56. *Glasgow Herald,* 13 July 1874 , 13 July 1875.
57. See McFarland, *Protestants First,* p. 197._
58. *Glasgow Herald,* 13 July 1886.
59. *Glasgow Herald,* 13 July 1887. Local Catholic clergy in Lanarkshire generally attempted to restrain their flocks from confrontation, not only warning them from the pulpit, but physically intervening in disputes: *Glasgow Herald* 13 July 1873; 13 July 1885.
60. *Glasgow Herald,* 13 July 1878; 1880.
61. *Govan Press,* 17 July 1886. *Partick Star,* 6 July 1889: one correspondent was in no doubt that 'noisy Irishmen', employed by the Tramway Department as cheap labour were the source of the problem.
62. *Glasgow Herald,* 13 July 1874.
63. Murdoch, 'Policing Public Processions', 99. Glasgow was not covered by the act and preferred effective policing and *post factum* policing, while Lanarkshire waited until 1912 until requiring permits to be obtained by the organisers of any demonstration involving music, flags or insignia.
64. See McFarland, *Protestants First,* pp. 78–88; 143.
65. *Glasgow Observer,* 16 July 1884.
66. *Glasgow News,* 4 November 1884; *Glasgow News,* 13 July 1877.
67. *Glasgow News,* 13 July 1877.
68. *Greenock Telegraph,* 5 November 1870.
69. *Glasgow Herald,* 13 July 1874.

70. *Glasgow Herald,* 16 July 1898.
71. See McFarland, *Protestants First*, pp. 115–36.
72. Ibid, pp. 190–209.
73. *Scotland on Sunday,* 28 May 1995.
74. J. Bradley, *Ethnic and Religious Identity in Modern Scotland* (Aldershot, 1995) p. 97.
75. *Scotsman,* 11 July 1989.
76. *Scotland on Sunday*, 28 May 1995.

5
Parades, Police and Government in Northern Ireland, 1922–69

Keith Jeffery

From the very start of Northern Ireland as an entity the issue of parading had particular political significance. Among the first enactments of the new parliament was the Civil Authorities (Special Powers) Act which came into effect in April 1922. This sweeping statute, designed, according to its preamble, 'to empower certain authorities of the Government of Northern Ireland to take steps for preserving the peace and maintaining order', came to represent the unacceptable, coercive face of the Ulster unionist regime. In February 1969, the People's Democracy, embodying much of early pressure for civil rights' reform, gave high priority to its abolition. Following the first demand on their manifesto – 'one man one vote' – came 'an end to repressive legislation and partial law enforcement by repeal of the Special Powers Act'.[1] Linked with this was the 1951 Public Order Act, which had superseded the Special Powers Act in the matter of regulating public demonstrations.

The 1922 act transferred to the new Northern Ireland government many executive powers which had been granted to the military authorities under the Restoration of Order in Ireland Act of 1920 which itself renewed powers provided for under First World War Defence of the Realm legislation.[2] Thus it may be seen that the lineage of the legislation lay in emergency powers acquired by the government in time of war, when the British state was under sustained military challenge. A sense of embattlement suffused the new polity and the response of the unionist administration to *any* political challenge, but especially from within the nationalist community, was coloured by a continuing sense that the state remained at war.[3] In keeping with this notion, the 1922 Act was explicitly framed as a temporary measure, to continue in force for only one year. Nevertheless, it was renewed annually until 1933 when its life was extended to five years. Indeed, emergency legislation relating to Northern Ireland, as Laura K. Donohue has note. sistibly took on a condition of 'temporary permanence'.[4]

Under the 1922 Special Powers Act, the Northern Ireland Minister of Home Affairs was empowered to make 'Regulations for Peace and Order' and a wide-ranging list of thirty-five such provisions was published with the original act. Regulation 4 related to public meetings:

> Where there appears to be reason to apprehend that the assembly of any persons for the purpose of the holding of any meeting will give rise to grave disorder, and will thereby cause undue demands to be made upon the police forces, or that the holding of any procession will conduce to a breach of the peace or will promote disaffection, it shall be lawful for the civil authority, or for any magistrate or chief officer of police who is duly authorised for the purpose ... to make an order prohibiting the holding of the meeting or procession.

The regulation was extremely permissive and left much discretion to the minister or his nominee. Although the criterion for the banning of a meeting was the possibility of 'grave disorder' – interestingly elaborated in terms of excessive strain on the police – that for a procession was much less stringent: 'conduce to a breach of the peace' (necessarily a hypothetical assessment) and 'will promote disaffection' could mean virtually anything. Since the implementation of this law was never tested in the courts, the government were effectively left with a free hand to deal with parades and demonstrations as they wished.

The Royal Ulster Constabulary (RUC) clearly had a major role to play in the application of the law. In 1925 the police chief (Inspector-General) was, in fact, formally given authority by the Minister of Home Affairs to make orders on his own behalf banning processions under regulation 4.[5] But the RUC was no ordinary police force.[6] It was born in violent circumstances: nationalist violence directed throughout Ireland against both its parent body, the Royal Irish Constabulary (RIC), and any other manifestation of the British administration of Ireland; violence specifically aimed at destroying the infant 'statelet' of Northern Ireland; and widespread communal violence, especially in working-class parts of Belfast, where the sectarian interface was marked by frequent bloodshed. This state of affairs indelibly marked the new Northern Ireland police force, and in particular, defined the attitude of its political masters towards its functions and control. For them, always, the primary duty of the force was the securing and protection of the new political *status quo*. For the police themselves, however, during much of the period between the end of the 1916–21 'Troubles' and the resurgence of violence in 1968–69, the violent threat to the state largely lay dormant, and their primary role lay in dealing with what has sardonically come to be known as 'ordinary decent crime' (as opposed to politically motivated lawbreaking). For half a century, therefore, a tension existed between the actual duties of the RUC as a police force and its symbolic status as the first coercive line of defence of the new polity, a tension abundantly illustrated in the matter of policing parades.

Between 16 June 1922 and 15 March 1950, the Minister of Home Affairs made ninety-one proclamations prohibiting meetings, assemblies and processions under Regulation 4 of the Special Powers Act.[7] The overwhelming majority of these bans concerned nationalist events. The Easter Commemorations of the 1916 Rising which began on the tenth anniversary attracted the highest member of prohibitions (49). Various other anti-partition meetings, and St Patrick's Day marches also feature on the list. In February 1940 protests against the execution in Birmingham of two republicans, Peter Barnes and Frank Richards, for their part in a bombing in Coventry in August 1939,[8] were similarly banned. But in many ways the most interesting bans under the act were the dozen or so events which were not nationalist, or at least not purely so. The challenge posed by, for example, labour or socialist organisations did not fit readily into the Manichean political world view of the unionist regime. Anything beyond the core political issue of Northern Ireland – that of the province's survival as a part of the United Kingdom – presented unusual challenges to the government, and exposed tensions akin to those affecting the police, between 'ordinary' political debate and the all-too-ready identification of *any* political challenge with republicanism and conspiratorial efforts to destroy the entire state.

This can be seen in the problem posed by a proposed march in October 1925 by unemployed workers from the Belfast city centre to the Northern Ireland parliament in its then temporary quarters at the Presbyterian Church Assembly's College a short distance away. The march was planned to coincide with the official opening of the new parliamentary session,[9] and to protest about government policy on unemployment benefit which was lower than in Great Britain. It came at a time, moreover, when the Northern Ireland Labour Party (NILP) were enjoying a modest degree of success. In the April 1925 general election the party had won over unionist voters in Belfast. At the end of September the head of the city police reported that a committee of labour MPs, Belfast city councillors and other trade union representatives under the auspices of the NILP, were planning a demonstration. In his opinion, he wrote, the event should be banned as it constituted a clear 'attempt to overawe Parliament and would amount to Treason' under section (3) of the Treason Felony Act of 1848.[10]

The RUC Inspector-General concurred and left the minister, Richard Dawson Bates, with the worry of how public opinion in general might view such a ban. Personally, he wrote to the attorney-general, he was 'very strongly of opinion that the procession should not be allowed', but on the other hand he thought 'we must try to avoid giving ground for the allegation that we are interfering with legitimate political agitation'. A further problem lay in the appropriate legislative means to deal with the demonstration. Bates noted that it could be dealt with by a 'proclamation' under the Criminal Law and Procedure (Ireland) Act of 1887 (popularly known at the Crimes Act), but that this was rather an 'elaborate' method. The 'simplest and most efficient' procedure would be to use the Special Powers Act, but this also entailed political risk. He had, he said, 'some reluctance' to use this act as it 'was originally passed for the purpose of dealing with disorder of a different kind, and I would like to avoid making it a bone of contention with the Labour Party'.[11] The matter went to the cabinet where the Prime Minister supported prohibition. The political sensitivities which Bates had expressed, and which in any case may have reflected more the opinions of his civil service advisers than his own generally fierce conservative views, were apparently ignored.[12]

There is evidence of some divergence of opinion towards processions between politicians, civil servants and police following the celebrated and uniquely non-sectarian 'outdoor relief' riots in Belfast in October 1932 sparked off by the increasingly unsatisfactory provision for the growing numbers of unemployed in the city.[13] The march which preceded the disturbances marked the first of a number of uses of the Special Powers Act against demonstrations of unemployed people in the 1930s. Evidently the scruples about using regulation 4 against other than nationalist demonstrations or parades which Bates had raised in 1925 had now entirely been abandoned. In January 1933, a 'Derry Unemployed Demonstration' to the city workhouse was banned, though meetings in Belfast and Newry by the same organisation to demand the release of republican prisoners (which were also banned) indicated that the concerns of the Derry Unemployed were not solely socio-economic.[14] Happily, from the government's point of view, this overt republican enthusiasm no doubt eased any residual concerns about employing the Special Powers Act.

In October 1933, a proposed march to mark the first anniversary of the outdoor relief riots was banned under regulation 4. Bates believed that the occasion was no more than an opportunity for southern nationalists to come North to make trouble. He had 'reason to believe that an assembly of certain persons from the Free State purporting to be members of the Irish Unemployed Workers' Movement is likely to take place' and that it would 'give rise to' disorder.[15] The following year a similar demonstration 'to commemorate the riots of 1932' was proposed for Belfast city centre. The RUC Inspector-General recommended prohibition, particularly since the trade union and labour movements were 'likely to be supported by the Republican Congress Party, Communist Party, Irish Labour Defence League, and similar organisations'.[16] This initial response, however, was modified after further consideration. Richard Pim, a former RIC man, currently attached as a civil servant to the Ministry of Home Affairs, and who was later to head the RUC (1945–61), took up the matter with Chief Inspector Gilfillan, the Inspector-General's representative. Gilfillan told Pim he thought that 'the demonstration this year will be of little importance' and was in fact 'rather doubtful that it should be prohibited'.[17] It is not clear whether the initiative against banning came from Pim or the police, but there is an indication here that someone at least was concerned about the over-promiscuous use of the Special Powers Act. Not only, perhaps, was there a renewed appreciation of the need to restrict the use of the act against what might be regarded as 'ordinary' political demonstrations, but there was also some sense that the banning of a comparatively insignificant demonstration might actually do harm in drawing more attention to the event than would otherwise have been the case. In the end, however, such speculations came to nothing as the minister pressed ahead with a ban under regulation 4.

While the banning of labour (or quasi-labour) demonstrations raised particular considerations, that of loyalist parades was naturally much more contentious for the unionist government. Under regulation 4, no loyalist gathering was ever exclusively prohibited,[18] but on three occasions (at least) between the wars, loyalist parades were halted. The first of these was in July 1932 when the police stopped an Orange procession in Coalisland, County Tyrone. Sectarian tension in Northern Ireland ran particularly high during the spring and early summer of that year. The coming of power of the pro-republican Fianna Fail under Eamon de Valera in the South in March 1932, coupled with what the Northern Ireland Cabinet the following month called 'the excitement, amounting almost to frenzy, caused by the Eucharistic Congress' stoked up loyalist passions which in turn led to sectarian clashes with police trying to hold the line between rival mobs. So much so that in several places loyalist crowds were baton-charged by the police.[19]

In these circumstances it is clear that the police in County Tyrone were generally apprehensive about the potential for further violence. On 10 July, an Orange lodge marching from their hall on their way to church was stopped by a force of police. The local RUC commander, District-Inspector Nevin, told the Orangemen that they could not march through Coalisland (a predominantly nationalist town). The legal basis for this action is unclear. No order under regulation 4 of the Special Powers Act was made on this occasion, but the district inspector told the Orangemen that 'he was authorised to close the road against the processionists and could not allow them to pass'. The Master of the lodge, Brother Thomas Neill, raised what in more recent times has become a familiar argument, that the route was a traditional one which had been 'used by the Coalisland and Newmills brethren for years'. He declared that the 'brethren considered it ... humiliating when they were prohibited from parading', and added with a hint of menace that 'the Government had been placed in power with the assistance of the Orange brethren, and if that Government could not afford them reasonable protection the sooner a change was made the better'.[20] Despite these trenchant opinions, the Orangemen accepted the direction of the police and proceeded by a different route to a church service at Newmills parish church.

At the 12 July area demonstration two days later, the Deputy County Grand Chaplain, the Reverend S. W. Thompson of Dungannon, reflected on these disturbing events. The matter, he thought, was one of civil liberties: 'He considered it a monstrous thing that any citizen of the British Empire carrying the Union Jack should be prevented from walking wherever he liked within the bounds of the Empire and under that symbol of loyalty and freedom.' As with Brother Neill, his main criticism was reserved for the government. Despite the fact that the decision to stop the parade had apparently been taken by a local police officer fearing possible disorder, Thompson was sympathetic to the RUC's plight. He said 'he did not want to find any fault with the police. The police must do their duty and obey orders, and they had been having a very trying time of late. It was the duty of the Orange brethren to support them in trying to keep law and order.' Like Neill he had a word of warning for the government which he evidently felt had been acting in an insufficiently democratic fashion. 'The authorities behind the police ought to remember', he said, 'that they were not autocrats. They ruled by the will of the people, and they could be deposed by the will of the people.'[21] These were striking sentiments indeed. It is a measure of the sense of betrayal felt by the Orangemen that the re-routing of just one parade should provoke such an extreme reaction, if only in rhetorical terms. The message for the government was clearly that the policing of loyalist parades had to be conducted with the very greatest delicacy.

This was confirmed by the controversy stirred up by a blanket ban on processions imposed under regulation 4 in June 1935. Again, the government were rightly worried about the possibility of sectarian violence. In May there had been rioting in the York Street area of Belfast and on 12 June a loyalist procession, organised by the ultra-militant and provocative Ulster Protestant League, was fired on in Donegall Street. This was followed by sporadic outbreaks of rioting and shooting in Belfast. Bates, after consulting with the police, issued a regulation 4 proclamation on 18 June banning all processions in the city of Belfast, apart from funerals.[22]

By issuing a blanket prohibition he no doubt wanted to evade criticism which would inevitably follow action exclusively against a loyalist group, but the ban ... which threatened to remain in force over the period of the 12 July Orange marches ... was immediately met with outrage throughout the unionist community. On 22 June the Orange County Grand Master of Belfast, Sir Joseph Davison, issued a direct challenge to the government:

> You may be perfectly certain that on 12th July the Orangemen will be marching throughout Northern Ireland and I shall be marching at their head in Belfast.
>
> I do not acknowledge the right of any Government, Northern or Imperial, to impose conditions as to the celebrations of the glorious anniversary of the victory at the Boyne, nor shall I acknowledge any authority to ban the celebration ...
>
> I have put that plainly to the Minister of Home Affairs in the name of the Orangemen of Belfast ... No funeral processions for us! Our banners will be waving; our colours will be worn, and our bands will be playing patriotic tunes.[23]

The following day, three illegal Orange meetings were held in Belfast. Already Bates's firm line was weakening: the police had been instructed not to interfere with loyalist processions so long as they kept away from 'hostile districts'.[24]

On 26 June, Bates buckled under the pressure and rescinded the ban.[25] While the prohibition had, in the precise terms stipulated by the Special Powers Act, been invoked because of the likelihood of 'grave disorder' and 'a breach of the peace', its revocation contributed mightily to the wave of violence which then afflicted Belfast, especially the nine days of serious rioting and shooting following the 12 July demonstrations. So serious was the disorder that on 13 July regular army troops were called out, for the first time since 1922, and remained on the streets until 24 July.[26] Many loyalists celebrated the government's capitulation with particular vigour. On 1 July, the loyalist Beresford Accordion Band, returning from a Battle of the Somme anniversary commemoration at the Belfast Cenotaph, was, according to initial reports in the unionist press, attacked by nationalists in Upper North Street. At the court proceedings which followed, however, a police district-inspector reported that when the band, which had been 'playing party tunes in a provocative manner', reached Upper North Street, it 'occupied ten minutes in covering a very short distance'. The 'mob' which accompanied the band were, moreover, 'shouting party expressions'. The procession had stopped at Carrick Hill where a section of the loyalist crowd broke through a police cordon and attacked the nationalist inhabitants. The police view was that the disturbances had been a direct consequence of the band's conduct.[27]

The precise circumstances of both the applying and revoking of the 1935 ban are not clear,[28] but it appears that the decision to invoke regulation 4 was made in the small hours of 18 June at a meeting between Bates and the Inspector-General in 'an embattled police station' in central Belfast.[29] The hard-line unionist MP, William Grant, told parliament that the RUC Inspector-General, Sir Charles Wickham, had pressurised Bates into making the order. The minister, he asserted, was 'too much under the influence of the Inspector-General, and it is time', he added, 'that that influence was broken down'.[30] Wickham, a public-school educated Yorkshireman with an army background, had in 1920 been appointed an RIC District Commissioner with special responsibility for the six-county area which became Northern Ireland. Although he had quickly established himself as a valued and trusted servant of the new state, when the government took unpalatable decisions, they could yet be blamed on the malign influence of the 'outsider' Wickham. Grant warned Bates that his political future could well be jeopardised by an undue reliance on Wickham's advice:

I want to suggest seriously to the Minister for Home Affairs that it was not the Inspector-General who put him into Parliament, but I would remind him that the Inspector-General may put him out of Parliament. ... Remember that the Inspector-General ... is an Englishman; he has queer ideas about Northern Ireland.[31]

Wickham was to survive as Inspector-General for another ten years, but the criticisms levelled by Grant illustrated the problem for the administration of balancing the basic function of any government to maintain law and order, with the sometimes more pressing party political requirement of keeping their own supporters sweet. In 1935 the advice of the police to impose a ban was initially followed and then, apparently, rejected under pressure from the unionist community at large. The police apprehensions concerning the public-order situation were fully vindicated, but they were overruled on the grounds of political expediency. A report by the National Council for Civil Liberties following the disturbances highlighted the RUC's dilemma in controlling the sometimes militant activities of the government's own supporters. 'It is difficult to escape the conclusion', it observed, 'that the attitude of the government renders the police chary of interference with the activities of the Orange Order and its sympathisers'.[32]

The third time a loyalist meeting was banned was late in 1938 on the occasion of a specially-organised counter-demonstration against a planned Ancient Order of Hibernians (AOH) anti-partition meeting in Newtownbutler, County Fermanagh. When the AOH scheduled their meeting for 20 November, local Orangemen responded by announcing a counter-demonstration for the same day. The government's initial response to the proposed AOH demonstration had been quite permissive. Although both the Minister of Home Affairs and the Inspector-General recommended banning the meeting, the Prime Minister was minded to let it go ahead as a harmless outlet for nationalist feeling. But once the counter-demonstration was threatened a ban was imposed on *all* demonstrations during the period in question. The pattern of proposed AOH meeting, Orange counter-demonstration and government ban was repeated over the next two weekends, prompting the reasonable complaint from nationalists that the loyalists were merely aiming to stifle legitimate and peaceful nationalist political expression.[33] In this case, of course, there was no unionist condemnation of the ban since the aim of preventing the AOH meeting was most satisfactorily met with the regulation 4 prohibition.

This loyalist tactic of counter-demonstration, which does not seem to have been much used between the wars, emerged again in 1948, when, with government attitudes towards nationalist demonstrations softening, it led to a interesting situation. Following the end of the Second World War, there was some feeling within the government that a more permissive line might be taken towards nationalist demonstrations and that the hitherto blanket bans on Easter commemorations might be modified. The initiative in this potential policy shift was taken by civil servants in the Ministry of Home Affairs. In 1946, after the Inspector-General had recommended 'the usual prohibition of Easter meetings', H.C. Montgomery, an assistant secretary in the ministry, argued 'whether anyone wants to hold commemoration meetings or not is doubtful and it might be good policy to do nothing in the way of a general prohibition'. Any individual meetings which were announced could be prohibited at short notice if necessary. Montgomery felt 'that undue publicity is given to "the anniversary" by the publication of the prohibition Order'.[34] But the moment was too soon for such a liberalisation and the minister decided to apply a general ban as before.

By 1948, however, it was agreed that unless there were 'unforeseen developments' no general ban on Easter meetings would be applied. But following controversy over the regulation 4 banning of an anti-partition meeting planned for Derry on St Patrick's Day, the RUC took the view that all Easter meetings should also be prohibited.[35] This time the minister, prompted by his officials, took the more moderate line. The official line repeated that of 1946: any orders 'should be in regard to individual meetings rather than a general prohibition'. The minister, Edmond Warnock, who had no particular reputation for liberality (and whose Belfast constituency, St Anne's, was in the strongly loyalist Sandy Row), agreed. 'It seems to me', he minuted, 'that the less "banning" we do the better'.[36] No prohibition was made and Easter 1948 passed off peacefully.

This modest shift in government policy on nationalist processions and demonstrations was too much for some sections of loyalist opinion. Particularly forceful opinions were expressed by the National Union of Protestants (Ireland) which became active in Northern Ireland during the late 1940s. Organised by an unemployed engineer, Norman Porter, it campaigned against any perceived encroachments on the dominant position of Protestant culture and provided the first public arena for the youthful evangelical firebrand, Ian Paisley, who was the movement's treasurer.[37] Early in September 1948, Porter wrote to the Minister of Home Affairs to warn that if he did not ban a planned commemoration in central Belfast of the 150th anniversary of the 1798 Rising they would meet the challenge of these rebels by organising a large Protestant demonstration at the same venue – a vacant bombsite in High Street, undeveloped since the war. He proposed, he added helpfully, to occupy the ground from early morning to late in the evening in order to let the world know that Northern Ireland was still a Protestant and British country.[38]

Having discussed the matter with both the Prime Minister and the Inspector-General, Warnock secured Cabinet approval to ban any meeting on the High Street site 'by either side' on Saturday 11 or Monday 13 September. Faced with a further planned parade organised by the 1798 Commemoration Committee and scheduled for the following Sunday, 19 September, under regulation 4, Warnock prohibited all processions in the city of Belfast except within a clearly-defined area of nationalist west Belfast.[39] This was obviously designed as a concession, in keeping with the gentle relaxation of government policy towards nationalist demonstrations. Warnock could declare that the 1798 march on 19 September was not being banned, merely restricted to parts of the city where it would not 'conduce to a breach of the peace'. But he – or perhaps his officials are to blame here – neglected to enquire if any other parades were planned for that day.

If it was unfortunate that the Cumberland Loyal Orange Lodge No. 685 annual service was planned for 19 September, it was doubly so considering that the chaplain of the lodge was none other than Ian Paisley. The officers of the lodge placed a notice in the *Belfast Telegraph* on the evening of 18 September postponing the parade but, as the police noted afterwards, there was 'no doubt whatever that enthusiastic support' for challenging the ban 'was forthcoming from the National Union of Protestants, and particularly from two of its leading members, the Reverend Paisley and Mr Porter, who are themselves Orangemen'. With perhaps a touch of *litotes*, the police added that 'the decision to postpone … was not very well received by some of the more militant members, who seemed determined to break the ban at any cost'. On the afternoon of 19 September an estimated four hundred Orangemen assembled at Albertbridge Orange Hall, marched to St Donard's Church, Bloomfield, and returned to Templemore Avenue. 'The irresponsible element in the Order', reported the police, 'was really responsible for organising the Parade in defiance both of the Civil Authorities' Order [regulation 4] and the decision made by their own Officers'.[40]

Although the law had clearly been broken by the Orange marchers on 19 September, Warnock decided that no prosecutions should ensue. He was very worried about the political ramifications of the affair. When parliament reassembled in October, he prepared to make a fulsome public apology and had a statement drawn up for use in the Commons: 'Having taken counsel with the Inspector-General and the City Commissioner [of the RUC] I decided that I would not prohibit the [1798 commemoration] procession, because I dislike the necessity of interfering with public assembly, but that I would direct the route of the procession to parts of the City where I felt that there was the least likelihood of any incidents.' When he had prohibited all other processions in the city he had not known that any others had been arranged. He had, of course, had no intention of catching the Cumberland Lodge march in the in ban and in pretty grovelling terms apologised for the mix-up:

I am, in fact, more to blame for this difficulty than anyone else. My Order was badly drafted and ... I feel a very considerable sense of personal responsibility for this situation. If I had suspected that any other procession had been arranged the Order would have taken a very different form and I must express to the House and to the public my regrets.[41]

In the event, Warnock was not challenged and was spared the indignity of having to read this public *apologia*. But the affair clearly illustrated the continuing sensitivity with which the government had to handle loyalist parades.

The slight liberalisation of policy on nationalist parades which was being promoted in the late 1940s was partly based on a pragmatic assessment of the political utility of the Special Powers Act regulation 4 procedure. In each case where a meeting or demonstration was banned a proclamation had to be made with, as had been noted in 1946, the risk of stimulating 'undue publicity'. Blanket bans were even more difficult to justify, and the quiet dropping of the annual comprehensive prohibition of Easter Commemorations had been managed without too much difficulty. But in some ways regulation 4 was a crude and over-elaborate mechanism for dealing with day-to-day demonstrations, and, as had been seen in 1948, its use against nationalist meetings could inadvertently affect loyalist ones as well. These problems were met with the Public Order Act of 1951.

The new statute gave greater responsibility to the police in the matter of public meetings. Anyone intending to organise a procession was required to provide at least forty-eight hours' notice to the RUC who were empowered to impose conditions on the march, or prohibit it altogether, if there were 'reasonable grounds for apprehending that [it] may occasion a breach of the peace or serious public disorder, whether immediately or at any time thereafter' (sec. 2(1)). The Minister of Home Affairs was additionally given power to ban all public processions or meetings in a specific location for up to three months at a time. (sec. 2(2)). There was no requirement to make a public proclamation concerning the banning of meetings, and, in contrast to the Special Powers Act, the onus with regard to demonstrations was placed on the organisers who had to seek specific permission for each event. But any 'public procession ... customarily held along a particular route' (sec. 1(1)) was exempt from the procedure. 'Stripped of legal language', what this meant, asserted the leader of the Nationalist Party, Eddie McAteer, was 'the permanent exemption of Orange processions from the necessity of giving 48 hours' notice to the police'.[42]

These legal changes, however, did not materially reduce the difficulties which the government continued to face in reconciling obligations for the maintenance of public order with their own political survival. In the 1950s a series of disputes about an Orange march over the Longstone Road which ran through a Catholic area near the village of Annalong, County Down, achieved great notoriety and 'passed into Ulster folk-lore'.[43] In June 1952, local Orangemen announced their intention to march along the road, but the Minister of Home Affairs, Brian Maginess (who had succeeded Warnock in 1949), banned the procession on RUC advice,[44] only to reverse his decision in the face of hard-line unionist pressure and allow a march to go ahead on 3 July. The political risks run by government ministers who offended Orangeism were demonstrated in the general election of October 1953 when Maginess was opposed in his County Down constituency by an independent unionist candidate. In the event, the minister won the seat, but only with a very greatly reduced majority. In the same election another liberal unionist, S.H. Hall-Thompson (a former Cabinet minister), was narrowly defeated by the Protestant evangelical campaigner, Norman Porter.

In April 1954 Maginess's successor, G.B. Hanna, banned another Orange march along the Longstone Road planned for Easter Monday. On this occasion the Cabinet were consulted and fully concurred in the decision.[45] But the issue had become a *cause célèbre* and the following 12 July parade was allowed to take place, despite the setting off on 11 July of three small bombs along the route. The next day an estimated 15 000 Orangemen marched, protected by some 300 RUC men. At Easter 1956, violent protests met the Orangemen along the Longstone Road, though again the police forced the march through.[46] The loyalist position, as repeatedly articulated by Norman Porter, was clear enough: any trouble associated with Protestant marches was the responsibility of the disaffected and disloyal minority. 'If it is provocative for the loyalists of the North of Ireland to parade in any part of Northern Ireland', he averred in May 1955, 'then I have lost all sense of who is responsible in the matter'.[47] The onus of keeping the peace 'really lies upon those who would be going to cause trouble and not upon those who would be marching'.[48] And the incidents along the Longstone Road had been of such importance, demonstrating 'a continuance of the kind of risings in Northern Ireland that have been detrimental to the progress of our country', that they should be included in the school history syllabus 'as well as the Battle of the Boyne and other events of that nature'.[49]

All the main issues associated with parades and parading, which so disturbed the unionist government in the late 1960s and have continued to present political, legal and policing problems to the successor regime in Northern Ireland, had emerged in the experience of the province before 1969. These issues included the need to establish a clear legal framework for the organisation and control of meetings and processions. In order to secure and retain the confidence of the whole community, the government, moreover, had to demonstrate fairness in the application of the law, a point which the Unionist government signally failed to do on a number of occasions. The crucial role of the police in the management of parades had also been established and was highlighted, for example, in June 1935 and (apparently) in June–July 1952, when police advice to ban loyalist marches was first taken and then rejected. But the unionist government were in an impossible situation. In order to keep their more extreme supporters in line they were compelled to favour loyalist marchers over nationalist protesters. It might be asserted that a satisfactory handling of a parade from the loyalist perspective was *by definition* unsatisfactory for nationalists. Even when a demonstration apparently came from outside the conventional unionist-nationalist political spectrum (as in 1934), the government tended to treat the challenge as if it were nationalist-inspired. When in the late 1960s the viability of the Northern Ireland political system was gravely, and perhaps fatally, undermined by parades and demonstrations which developed into extensive civil unrest, the very novelty of the challenge made it all the more difficult for the administration to cope. In the autumn of 1969 the Cameron Commission, appointed to investigate the causes of the recent disturbances in Northern Ireland, remarked on this very point. 'It is', it reported, 'one of the novel circumstances of recent demonstrations that they do not fit into the accepted or traditional pattern, and therefore have presented an entirely new problem for solution by the police and the authorities'.[50] As was abundantly shown, the traditional methods of 1922 onwards which had, it seemed, served the unionist regime so well, were found sadly wanting after 1968–69, ultimately at the cost of the regime itself.

Notes

1. Paul Arthur, *The People's Democracy 1968–73* (Belfast, 1974), appendix C, p. 119.
2. The most complete legal analysis of this legislation is in Colm Campbell, *Emergency Law in Ireland 1918–1925* (Oxford, 1994). The political and military context may be followed in Charles Townshend, *The British Campaign in Ireland 1919–1921* (Oxford, 1975).
3. This is a longstanding feature of unionist *mentalité*. See Keith Jeffery (ed.) *'An Irish Empire'? Aspects of Ireland and the British Empire* (Manchester, 1996), pp. 15, 82–3, 155; Bryan A. Follis, *A State under Siege: the Establishment of Northern Ireland 1920–1925* (Oxford, 1995); and Arthur Aughey, *Under Siege: Ulster Unionism and the Anglo-Irish Agreement* (Belfast, 1989).
4. See the examination of this phenomenon in the excellent study: Laura K. Donohue, 'Emergency Legislation in the Northern Irish Context' (unpublished PhD dissertation, Cambridge University, 1997).
5. 2 October 1925, minute by R. Dawson Bates (Public Record Office of Northern Ireland (PRONI), HA/32/1/465).
6. This paragraph draws on my essay 'Police and Government in Northern Ireland, 1922–1969' in Mark Mazower (ed.), *The Policing of Politics in the Twentieth Century: Historical Perspectives* (Providence and Oxford, 1997), pp. 151–66.
7. These occasions are individually listed in Donohue, 'Emergency legislation', Figure 3–2 (between pp. 90 and 91).
8. See Tim Pat Coogan, *The I.R.A.* (London, 1971), pp. 167, 172.
9. Paddy Devlin, *Yes We Have No Bananas: Outdoor Relief in Belfast, 1920–39* (Belfast, 1981), says that the banned march was to go to the workhouse, to coincide with the holding of a Poor Law Guardians board meeting (p. 95), but there is no mention of this is the relevant Cabinet and Ministry of Home Affairs files on the incident.
10. 30 September 1925, Commissioner RUC, Belfast, to Inspector-General (PRONI, HA/32/1/465).
11. 1 October 1925, Bates to Anthony Babington (ibid.).

12. 2 October 1925, Cabinet conclusions (PRONI, CAB 4/151).
13. The protestors had to agree on non-sectarian songs to sing on their march, hence the title of Paddy Devlin's splendid book on the topic: *Yes We Have No Bananas*.
14. See Ministry of Home Affairs memoranda, January 1933 (PRONI, HA/32/1/465).
15. 4 October 1933, proclamation banning demonstration planned for 8 October (PRONI, HA/32/1/466).
16. 2 October 1934, R. Gilfillan (for I-G, RUC) to Ministry of Home Affairs (ibid., HA/32/1/469).
17. 4 October 1934, memo by Pim (ibid.). For Pim's career see Chris Ryder, *The RUC: a Force Under Fire* (London, 1990), pp. 79–80.
18. Donohue, 'Emergency Legislation', p. 92.
19. Philip L.F. McVicker, 'Law and Order in Northern Ireland, 1920–36' (unpublished PhD thesis, CNAA (University of Ulster), 1985), pp. 198–200 (Cabinet quotation from Cabinet conclusions, 22 June 1932 (PRONI, CAB 4/303/1)).
20. *Belfast News-Letter*, 11 July 1932.
21. Ibid., 13 July 1932.
22. McVicker, 'Law and Order', pp. 219–21. The proclamation was published in the *Belfast Gazette*, no. 730, 21 June 1935.
23. *Belfast News-Letter*, 24 June 1935, quoted in McVicker, 'Law and Order', pp. 222–3.
24. Ibid., p. 223.
25. *Belfast Gazette*, no. 732, 5 July 1935.
26. A.C. Hepburn, 'The Belfast Riots of 1935', *Social History*, vol. 15, no. 1, 1990, pp. 75–96.
27. McVicker, 'Law and Order', pp. 223–5, quoting reports in the *Belfast News-Letter*, 2 and 11 July 1935.
28. Some security-related papers in the Public Record Office (NI) remain closed. The Ministry of Home Affairs files on 'Orders Prohibiting Meetings and Demonstrations' cover 1925–33 (HA/32/1/465) and 1938–42 (HA/32/1/466), but not 1934–37. One relevant file in the Cabinet papers, '1935 Disturbances in Belfast' (CAB 9B/236/1), although formerly available to the public and consulted by A.C. Hepburn (see Hepburn, 'The Belfast Riots', p. 75), is currently (1997) closed for 75 years.
29. Hepburn, 'The Belfast Riots', p. 79.
30. *N.I. Parl. Deb. (Commons)*, 10 July 1935, col. 2427–8.
31. Ibid., col. 2428 and 2431.
32. Quoted in Ryder, *The RUC*, p. 71.
33. Donohue, 'Emergency Legislation', pp. 97–8.
34. 1 April 1946, memo. by Montgomery (PRONI, HA/32/1/467).
35. Ministry of Home Affairs minutes, 4 and 9 March 1948 (ibid.).
36. Ibid., 11 March 1948.
37. Steve Bruce, *God Save Ulster! The Religion and Politics of Protestantism* (Oxford, 1986), pp. 38–9; Ed Moloney and Andy Pollock, *Paisley* (Swords, Co. Dublin, 1986), pp. 24–9. Paisley was born on 6 April 1926.
38. Porter to Warnock, 4 September 1948 (PRONI, HA/32/1/467).
39. Minutes, 8 and 9 September 1948 (ibid.).
40. Police reports, 25 and 30 September 1948 (ibid.).

41. Draft statement, October 1948 (ibid.).
42. *N.I. Parl. Deb. (Commons)*, 19 June 1951, col. 1545.
43. Brian Faulkner, *Memoirs of a Statesman*, ed. John Houston (London, 1978), p. 25.
44. It is not possible fully to assess this advice since the Ministry of Home Affairs papers for this period and on this subject were not available at the time of writing.
45. Cabinet conclusions, 15 April 1954, Public Record Office of Northern Ireland (PRONI CAB 4/936/7). This was, apparently, the only time the Cabinet formally discussed the Longstone Road parades.
46. Farrell, *Orange State*, pp. 207–8.
47. *N.I. Parl. Deb. (Commons)*, 25 May 1955, col. 1539.
48. Ibid., 28 June 1956, col. 2284.
49. Ibid., 3 May 1956, col. 1130.
50. *Disturbances in Northern Ireland* (Cameron Report), Cmd. 532 [NI] (Belfast, 1969), para. 25.

6

Green Parades in an Orange State: Nationalist and Republican Commemorations and Demonstrations from Partition to the Troubles, 1920–70

Neil Jarman and Dominic Bryan

Parading is seen as a practice that is central to the Northern Irish Protestant culture and one that defines that community in distinction to the nationalist community. While it is acknowledged that nationalist organisations do hold commemorative and other parades, these are regarded as either little more than a pale reflection of their Orange counterparts or as part of a political strategy which could be easily abandoned. Parades are not seen as part of nationalist culture in the way that they are a part of unionist culture.[1] They are not imbued with the weight of tradition. Yet parades have been a part of Irish social, cultural and political life since at least the fifteenth century, and during the late nineteenth century were as much a vehicle for mobilising and defining an Irish nationalist identity as they were for defining a Protestant British identity.[2] For instance, from the 1890s to the First World War, the Fifteenth (Lady's Day, 15 August) was treated by the *Irish News* as comparable to the Twelfth, the Ancient Order of Hibernians (AOH) rivalled the Orange Order, and Derry nationalists paraded the city walls each St Patrick's Day.[3]

Parades were always an important part of the nationalist calendar, but the right of nationalists to demonstrate was contingent on the local balance of demography and power. Prior to partition the state authorities did try to uphold the rights to parade of both communities but were also always more concerned about public order. As a result attempts to parade in Belfast and Lurgan were usually restricted to

perceived nationalist areas, while no nationalist parade was ever possible in Portadown. Nevertheless, a culture of parading was part of
Catholic religious, social and political life. However, the establishment
of a local parliament for Northern Ireland in 1921 significantly
changed the balance of power in the six counties. The new state contained a clear Protestant majority and that majority was now in an
unprecedented position of power; yet the perceived threat to the
union from Irish nationalism remained a preoccupation of the administration, Ulster Unionist politicians encouraging the perception
regardless of how real that threat was. As such, any public manifestations of Catholicism and Irish nationalism could be represented as a
threat to the state and therefore dealt with accordingly. The
ramifications of the new relationships of power in terms of public
political expression were most obvious in the use of emergency powers
under the Civil Authorities (Special Powers) Act of 1922 and through
the practice of policing.[4] Put simply, unionist control of the legislature
and Protestant domination of the police force was reflected in the
ability of the Protestant community to hold parades and demonstrations when they wished and at the same time impose restraints on
political expressions of the nationalist community. The expansion of
the Orange parading 'tradition' and the lack of a comparable Green
'tradition' were closely linked to the differentials of power within the
northern state as the new political entity aimed to consolidate its identity as both Protestant and British.

The Ancient Order of Hibernians grew dramatically in size and
importance in the early years of the twentieth century, but after 1916
constitutional nationalism was eclipsed by republicanism and the
political influence of the Hibernians declined rapidly in the period following partition.[5] However, the organisation maintained a large membership in the north and continued to parade each March on
St Patrick's Day and in August on Lady's Day. Threats to the rights of
the Hibernians to continue their parading traditions were uncommon,
but not unknown. In general, the Hibernians did not seek out confrontation, and the venues that they chose for the main parades were
largely limited to predominantly Catholic villages or towns. Hibernian
parades could be tolerated in areas with a large Catholic population
but were less readily accepted in areas deemed to be Protestant. The
very challenging of such displays reaffirmed that an area was truly
Protestant. The village of Moy, County Tyrone, can be used to illustrate
this point. The local Hibernian Division had paraded in the village in
the period before partition and in 1904 Moy had been the venue for a

major Lady's Day parade.[6] But after partition the Hibernians were less welcome in the village. In 1927 members of the local Division were fired upon while parading through Moy prior to the main Lady Day demonstrations in Lurgan,[7] and the AOH responded by announcing that one of their main St Patrick's Day parades would be held in the village the following year. However, when local Protestants claimed that such a parade would be provocative, the government agreed and invoked the Special Powers Act to restrict the gathering to a small section of the village. Extra police were brought in to ensure the law was enforced.[8] While this action was designed to send a clear message to the Hibernians with regard to their status in the village, it also confirmed to loyalists that the police would support their protests at nationalist displays. Furthermore, loyalists then organised a meeting to commemorate the Relief of Derry in the village in August to re-affirm its Protestant status.[9] When the Hibernians paraded again in August 1935, extra police were brought in to maintain order,[10] and two years later the Moy Division were stoned at the St Patrick's Day parade in nearby Dungannon.[11] After these confrontations it was twenty years before the Hibernians again organised a parade in Moy. It is also interesting to note that the Hibernians had planned to hold their main Lady's Day parade in the village in 1996, for what would have been their first visit since 1957. But this was cancelled in response to the violence that had been provoked by the banning of the Orange Order's Drumcree church parade. In spite of assurances by local people that they would be welcomed, the parade was relocated to Ballybofey in County Donegal. Moy was far from unique as a site of local conflict in the early years of the Northern Irish state but does serve to illustrate how the combination of local protests and state interests could coincide to restrain nationalist political expression.

The Hibernian parades were a continuation of a tradition that had been established in the nineteenth century, but republican commemorations of the Easter Rising, had no such history behind them and they were also more overtly antagonistic to the state. As the IRA had effectively stood-down as a military force in the north by the late 1920s and Sinn Fein maintained a low political profile, the Easter commemorations became the major public manifestation of the republican movement. Regular commemorations were held to mark the anniversary in Belfast, Derry and Newry but many events involved no more than a few hundred people. However, the Special Powers Act was widely used by the authorities to try to stop processions and meetings that might take place on Easter Sunday and this produced a variety of responses.

In 1930 a heavy police presence ensured that no public gatherings took place in either Belfast or Derry but large numbers of people were able to visit graves at the Milltown and Brandywell cemeteries in the two cities.[12] The following year, the police placed a guard on any likely venue for a commemoration, breaking up an attempted procession to Milltown, arresting three republicans for laying wreaths in Newry, and removing cards and Irish Tricolours from wreaths at Brandywell.[13] In 1933, 5000 people made their way to Milltown and when they were stopped they knelt on the road outside and recited the Rosary. In 1937 there were serious disturbances along the Falls Road when police baton charged the crowds that had gathered.[14]

Although there was a wide ideological gulf between the constitutional nationalism and republicanism, in practice loyalists readily ignored differences. Hibernian parades, Easter commemorations and Catholic religious displays were all regarded as no more than shades of Green, and therefore as a threat or a challenge to the Union. The main opposition to nationalist parades came from the state, but as we have seen, local opposition was also a significant factor, and confrontation over parades could easily lead to more widespread sectarian violence. This became a recurrent factor through the 1930s when parades became both a focus of localised disputes over territorial control and a proxy to more violent clashes over the border.

Orange parades had initially continued in the border counties but in 1931 became a target of IRA threats. When in August that year a crowd gathered to stop a Black parade, described as an 'Imperialist-led Orange demonstration', from passing through Cootehill, County Cavan, loyalists responded by confronting Hibernian parades in Armagh and Portadown. The B Specials were mobilised to deal with the disturbances in Portadown, while rioting also broke out in Armagh and Lisburn.[15]

Cross-border tension increased after Fianna Fail's election victory in 1932 and provoking further reaction to nationalist parades and demonstrations in the north. There were disturbances in Enniskillen when Fianna Fail supporters tried to celebrate their election victory and two members of the Hibernians were shot and injured in Ballinderry Bridge, near Lisburn, on St Patrick's Day a few weeks later.[16] Loyalists also reacted violently to the rise in religious fervour which accompanied an international Eucharistic Congress in Dublin at the end of June. Extensive decorations were erected in Catholic areas in the north: bunting was hung across streets, arches erected and shrines built and thousands of pilgrims travelled to Dublin for the Congress. But on their return trains and buses were attacked in Banbridge, Ballymena,

Coleraine, Donemana, Kilkeel, Larne, Lisburn, Lurgan, Loughbrickland and Portadown.[17] A few days later protesters tried to stop a Hibernian band from parading in Caledon on its way to a church service, and in retaliation a loyalist band returning from a Somme commemoration was attacked on the Crumlin Road in Belfast. Tension was such that the police were forced to re-route an Orange church parade in Coalisland on 10 July, although on the Twelfth the local Orange lodge was allowed to march through the town.[18] There were yet more disputes on Lady's Day, the most significant being in Caledon where a 'drumming party' occupied the centre of the village and the police stopped the local Hibernian Division from holding their parade.

In Belfast sectarian violence had been increasing through the 1930s particularly in the densely packed terraces around the Docks. These clashes reached their peak in 1935 with some of the worst rioting Belfast had ever seen. Many of the disturbances were sparked by parades and by mid-June the authorities had become concerned enough to ban all parades in the city. However, the Orange Order organised an illegal parade in protest at the ban and four days later the restriction was lifted. The parades on the Twelfth led to nine days of riots which resulted in the death of seven Protestants and three Catholics and to over two thousand Catholics being forced from their homes.[19]

While constitutional nationalists were able to continue to hold their parades after partition, this was accepted only so far as they did not transgress into areas perceived as Protestant. Their limited rights to political expression were a function of their ambiguous position within the new state. However, there was no ambiguity in the relationship between the state and the republican movement and their political displays were strongly opposed. Nevertheless, it is important to place these restrictions within a wider historical context and compare the actions of the northern state with those of its neighbours in the same period. Unionist politicians increasingly defined Northern Ireland as a Protestant state but did so at a time in which the Free State under de Valera increasingly defined itself in terms of Catholicism. Many within the Protestant community saw the entire Catholic population as a real threat to their existence and reacted to any assertive public expressions from that community. This not only led to constraints on nationalist parades but also to an escalation of Orange parades. Much of the contemporary Orange tradition derives from this period. The Last Saturday parades date from the 1920s and during the 1930s the Apprentice Boys and the Junior Orange Order established new parading days over the

Easter period in an attempt to 'recover' the holiday, which they saw as being 'hijacked' by republicans, for Protestants.[20]

But it was not only the northern state that saw a threat in republicanism; so, too, did the Free State. For example, in 1931, Free State troops were present at Bodenstown to stop the IRA issuing military orders at the Wolfe Tone commemoration. Under de Valera, from 1932, the government encouraged the Easter commemorations and Fianna Fail politicians took centre stage at Bodenstown. However, the resurgence of a more militant and violent IRA and persistent street clashes with the right-wing Blue Shirts generated increasing government concern. In 1939 they introduced the Offences Against the State Act which gave them wide powers to deal with political opponents and a few days later the IRA was declared an unlawful organisation and the Bodenstown commemorations were banned.[21] The example of the actions of the Free State towards public political expression illustrates the point that it is a common enough reaction for governments to ban public events by those opposed to the state. During the same period the British government was similarly concerned with threats to the state and public order. In the 1930s the threat of Fascism led to calls for greater controls on demonstrations and the wearing of uniforms in parade. In 1936 the first Public Order Act was passed despite arguments by civil libertarians that state was gaining undue powers.[22] In that sense the government of Northern Ireland acted as its neighbours did, to protect its interests, the difference being that in this case the threat to the state was seen as coming from a community that made up around a third of the population.

The post-war period is fondly remembered by many in Northern Ireland, particularly unionists, as relatively trouble free. It is seen as a time when Catholics would come out to watch Orange parades; when Orangemen and Hibernians would share band instruments or banner poles; a period with neither parade disputes nor major civil disturbances, and IRA activity was largely confined to the ineffectual border campaign of 1956–62. A greater sense of confidence amongst unionists seems to have made major anniversaries such as the Twelfth and Derry Day less assertive events, and there is some evidence that Orange parades were more relaxed affairs which contained fewer overt expressions of sectarianism.[23] The recollections that people have about the post-war period are important because they influence the way they view the parade disputes that have taken place since the early 1980s. Since many of those involved in the recent disputes were brought up in the 1950s and 1960s, their memories of this time frame their understandings of the norms and meanings of their cultural practices. But this period also witnessed a growing confidence within the nationalist community over the issue of public displays of their political identity. This manifested itself in two main ways. First a desire to commemorate a wider range of events than previously, and second to begin to challenge the apparent unionist assumption that they could parade wherever and whenever they so desired. The Northern Ireland government responded to these developments in two ways. They allowed more nationalist demonstrations but focused their attention more on the symbols being displayed than the body of marchers. Second, they introduced new legislation to deal with parades and symbolic displays: the Public Order Act (NI) was introduced in 1951; and the Flags and Emblems (Display) Act (NI) in 1954.

Ironically, this post-war 'Golden Age' was ushered in on a wave of street violence and disputes over parades which has since been largely forgotten. The end of the war was marked by the appearance of a new constitutional nationalist organisation, the Anti-Partition League (APL), which brought together farmers and the professional and middle classes in opposition to the northern state. As well as contesting local and Westminster elections, the APL took their politics onto the streets, organising a series of parades and demonstrations to mobilise support. The government responded to this resurgence of public displays by banning a wide range of nationalist gatherings. As well as the longstanding (but widely ignored) prohibition on Easter commemorations, St Patrick's Day parades in Derry were banned in 1948 and 1949, as were rallies in Belfast to mark the anniversary of the United Irishmen in September 1948. Furthermore, during a particularly violent election campaign in February 1949 a number of public meetings in Belfast were attacked and broken up by police or loyalists, while three Orange bands were at the head of a crowd which broke up a rally in Garvagh. Over the next two years violent clashes occurred between police and nationalists at a range of parades and rallies, including trouble at Hibernian parades at Aughnacloy and Moneymore in 1950, and once again in Derry on St Patrick's Day in 1951.[24]

The Northern Ireland government responded to this increase in violence by introducing new legislation to control parades. The 1951 Public Order Act was similar to the British Public Order Act of 1936 in so far as it gave the police power to re-route or impose conditions on a parade if there was a possibility of serious disorder and the Minister of Home Affairs could also ban parades for three months. There was no right of appeal to either decision. But the new law differed from the

British law in so far as it also required that the police be given forty-eight hours' notification of a parade unless the procession was 'customarily held along a particular route'.[25] These changes were clearly aimed at giving the police greater power and flexibility to control the growth of parades by nationalist organisations since they effectively exempted the loyal orders from any requirement to give notification for their traditional parades. In so doing they legalised the inequalities of power which had allowed a continuity for Protestant-unionist 'tradition' while the consolidation of Catholic-nationalist 'traditions' had been restrained as a result of opposition by loyalists and the police.

Nationalists initially reacted angrily to these changes and there were violent clashes at one of the first events after the new law came into force when police tried to remove a Tricolour at a Hibernian parade in Enniskillen on Lady's Day 1951. There was further trouble in Derry on St Patrick's Day the following year, once again sparked by police seizing a flag.[26] It is not clear how extensively the law was ever used to restrict or control parades and demonstrations. By the time the new law was passed, the APL was already beginning to decline and the impetus for more overtly politicised parades and demonstrations was lost. Furthermore, it was still the case that extra-legal activity was just as effective at stopping nationalist parades if the police were not willing to defend them. Three days after the police broke up the Enniskillen Lady's Day parade, a large crowd of loyalists took the law into their own hands and stopped a local Catholic band from parading through nearby Tempo.[27] But once again this appeared to be less a part of a systematic strategy than a localised response to nationalist assertiveness.

Nevertheless, the passing of the Public Order Act was something of a watershed. But rather than marking the beginning of a sustained assault on nationalist political expression, there seems to have been some acknowledgement of the legitimacy of their commemorations. Instead of confronting nationalist parades, greater concern was given to the growing prominence given to symbolic displays of the Tricolour. The annual Hibernian parades began to grow in scale and significance, with at least two main parades held each March and August and more prominent political speeches were made at the field. In this same period nationalists and republicans were also able to extend the range of their commemorations, albeit as long as they were confined to remote areas where they would not offend loyal Protestants. In 1949, the Antrim branch of the National Graves Association erected a memorial to Roger Casement in Glenariff and on 6 August 1950 the same branch attracted a large crowd for the unveiling of another memorial at Cushendun.[28] In 1955, the anniversary of Casement's execution (3 August 1916) was marked by a commemoration on the first Sunday of August at Murlough Bay, in north Antrim. This continued to be held on an annual basis until the early years of the Troubles. Other anniversaries were marked on a one-off basis. Although the 150th anniversary of the United Irishmen Rising had been banned from the centre of Belfast, commemorations did take place on the Falls, and the 150th anniversary of Robert Emmett's Rising in September 1953 was marked by large parades in Belfast and Downpatrick. In Downpatrick the processionists carried a green and white flag and a placard proclaiming 'Orange forbidden in the Six Counties' after they had been prevented from carrying a Tricolour. In contrast, the parade along the Falls Road was bedecked with Tricolours and banners.[29]

As this last example illustrates, the reaction of the police to republican displays was somewhat inconsistent, apparently based on the attitudes of local police officers rather than any notion of civil rights, or even public order. In Newry in 1951 an estimated 10 000 people took part in an Easter commemoration parade, which involved members of Newry Council, the Anti-Partition League and the Transport and General Workers Union as well as republicans. Reports suggest that on this occasion the police took no action at the flying of Tricolours and did not interfere with the procession.[30] But at other times, such as at the Easter parades in Lurgan in 1952 and 1953, they confiscated flags and made arrests.[31] Sometimes people were prepared to accept the police instructions but on other occasions the police activity seems to have been a deliberate attempt to provoke an otherwise peaceful procession and people responded violently.

In February 1954 the government introduced the second piece of legislation related to public displays: the Flags and Emblems Act. In part this was a response to the persistent disputes over displays of the Tricolour, but it was also in part a response to problems which had occurred over the flying of the Union Flag during the celebrations of the Coronation of Queen Elizabeth II in the summer of 1953.[32] Unionist decorations were not only put up in Protestant areas but they were also erected in some Catholic areas. Disputes arose over displays in Cookstown and Newry and there were numerous incidents elsewhere involving bunting and flags being torn down, of Tricolours replacing Union Flags and vice versa. The police were forced to intervene in a dispute in Derrymacash outside Lurgan when neighbouring households displayed the rival national flags, and to ensure the dispute did not escalate it was agreed that all flags in the village should be taken down.[33] The 1954 Act made it an offence to interfere with the Union Flag and empowered police officers to remove flags that might cause a breach of the peace. The Tricolour was not named in the act but the intention was clear. Although, as Bryson and McCartney point out, in many ways this did not add to the powers which the police already had available to them under the Special Powers Act, the very existence of the new law further angered nationalists.[34] It also failed to stop disputes over flags. In August 1954, a few months after the law was introduced fifty two people were injured in Pomeroy when the RUC tried to remove a Tricolour from a procession to welcome the return of abstentionist MP Liam Kelly after his release from prison.[35] In 1957, arrests were made in Newry over the carrying of Tricolours at the Easter commemoration and the following year the parade was banned, although this was ignored.[36] Again it was the perception of unequal treatment of the two communities that cause offence and anger. Lurgan in particular was one town where Catholics had been consistently denied the same opportunities to parade as Protestants and in June 1957 there were further clashes when a loyalist band from Kilkeel were allowed to parade with a Union Flag in a Catholic part of the town.[37] Yet in August 1959 the AOH were refused permission to walk along the main street on Lady's Day 'due to the threat of disorder'.[38]

The police generally ensured that loyalist parades were able to go where they so desired and in fact most parades by the loyal orders were unproblematic and provoked no overt opposition. However, a number of disputes did occur during this period: in Bellarena and Dungiven in County Londonderry and on the Longstone Road in County Down. The ways in which these issues were dealt with indicates that on occasion the RUC and the government were concerned about the effect that assertive loyalist parades had on community relations. But the way in which they were eventually resolved also illustrates the political power of the loyal orders at this time. Through 1947 and 1948 there were confrontations between Orange and nationalist bands at Bellarena, local RUC officers initially stopped the loyalist band from parading their desired route. However, under pressure from senior Orangemen, the Home Affairs Minister, Edmond Warnock, told the RUC to let the band hold their parade.[39] A similar process was played out on the Longstone Road in 1952. A parade planned to go to a new Orange Hall in a predominantly nationalist area was banned by the Minister of Home Affairs, and the decision was upheld by his replacement, G.B. Hanna, in 1954. But once again, pressure from within the

Unionist Party and the Orange Order was such that the ban was lifted to enable a parade to take place on the Twelfth in 1955.[40] The dispute arose in Dungiven when a loyalist band tried to march through the town to celebrate the Queen's Coronation in 1953. Nationalists protested in part because of the continued banning of nationalist parades in Derry. The issue arose again in 1958 when the same band marched through the town without warning, and a few days later a Union Flag was hung in the grounds of the Catholic church. The government feared that violence in Dungiven might boost the IRA's campaign and the Minister, W.W.B. Topping, banned an Orange parade through the town the next year. However, at the Twelfth that year Topping and other ministers were heckled and a few months later he resigned. The following year the new minister, Brian Faulkner, allowed the parade to take place.[41] It was clearly dangerous to a minister's political life to attempt to stop an Orange parade.

Disputes over nationalist parades and symbolic displays continued into the 1960s. But despite this undercurrent of conflict, community relations at this time were possibly better than they had been, or would be, at any point in the century. There were discussions within the unionist administration of the need for economic and social reforms, and the Dublin government was keen to foster good relationships with the government in Northern Ireland. Talks were held between the Grand Master of the Orange Order, Sir George Clark, and a National Vice-President of the AOH, Gerry Lennon, in 1963 and in January 1965 the Prime Minister, Terence O'Neill, and the Taoiseach, Sean Lemass, met in both Belfast and Dublin. There is a question over how far O'Neill was prepared to go in reforming Northern Ireland, but his actions nevertheless had a significant effect on the Protestant community. A 'liberal' shift by Unionist politicians left them open to accusations of disloyalty, of putting the Union at risk, leaving fertile ground on which hard-line politicians could move. At the Twelfth in 1965 shouts of 'Lundy' were hurled at George Clark because of his willingness to talk with the Hibernians. Amongst the more hard-line unionists, the Reverend Ian Paisley was proving to be the most adept at campaigning. In part this was due to his skills within the sphere of public political expression and exploiting the type of situations which we have been discussing. The most contentious example took place on 27 September 1964 when Paisley threatened to walk up the Falls Road to remove a Tricolour from offices of the Republican Party. The following day the RUC decided to remove the 'offensive flag'. When it was replaced a few days later, the police smashed windows to gain access to it and serious street disturbances broke out, the worst since 1935.[42] Because of the relationship of the institutions of the state with public political displays through legislation and the actions of the police, it was relatively easy for hard-line politicians to engineer incidents by threatening demonstrations or counter-demonstrations. Despite, or perhaps because of, the restrictions placed upon the rights of nationalists to express their political identity, inaction by the police or courts was depicted by some unionists as a sign of weakness.

The 50th anniversary of the Easter Rising coincided with growing concerns within the unionist community at both the apparent reforms being considered by the government and the growth of nationalist assertiveness. On 31 March, Gerry Fitt, standing as a Republican Labour candidate, won the seat of West Belfast in the Westminster General Election and over the following weeks large Easter commemorations were held across the north. The government mobilised over 10 000 B Specials as a precaution, but apart from confiscating Tricolours in a number of areas the events passed without major incident.[43] The main commemorations took place in West Belfast. On 3 April, a pageant was held in Casement Park, while on 10 April 5000 people walked from Beechmount Park to Milltown, carrying Tricolours and other republican flags, while an estimated 20 000 were reported to have lined the route.[44] Despite their previous concerns over security, the government actually expressed its approval over the co-operation that organisers of the commemorations had given.[45] A week later, on 17 April, one of the biggest ever parades was expected on the Falls. But when Paisley announced that he would hold a counter-march from the Shankill to the Cenotaph and the Ulster Hall, which would pass close to where the republican parade was to start, the government was forced to consider potential public order problems. Rather than ban Paisley's rally, they focused their attention on supporters of the republican cause. A special train bringing people from Dublin was banned, stringent checks on vehicles were made at border crossings and more extensive security measures were placed upon the parade on the Falls Road.[46] In spite of these restrictions, up to 20 000 people paraded to Casement Park and tens of thousands turned out to watch. Taking part in the parade were representatives of many strands of the nationalist movement, including the Belfast Trades Council, a number of individual trade unions, the old IRA, the Wolfe Tone Clubs, the Irish National Foresters and the GAA. The day passed peacefully but in spite of the heavy security presence a small bomb exploded in a telephone box near the Milltown Cemetery.[47] These large and assertive Easter commemorations reflected the developing politicisation of the Catholic community, but growing inter-communal tensions revealed themselves in a catalogue of attacks on churches, schools and other significant buildings and stories of intimidation directed at residents in various areas of Belfast.[48] On 6 June, Paisley organised a demonstration against the 'Romanising tendencies' of the Presbyterian church past the Catholic Markets area and left a riot in his wake. This time the government was forced to act. On 20 July, Paisley was jailed for his part in the parade and non-traditional parades were banned for three months.

The Easter commemorations of 1966 set a pattern for the years that followed with larger and more militant nationalist commemorations taking place in the context of the emergence of the civil rights movement and worsening communal tensions. There is no need to repeat the details of the civil rights movement as it has been adequately recounted and discussed elsewhere.[49] The discontent around which the different strands of the civil rights movement coalesced were housing, employment and political representation, but the way this discontent was manifested was through demonstrations. The result was that the area of inequality that was most directly challenged was over rights of public political expression. It was difficult to directly challenge housing policy and employment practice but the right to march could be physically contested. The civil rights movement directly challenged the control that the institutions of the state had placed upon political expression which sought to oppose unionist power. In many ways the civil rights campaign was a dispute over the right to march, a dispute that had, in one form or another, continued since partition.

Disputes over civil rights parades in Derry, Dungannon, Newry, Armagh in 1968 and 1969 led to serious violence as loyalists and the state sought to constrain the rights of Catholics to march in the centre of the major towns. It mattered little that they were arguing for a reform of the northern state rather than the republican demand of a United Ireland, the civil rights marches questioned the state's control of public space and the forces of the state reacted violently. In largely Catholic areas such as Derry the limitations of the police to impose control became clear despite their increasing use of physical violence. As a result, political and social spaces were created within which the republican movement could develop with new vigour.[50] After the February 1969 election, a now divided Unionist administration introduced a new Public Order Bill, which required a longer notice for parades (72 hours); made participating in an illegal parade an offence; made illegal counter-demonstrations that attempted to stop a legal parade; and gave greater power to ban specific parades. However, traditional parades were still exempt from these constraints.[51] Even as the Bill passed into law there were protests at Stormont and around the country.

Civil Rights demonstrations and street clashes continued throughout 1969 and climaxed in Derry on 12 August at the Relief of Derry parade. There had been many calls for the parade to be banned or re-routed and despite meetings between the Apprentice Boys and the Derry Citizens' Defence Association the parade went ahead. The day soon degenerated into running battles between residents of the Bogside and the RUC and loyalists. The battle of the Bogside, widely seen as the start of the Troubles, had begun. On 13 August, two days before the AOH parades and with all but the Last Saturday Black parades completed, the Government announced a six-month ban on parades. *The Times* argued that 'by waiting until now to ban the parades, the Stormont Government convicts itself of partiality in the eyes of the minority'.[52] In the end an AOH parade was held in Dungannon, although another in Lurgan was cancelled as were the Black parades, while the Apprentice Boys celebrated the Burning of Lundy in December without a major parade.[53] By the end of the year many working class Catholic areas in Derry and Belfast had become No-Go areas for the security forces. What had started as a non-violent campaign that questioned the control of public space by unionism had developed into an armed challenge to the existence of the state. The crisis that followed led, among other things, to the introduction of direct rule from Westminster and changes to policing in Northern Ireland. Relations of power altered significantly. By the mid-1980s a number of Orange parades in nationalist areas were rerouted and in 1993 a republican march commemorating Internment was allowed into the centre of Belfast. Nationalist parading seemed to have come of age.

Notes

1. Neil Jarman and Dominic Bryan, *Parade and Protest: a Discussion of Parading Disputes in Northern Ireland* (Coleraine, 1996).
2. Neil Jarman, *Material Conflicts: Parades and Visual Displays in Northern Ireland* (Oxford, 1997).
3. Neil Jarman and Dominic Bryan, *From Riots to Rights: Nationalist Parades in the North of Ireland* (Coleraine, 1998).
4. R. Weitzer, *Policing Under Fire: Ethnic Conflict and Police-Community Relations in Northern Ireland* (Albany, 1995); and Keith Jeffery in Chapter 5 of this volume.

5. M.T. Foy, 'The AOH: an Irish Politico-religious Pressure Group, 1884–1975' (unpublished MA Thesis, Queens University Belfast: Belfast, 1976).
6. *Irish News*, 16 August 1904.
7. Ibid., 7 August 1927.
8. Ibid., 19 March 1928.
9. Ibid., 13 August 1928.
10. Ibid., 16 August 1935.
11. Ibid., 18 August 1937.
12. Ibid., 19 April 1930 and 21 April 1930.
13. Ibid., 6 April 1931.
14. Ibid., 29 March 1937.
15. Ibid., 17 August 1931; *News Letter*, 13 August 1931, 17 August 1931, 18 August 1931.
16. *Irish News*, 18 March 1932; see also Jonathan Bardon, *A History of Ulster* (Belfast 1992) p. 535.
17. *Irish News*, 27 June 1932, 28 June 1932; see also Bardon, *A History of Ulster* pp. 537–9; and Michael Farrell *Northern Ireland: the Orange State* (London, 1980) pp. 136–7.
18. *Irish News*, 11 July 1932; *News Letter*, 11 July 1932.
19. A.C. Hepburn, *A Past Apart: Studies in the History of Catholic Belfast 1850–1950* (Belfast 1996) pp. 147–203.
20. Neil Jarman, *Material Conflicts*, p. 73.
21. Tim Pat Coogan, *The IRA*. London (London 1987).
22. Charles Townshend, *Making the Peace: Public Order and Public Security in Modern Britain* (Oxford, 1993) pp. 80–111.
23. Dominic Bryan, 'Ritual, Tradition and Control: the Politics of Orange Parades in Northern Ireland' (Unpublished PhD Thesis, University of Ulster: Coleraine, 1996).
24. Michael Farrell, *The Orange State*, p. 199.
25. Tom Hadden and Anne Donnelly, *The Legal Control of Marches in Northern Ireland* (Belfast, 1997) pp. 19–21.
26. Michael Farrell, *The Orange State*, p. 203.
27. Ibid., p. 200.
28. *Irish News*, 7 August 1950.
29. *Irish Independent*, 14 September 1953; 21 September 1953.
30. *Irish News*, 26 March 1953.
31. Ibid., 6 April 1953.
32. Lucy Bryson and Clem McCartney, *Clashing Symbols: a Report on the Use of Flags, Anthems and Other National Symbols in Northern Ireland* (Belfast 1994) p. 145.
33. Ed Moloney and Andrew Pollack, *Paisley* (Dublin, 1986) pp. 62–3.
34. Bryson and McCartney, *Clashing Symbols*, pp. 144–56.
35. *Irish News*, 20 August 1954; see also Farrell, *Orange State*, p. 206.
36. *Irish News*, 22 April 1957; 7 April 1958.
37. Ibid., 17 June 1957.
38. Ibid., 13 August 1959.
39. Henry Patterson, 'RUC and Orange Order Frequently at odds', *Irish Times*, 11 July 1997.
40. Michael Farrell, *The Orange State*, pp. 107–208.

41. See Keith Jeffery, Ch. 5; Farrell *The Orange State*, p. 222; Moloney and Pollak, *Paisley*, pp. 90–3.
42. Bardon, *A History of Ulster*, p. 632.
43. Moloney and Pollak, *Paisley*, p. 130.
44. *Irish News,* 11 April 1966 and 12 April 1966.
45. Ibid., 13 April 1966.
46. Ibid., 15 April 1966, 16 April 1966 and 18 April 1966, see also D. Boulton, *The UVF, 1966–73: an Anatomy of Loyalist Rebellion* (Dublin, 1973) and Moloney and Pollak, *Paisley*, pp. 130–1.
47. *Irish News,* 18 April 1966.
48. B. Purdie, *Politics in the Streets: the Origins of the Civil Rights Movement in Northern Ireland* (Belfast, 1990) p. 32.
49. Eamon McCann, *War and an Irish Town* (London, 1980); Farrell *The Orange State*; Sarah Nelson, *Ulster's Uncertain Defenders: Loyalists and the Northern Ireland Conflict* (Belfast, 1984); N. O Dochartaigh, *From Civil Rights to Armalites: Derry and the Birth of the Irish Troubles* (Cork, 1997).
50. O Dochartaigh, *From Civil Rights to Armalites*, pp. 41–2.
51. Haddon and Donnelly, *The Legal Control of Marches in Northern Ireland*, p. 20.
52. *Irish News,* 14 August 1969.
53. Ibid.

7

Wearing the Green: a History of Nationalist Demonstrations among the Diaspora in Scotland

Joseph M. Bradley

During the late nineteenth and early twentieth centuries, there was significant Irish-oriented cultural and political activity among the immigrant Irish Catholic community in west-central Scotland. Along with a plethora of Catholic religious and social bodies, Irish organisations were vibrant wherever large numbers of the Irish diaspora in Scotland settled: an estimated 100 000 in the years during and after the Great Famine of the mid-nineteenth century, and even more in the latter nineteenth and early decades of the twentieth centuries.[1] By the first decade of the 1900s, the Gaelic League had seventeen branches in the Glasgow district and over the course of the following years, numerous other branches in and around Lanarkshire, Paisley, Ayrshire, Dumbarton and several other areas of west-central Scotland.[2] This expansion of League activities was also significant in relation to the evolution of gaelic athletic clubs, the first one, Red Hugh O Neill's, being founded in the east end of Glasgow in 1897. Almost one hundred such clubs have been founded during the course of the twentieth century.[3]

In relation to aspirations to an independent and united Ireland, some Irish political activity was established throughout the nineteenth century. As early as 1823, the few thousand Irish who lived in the Glasgow area formed an offshoot of Daniel O'Connell's Catholic Association, which identified with the political nationalism then stirring at home. After a generation or more of cultural and political decimation in the wake of the Great Famine, and a resultant emphasis on human survival, by the 1870s stronger Irish political feelings began to make a significant impact. In November 1871, a Glasgow branch of the Irish national movement, then known as the Home Government Association, was formed and its leader, Isaac Butt MP, was on hand to

111

deliver the local body's inaugural address. In 1893 Ulster Protestant immigrant and nationalist Home Ruler, John Ferguson, was elected to Glasgow Council. In 1898, the United Irish League emerged in Scotland 'which was able to mobilise the bulk of votes in strongly immigrant neighbourhoods right up until the First World War'.[4]

In 1908, three years after the founding of Sinn Fein in Ireland, a branch of the organisation was formed in Glasgow. It is estimated that the number of Sinn Fein branches in Scotland rose to around eighty in the years following the 1916 Rising, while the number of people who directly became involved in the developing Irish Republican Army was around three thousand in the Glasgow area alone.[5] The political situation in Ireland dominated within the Irish community during these years, indeed, it was a pre-eminent issue among the general population. So much so, that Eamon de Valera later revealed that the Irish in Scotland had contributed more money to the republican struggle than any other country, including Ireland itself.[6] Gallagher's work on Glasgow has confirmed the central role of Irish radicalism in the development of the Labour party in Scotland.[7] This radical, anti-establishment content of Irish nationalist politics meant that the Irish were amongst the most important sections of the general population for the evolution of the Labour party. They were at the forefront of the mass of the working class ripe for class politicisation.

This period also marked the zenith of active nationalist support in Scotland. The years 1922–23 saw the eruption of the fratricidal conflict of the Irish Civil War. Gallagher believes that the Irish in Scotland became confused and 'war wearied' as the fight in Ireland became less straightforward.[8] Confusion over the situation in Ireland, along with British anti-subversive actions, also contributed to many in the immigrant community becoming less inclined in their political Irishness. Although in 1925 in the Lanarkshire town of Coatbridge, Sinn Fein was instigating meetings in an attempt to revive the organisation,[9] the political parties which emerged in the new and independent Irish Free State had less need to create a British dimension than had their forebears in the Parliamentary Party and Sinn Fein. Irish parties began to weaken in Britain as Ireland played a less significant part in the British political agenda. In Britain, the Labour Party and trade unions served as incorporatist agents by diverting the attentions of the Irish towards matters immediately relevant to their everyday experiences. With the Irish Free State adjusting to its recently found independence, the new Northern Ireland state developed as a violent sectarian entity, largely hidden from the eyes of the general public. As a result Ireland's historical struggle declined in the immigrant mind.

Although many Irish in Britain became involved in bodies such as the Anti-Partition League, Irish politics ceased to stir the same level of activity as in pre-partition days. Allied to this, immigration from Ireland to Scotland declined dramatically after the First World War and many of the Irish and their offspring began to acquire new party political allegiances which were the product of their immediate circumstances. Despite affinity with and loyalty to Ireland, many Irish gradually recognised that politically they could be more influential in a local setting. The extension of the franchise during this period also contributed towards a more progressive view of Labour. So began the Labour Party's deep reliance on the Irish in west-central Scotland. Early relations between both bodies were often tense but gradually the Labour Party became the main beneficiary of Irish immigrants' changing political experiences and perspectives: this in direct relation to the decline in Irish nationalist political activity.

Although the struggle for independence for Ireland became more complex during and after the 1920s and the vibrant Irish nationalist activities of the diaspora in Scotland subsequently weakened, the tradition of 'the cause' of Ireland, remained. This was particularly evidenced within the environs of Celtic Football Club. Immigrant Irish Catholics built and sustained Celtic and there was an interlocking of spirit between the club and the immigrant diaspora in west-central Scotland in particular. During its first decades of existence, Celtic officials and players were significantly involved in Irish patriotic activities, much like many others in the community which they represented. Although unlike in the pre-partition period, there are few post-1920s references to involvement in Irish politics on the part of Celtic directors or players, the wider Celtic 'community' remained politically minded with respect to Ireland. The eruption of 'the Troubles' in Northern Ireland almost half a century later, and the alignment of many supporters with the nationalist cause, reflected the part Irish nationalism continues to play in being a Celtic follower.[10]

During the latter nineteenth and early twentieth centuries, therefore, the tradition of 'the cause' of nationalist Ireland found a number of avenues for expression amongst the Irish in Scotland. Apart from political associations, meetings, activities, electoral behaviour (and through Celtic Football Club), Irish nationalism was also expressed in street demonstrations and marches. The O'Connell Association in the nineteenth century organised a number of marches, while during the

O'Connell centenary celebrations in the Partick area of Glasgow in August 1875, the Home Rulers were attacked by hundreds of Orangemen and fighting lasted for days.[11]

The Irish National Foresters (INF) was one of the most significant organisations which incorporated major parades into its calendar of events, this at a time when such demonstrations were viewed as integral to many contemporary cultural practices. The Foresters functioned as an insurance, welfare, friendly and political association, and was one of the most obvious manifestations of Irish identity in Scotland continuing links with home and heritage in Ireland. A vast number, if not the majority, of Catholic families amongst the diaspora in Scotland contained members of the Foresters. Towards the end of the nineteenth and throughout the early decades of the twentieth centuries, the INF was a primary Irish organisation in Scotland.

In 1903 the INF held a well-attended sports day at the Glasgow home of the immigrants' sporting heroes, Celtic Football Club.[12] However, ten years later the annual demonstration of the INF was viewed as being partly responsible for inhibiting a greater attendance at the Glasgow/Scotland versus Kilkenny exhibition GAA hurling match also held at Celtic Park. On the same day, at Whifflet in Coatbridge, ten miles east of Glasgow, a Foresters' demonstration took place and many thousands of Irish Catholics attended. With an estimated 100 000 members in Scotland on the eve of the First World War, men women and juniors, the INF held the allegiances of many members of the Catholic community. It is not surprising that a minority sporting occasion, Irish or otherwise, had failed to attract widespread interest amongst the immigrants.[13]

Large Irish and Catholic cultural and political demonstrations in Scotland continued throughout the early twentieth century. In 1921, barred from entering Glasgow, the nationalist-minded Archbishop Daniel Mannix, an Irishman who resided in Melbourne, Australia, spoke to the expatriate Irish community of west-central Scotland. His open-air rally held in Whifflet, Coatbridge, attracted over 50 000 people.[14] Coatbridge had also received attention in 1910 when Belfast MP, Joseph Devlin, visited Scotland during the St Patrick's celebrations. When Devlin visited the Lanarkshire town, Dr Charles O Neill, the Coatbridge-based MP for South Armagh, was encouraged to welcome Devlin to a United Irish League meeting in the Theatre Royal. O Neill commented that Devlin:

> would not need any pressure to force him to come there to witness such a demonstration of Irish power and loyalty.[15]

Even the Catholic Boys' Guild in Scotland held major marches. In 1928 and 1929 it was reported that 10 000 boys walked with the organisation.[16] A few years earlier, in 1921, the Catholic Knights of Saint Columba had 10 000 attend its parade. Although this body, like the Boys' Guild, was more of a Catholic spiritual organisation, such massive involvement of members of the immigrant community in marching and parading demonstrates the extent that this practice held during the period.[17]

The INF remained important amongst the plethora of Catholic and Irish bodies in Scotland until at least the Second World War. By 1936, the Foresters still retained over 5000 in its juvenile section alone.[18] Nevertheless, the growth of the Ancient Order of Hibernians (AOH) in Scotland rivalled the strength and marching prowess of the Foresters, although membership of both organisations frequently overlapped. Despite being a distinct organisation, the AOH at this time was similar to the Foresters, at least in relation to its members' Catholicity, politics and Irishness, as well as its friendly status. Both organisations' demonstrations served a number of functions and they allowed the Irish to congregate, to maintain a sense of community and celebrate their Irishness and Catholicity. At the annual demonstration of the AOH in Hamilton in 1912, over 30 000 nationalists were reported to have taken part. Resolutions were passed congratulating Redmond and the Irish National Parliamentary Party, and the meeting resolved to assist them by every means in its endeavours to place the government of Ireland in the hands of the Irish people. After the march:

> the procession of the different contingents, headed by their bands and banners, through the town formed an imposing spectacle, which was witnessed by thousands of spectators. Forty-five different bodies marched in the procession which was led by the famous O Neill War Pipe Band, Armagh.[19]

A year later, 50 000 Hibernians took part in a procession in Kilmarnock, before being addressed by their national president, Joseph Devlin.[20] Many of the bands which participated in Hibernian and similar demonstrations were Church and Catholic parochial associations and bodies.

In 1919, in the Lanarkshire village of Glenboig, twenty-nine male divisions and fourteen female divisions marched for the annual demonstration of the Lanark County on 30 August.[21] Even in the east of the country, where far fewer Irish settled, a crowd of 500 marched during the summer of 1920. In Fife, AOH divisions from Cowdenbeath,

Lochgelly, Lochore, Dunfermline, Methil, Kelty, Inverkeithing and Cardenden were headed by the Lochgelly Flute Band, political speeches were heard and finance was raised for the Cowdenbeath Church Building Fund.[22]

In 1929, 35 000 people took part at an AOH parade in Dumbarton, 40 000 took part in Hamilton in 1930, 10 000 participated at a rally in Edinburgh in 1931 and 30 000 walked in a demonstration held in the Lanarkshire town of Blantyre in 1932.[23] At one of the last major rallies held in Scotland shortly before the outbreak of the Second World War, 40 000 people collected to march in the strongly Hibernian village of Carfin, Lanarkshire, in west-central Scotland.[24]

Although significant numbers of the Irish diaspora in Scotland attended these later marches, the inter-war period was also a time when many Catholics' Irishness became increasingly privatised due partly to the political and cultural climate of the time. This period was also crucial to expressions of Irishness for many decades thereafter.

Cooney asserts that as late as 1938, the Church and Nation Committee of the Church of Scotland emphasised; 'the elementary right of a nation to control and select its immigrants'.[25] The debate which had resulted in such a way of thinking was conducted solely with Irish Catholics in mind. Brown states that from around the time of the Education Act (Scotland) 1918, until the outbreak of the Second World War, there was an 'official' Presbyterian campaign against the Irish Catholic community in Scotland.[26] This campaign was both institutional and popular, and is viewed by Brown as an attempt at 'marginalising, and even eliminating an ethnic minority whose presence was regarded as an evil, polluting the purity of Scottish race and culture'.[27]

This period was a fertile one for such activities as well as a time when they were acceptable to and supported by many people in the wider society. Such sentiments found expression in popular literature, for example in the works of Andrew Dewar Gibb (later to become Regius Professor of Scots Law at Glasgow University) and of journalist George Malcolm Thomson.[28] Political activists, like Alexander Ratcliffe in Glasgow and John Cormack in Edinburgh, gained success at the ballot by declaring similar anti-Irish and anti-Catholic opinions. Other significant political figures at the time reflected these widespread feelings regarding the Irish in Scotland. Conservative member of Parliament, Lord Scone, believed that:

> culturally the Irish population ... has not been assimilated into the Scottish population. It is not my purpose to discuss now whether

the Irish culture is good or bad, but merely to state the definite fact that there is in the west of Scotland a completely separate race of alien origin practically homogeneous whose presence there is bitterly resented by tens of thousands of the Scottish working-class.[29]

Such attitudes towards the Irish were conceived within a context of Britain's historic relationship with the island of Ireland as well as by established anti-Catholicism which dominated or filtered through many areas of Scottish society. Although this encounter was complex and multi-varied, and despite a number of Scots making no contribution to it, antagonism characterised many individual and popular perceptions.[30]

The anti-Catholic and anti-Irish nature of significant areas of life during the 1920s and 1930s made a critical impression upon the self perceptions and images of the immigrant diaspora in Scotland gradually ebbing at its self-confidence and expression. Irishness remained important to many within the community, as is reflected in the strength of Irish identity in the late twentieth century, a clear indication of elements of this identity being passed through generations. However, this period also helped create one of the strategies constructed by the Irish to contend with adversity in Scotland. Thus, becoming less obviously Irish was an important part of a strategy which many consciously or unconsciously embarked upon. If such campaigns against the Irish in Scotland had met with more obvious success, for some, the result might have been deportation. At the very least, members of the Irish Catholic community in Scotland were concerned about the widespread overt and well-supported hostility with which they were being confronted. In the context of such negative portrayals, it seems an obvious question to ask, who in society wished to be openly associated with Ireland or the Irish? For others who were varyingly anti-Irish, a less distinctive Irish identity and community within Scottish society might not have dampened some of their antagonism, but it may have relieved its worst features. If the Irish were there to stay and could not be viably rejected, then rather than negatively effect a perceived purity in the Scottishness of the host community, they would have to be assimilated. Irishness remained largely unacceptable, but the Irish might be more acceptable if they became less Irish and more Scottish.

Partly as a response to such ethno-religious circumstances, from the 1930s Catholic identity, in relation to a diminishing Irishness, became the predominant feature of the immigrant community. A change amongst the Irish, which manifested itself in a less visible Irish identity, was reflected in an increasing Catholic emphasis in the Irish political, cultural and religious organ, *The Glasgow Star and Examiner*. Irish politics and cultural activities continued to be reported in Catholic newspapers but as they receded in prominence, they did so at the expense of purely Catholic or religious matters. Newspapers such as *The Glasgow Star* became less partisan and engaged in a struggle to be viewed as impartial in things Irish and political: more often than not, ignoring Irish and political affairs altogether. A product of this process was the gradual diminishing of news in relation to Ireland and the Irish in Scotland. *The Star* was one newspaper which began a trend amongst Catholic newspapers in Scotland reflecting a gradual shift towards reporting articles Scottish rather than matters Irish as was previously the case. Finally, with the death in 1934 of Derryman Charles Diamond, owner of much of the Catholic and Irish press in Britain, a new era for Irish ethnic newspapers dawned. By 1935, *The Glasgow Star* announced its forthwith 'strictly non-political' position whilst its 'aims and ideals [were subsequently] devoted entirely to the Catholic cause'.[31]

In many ways, Ireland and being Irish became less accessible. In addition, for some of the Irish community in Scotland, to be viewed as Scottish was a mark of success. For some immigrants, Ireland represented the poverty and oppression of the past. A perception existed that to be seen as Irish was to be viewed as parochial, ignorant and permanently ghettoised.[32] A less visible Irishness amongst Irish immigrants in Scotland and the steady adoption of a new framework of identity for some immigrants, has since characterised many of the offspring of the Irish. Antagonism and hostility on the part of a variety of institutions, organisations and individuals throughout Scottish society, helped create and sustain an atmosphere where to be seen as Irish meant that life chances were perceived as being limited. Almost inevitably, part of the Irish Catholic response to this hostility was a privatisation as well as dilution of Irish identity.[33]

With the social climate during the inter-war years perceived as unfavourable towards things Irish as well as Catholic and with a growing militancy amongst numerous Protestant associations in Glasgow and Edinburgh in particular, added to the number of disturbances associated with Hibernian parades during the 1930s, the membership of the AOH imposed on themselves a marching ban which effectively lasted until the 1960s. For one observer, two things emerged from a 'no-parades policy':

One was an almost overnight end to Irish marching bands (Glasgow had at least twenty fine Irish pipe bands) and the other the start of the gradual run-down of the biggest Irish organisation Scotland had ever seen.[34]

By the time the Hibernians began to re-emerge in the late 1950s and early 1960s, the social, economic and political landscape in Scotland had changed dramatically: the introduction of the Welfare State and re-locations of local populations which resulted from the building of Scottish new towns being two of the non-political and secular influences which helped induce a different view of the Order, which had virtually lost a generation of potential members due to its self-imposed ban. Despite claims of forty-six divisions in 1952 and fifteen to twenty by the early 1960s, in reality many local AOH divisions had disappeared. Its musical prowess was lost amidst the previous generation and most of its properties were sold off, sometimes to the Catholic Church or the local Labour Party for small amounts of money.[35] By this time, the only substantial marching organisation in Scotland for a generation was the Orange Institution.

By the 1960s, many of the perceptions within the Catholic community were governed by a perspective that Catholic involvement with the Hibernians was simply a mimicking of the perceived bigotry of their Orange counterparts: Green, as opposed to Orange Walks, were no more acceptable to many of them.[36] Accordingly, a view began to dominate within parts of the 'practising' Catholic community (then in a majority) that the kind of Irishness portrayed by the 1960s and 1970s Hibernians was of a degenerate nature, more inclined and characterised by social activities in drinking clubs, shoddy and pathetic demonstrations and less distinguished by serious politics or Catholic spirituality and piety. For many Catholics, the AOH was increasingly negatively labelled because of a perception of members' lack of Church attendance and respectability, this during a time of increasing Catholic social confidence and progress. These views were further exacerbated by the negative images of Ireland, particularly Northern Ireland, which were becoming part of the everyday diet of the British media as 'the Troubles' began to make a greater impact on people's lives. Indeed, the AOH cancelled its annual demonstration at Carfin in case it was construed as inflammatory. Likewise, between 1970 and 1974, the AOH leadership in Ireland also cancelled its annual demonstrations due to continuing conflict.[37]

By the late 1990s, the Hibernians consisted of a limited membership: the organisation failed to revive itself, both in terms of participants and supporters. At most there were 500 members attached to Hibernian social clubs in Carfin and Port Glasgow. Approximately one hundred people were active Hibernians in Coatbridge, Hamilton, Airdrie and Dundee: their main marches being twice a year, St Patrick's Day and an annual demonstration in June. A number of marching bands was also attached to each of these divisions.[38]

Although the Hibernians again emerged on the streets in the 1960s and 1970s, the time lapse in activity proved a watershed for the movement and the wider diaspora in Scotland. Apart from external perceptions of the AOH (which inhibited potential new members), internally, the organisation lacked the type of membership for its effective co-ordination as well as promotion. Partly arising from a lack of organisation and poor management, within a context of the re-emergence of the troubles in Northern Ireland, a number of disillusioned Hibernians formed the first modern Republican marching group in Glasgow, the James Connolly Flute Band, during 1975–76.[39]

During the 1970s, many young Hibernians, as well as other potential members, also became disillusioned with the perceived political inactivity and 'conservatism' of older and more traditional members. This was especially in light of events occurring in Northern Ireland, with the 'dirty protest' campaign in Long Kesh/Maze Prison for the reintroduction of political status for Republican prisoners, and, in particular, in relation to the Hunger Strike of 1981. Throughout the 1970s Irish nationalist and republican feelings towards Northern Ireland had become apparent among second- and third-generation Irish in Scotland and for those who wished to publicly demonstrate these sentiments, the AOH was not capable of appropriate organisation or leadership. Earlier, these problems had also become manifest for the Hibernians when at a AOH demonstration in 1976, the James Connolly Flute Band was refused permission to parade on account of its alleged pro-IRA sympathies. This band subsequently contacted Republicans in Ireland who invited it to partake in the 1977 annual demonstration in Belfast to commemorate the reintroduction of internment.[40]

By 1979, other 'republican' bands in Glasgow and Lanarkshire began to defect from the Hibernians and around this time some contact was made with left-wing organisations. This was not a one-way process as left groups also saw potential in building links with other radical-minded bodies. Highlighting their emphasis on perceived left-wing activity rather than cultural, ethnic or religious 'Irishness', these bands also increasingly made it clear that they were not to be considered as 'Catholic', so as to reject their opponents labelling them as sectarian.

Finally, in response to an AOH rally held in Coatbridge in 1981, at which platform speakers were jeered by young republicans for their refusal to acknowledge and support the Hunger Strike then underway in Northern Ireland, the younger cohort set up the Republican Band Alliance (RBA) in Glasgow in July of that year.[41]

Unlike the Hibernian bands which have taken their names from saints and more traditionally recognised Irish heroes, the twelve to thirty band Republican Alliance which has existed since the early 1980s, have adopted names which have strong associations with the Republican campaign of the 1970s to 1990s period.[42] Since 1975, almost fifty of these bands have existed, sometimes for short periods of time.[43] In the main, these groups have originated in Lanarkshire and the Glasgow area although some have also emerged in Dundee and Edinburgh.

Since the early 1980s such bands (averaging around three-dozen strong) have taken part in local parades commemorating favoured Irish political events and figures, like the Rising of 1916 or the 1981 Hunger Strike. One group, the Billy Reid Flute Band from the Parkhead area of Glasgow, travelled to New York as guests of the Republican support organisation, Noraid, to march in the St Patrick's Day Parade of 1984. A number of these marches in Scotland have been confronted by loyalist, Orange and National Front supporters, aiming to drive the 'Troops Out' demonstrators off the streets and this has resulted in violence and police arrests.[44] However, the vast majority of these marches have passed without incident.

The RBA states that it supports the Irish nationalist community in 'occupied Ireland', while it has as its main aim a raising of political awareness among its young band members.[45] Politically it has been highly active, supporting not only Republican events in Ireland and Britain but perceived anti-imperialist ones, including pro-Palestinian and pro-ANC events in the 1980s. Some members view band activity as an opportunity to live out an Irish identity, one strongly characterised by its political fervour which emphasises Republicanism and anti-British imperialism. For a small number of members, it is also an Irish–Scottish phenomenon, because of its anti-British and anti-English dimension.[46] Ironically, bands from Scotland led to the emergence of a number of similar ones in Northern Ireland. This helped give Republican demonstrations in Ireland a more militant approach, one that had previously been missing.

The RBA is marked out by its leftist and working-class character. Relations have frequently been built with groups such as the 'Troops Out Movement', the 'Revolutionary Communist Party' and the 'Labour

Committee on Ireland', while a few bands have even became involved on occasion with the 'Scottish Republican Socialist Party' and several mainstream Scottish nationalist rallies.[47] One Catholic Bishop in Scotland condemned the bands, calling on Catholics not to be fooled by the playing of traditional tunes because these bands were 'belting out a hard left wing message'. He added, that he was not condemning the 'truly traditional bands of either the Orange Order or the AOH'.[48] Such criticism has been customary when the RBA or any of the individual bands have marched, or when they have been confronted by loyalist groupings. In this regard, Scotland's largest selling newspaper, *The Daily Record*, has been unambiguous and has vehemently criticised the RBA. The *Record* considers the Republican marchers as a sectarian menace on the streets.[49]

Republican marchers have been widely condemned by many religious persuasions in Scotland, not least from within the Catholic Church. In 1988, the Press Officer for the Archdiocese of Glasgow stated:

> In attempting to arouse sectarian or nationalistic emotions they are a threat to the good order of the community and as such should not be permitted.[50]

Similarly, Bishop Devine of Motherwell, stated that the bands were:

> importing sectarian strife into areas and recommended that Catholics should have nothing to do with them.[51]

During the 1980s, Strathclyde Chief Constable, Andrew Sloan, expressed his concern that the increase in annual walks by Protestant and Catholic organisations, was dividing the community.[52]

Confrontations between demonstrators and counter-demonstrators led to a number of violent incidents during this period: in Dumbarton, Glasgow, Coatbridge and Wishaw, and particularly in Edinburgh throughout the 1980s and 1990s. Such events have parallels with other conflicts between young left- and right-wing demonstrators which increased in frequency around Britain during the 1980s, principally in areas of England where 'racism' is seen as a problem. Including marchers, the events in Scotland usually attract crowds ranging from two hundred to two thousand people, though by the 1990s, attendances were frequently smaller.

Apart from RBA marches for the 'H-Block Hunger Strikers', 'Free the Guildford Four' and the 'Time To Go' campaign and other related low-

level Irish nationalist and 'republican' activity, there is little other contemporary evidence of the once vibrant political 'activity' in traditional
Irish influenced areas of the west of Scotland. In fact no community
initiative from within the Catholic Church in Scotland on the 'Free the
Birmingham Six' campaign (which attracted people from all walks of
life as a 'human rights' as well as an Irish issue) was organised until the
final year of its existence (1991).[53] Even in Labour Party circles, these
issues, as with most Northern Ireland-related ones, have often been
marginalised by party members either due to fear of being labelled religious or sectarian or because even Irish human rights issues have the
potential to divide its membership – such has frequently been the con-
tentiousness of the 'Irish Question' in Scottish/British politics.[54] The
key point is that while Irish identity and pro-Irish political attitudes
can be important for many of the diaspora in Scotland, pro-Irish political activity is much less evident.

Since the partition of Ireland, but particularly since the period of the
Second World War, many, if not most politically minded Catholics have
immersed themselves in Labour politics: only a few have involved themselves in further political activity in relation to Ireland and the Northern
troubles. Clearly, this results partly in relation to the time lapse between
the creation of the Free State and the eruption of the present conflict: for
almost half a century hostilities in the area were contained and largely
unreported. Many people are also deterred by the seemingly constant
violence attached to Northern Irish politics or by an atmosphere of fear
which has often paralysed political debate on the issue. As far as the RBA
is concerned, the first band did not take part in a major Glasgow Irish
demonstration concerning the Troubles until over ten years after they
began.[55] In addition, an atmosphere of fear was also generated within the
RBA itself when it was reported that the Prevention Of Terrorism Act and
Special Branch were being used to infiltrate and subdue band activity in
Scotland and the RBA's travels to Northern Ireland.[56]

Even though Irish political activity today is limited if compared to
the past, such political support remains a characteristic among all generations of the Irish immigrant diaspora. Irish nationalist and republican political activity generally (as distinct from those of a purely
left-wing background) involves only a few thousand people.
Nonetheless, the legacy of the Irish nationalist immigrant mind-set has
lasted throughout the period of immigration and cultural integra-
tion/assimilation. Support remains strong for a united Ireland independent from Britain. Survey figures for all types of Catholic opinion is
evidence of this support.[57]

Despite a general Catholic distaste for violence in Northern Ireland, but seemingly in contempt of dominant British interpretations of the northern troubles, an Irish nationalist identity persists among the offspring of the Irish in Scotland. Some of these Catholics have a passionate, but more have a passive, attachment to an Ireland united and detached from a British military and ruling presence. However, regardless of the patriotic clothes worn by the offspring of the immigrants, and indeed, despite its significance within the community, this characteristic should not be over-emphasised at the expense of other factors of Catholic life in Scotland. For over half a century the main political concerns of the Catholic Irish have been born out of their everyday circumstances and aspirations. Over the past three generations many of the politically aware or dynamic within the immigrant community have submerged themselves in Labour Party activity, and the 'Irish question' has been marginalised.

Nonetheless, the contemporary phenomenon of Republican bands in Scotland can be viewed partly as a re-emergence of an earlier form of political and cultural identity for some working-class youth of Irish origin. This activity, although occasionally headline making, is low level and, in reality, for many Catholics of the Irish diaspora, lacks the positive attributes which make up the movements that many of their forebears were part of. Indeed, despite only being two or three generations gone, much of this heritage has been lost or confined in an unspoken part of the community's past, primarily due to anti-Catholic and anti-Irish hostility in Scotland as well as because of perceptions of Northern Ireland troubles. Ireland's contentious relationship with Britain has provided much of the context for Irish identity in Britain itself. It is also an area of the Irish community's history in Scotland which is tense and contentious. This is largely a result of the immigrants' experience and the strategies which the Irish community has adopted to negotiate this encounter.

In recent years, many bands have collapsed within a few months or years of their foundation. They have lacked support from the traditional community, within which many more actually oppose them. Many have been unable to maintain their membership and most have experienced an enormous turnover in personnel, most bands having had hundreds of members throughout their short histories.[58] Few have given rise to a commonly perceived respectable, responsible and educated leadership. Their context of mobilisation has been one of a perceived ghetto mentality, further disabled by the media's reporting of events in Northern Ireland. Many of those traditionally viewed as recruits for an Irish nationalist movement in Scotland have dismissed or privatised their Irish political identity, asserted it in the perceived safety of numbers through their support for Celtic Football Club, become Labour Party activists or had their organisational leanings attracted by membership of more 'respectful' Catholic-minded institutions such as the Knights of St Columba.

However, since the 1980s and the general re-emergence of Irish identity among many of the diaspora in Scotland, much Irish nationalist sentiment has manifested itself significantly in the pub and social club scene. Whereas Irish political identity seems to have had only a few outlets for expression, has disappeared or been concealed or suppressed until the early 1980s, it has re-gained popular and widespread appeal amongst many offspring of Irish immigrants in west-central Scotland. Nevertheless, there is little likelihood that this will manifest itself in the kind of nationalist political activity which once characterised the Irish in Scotland. For many Scottish-born Irish, the practice of street demonstrations has long held little appeal: most perceiving such activity as the apeing of Orange demonstrations, with all the sectarianism, bigotry and racism which they perceive in that context.

Although Irish political consciousness in Scotland is maintained throughout areas where the diaspora has settled, such identity depends not on any marching tradition, but on family experience, local oral history, opposition to extreme Protestant and Orange identities, political education and the effects of a number of other Irish and Catholic cultural influences: continuing legacies of being part of the Irish diaspora in Scotland.

Notes

1. Handley estimates that 100 000 arrived in Scotland over the course of the Famine period. See J. Handley, *The Irish in Scotland* (Glasgow (this book incorporates both 'The Irish in Scotland, 1798–1845', and 'The Irish in Modern Scotland, 1943 and 1947' respectively, both Cork University Press), 1964.
2. See J.M. Bradley, *Sport, Culture, Politics and Scottish Society: Irish Immigrants and the Gaelic Athletic Association* (Edinburgh, 1998).
3. Ibid, p. 175.
4. T. Gallagher, *Glasgow: the Uneasy Peace* (Manchester, 1987), pp. 63–8.
5. Ibid, p. 90.
6. K. O'Connor, *The Irish in Britain* (Dublin, 1970), pp. 141–2.
7. Gallagher, pp. 94–7.

8. Ibid.
9. *The Star*, 9 January 1925.
10. See J.M. Bradley, 'Facets of the Irish Diaspora', *Irish Journal of Sociology*, vol. 6, 1996, pp. 79–100.
11. Handley, p. 257.
12. *The Glasgow Star and Examiner*, 26 July 1903.
13. Ibid., 7 August 1914.
14. See Gallagher, pp. 93–4.
15. *The Star*, 18 March 1910.
16. Ibid., 2 June 1928 and 1 June 1929.
17. Ibid., 25 April 1921.
18. Ibid., 25 April 1936.
19. M. Mitchell, 'The Catholic Community in Hamilton, c1800–1914', in *St Mary's Hamilton: a Social History, 1846–1996*, ed. T.M. Devine (Edinburgh, 1995), pp. 31–70.
20. *Glasgow Observer*, 6 September 1913.
21. Ibid., 26 July 1919.
22. *The Star*, 17 July 1920 and 21 August 1920.
23. Ibid., 7 September 1929, 6 September 1930, 5 March 1931, 3 September 1932.
24. Ibid., 18 August 1938.
25. J. Cooney, *Scotland and the Papacy* (Edinburgh, 1982), p. 19.
26. S.J. Brown, 'Outside the Covenant: The Scottish Presbyterian Churches and Irish Immigration, 1922–1938', *The Innes Review*, Vol. XL11, No. 1, Spring 1991, pp. 19–45.
27. Ibid.
28. Gallagher, pp. 168–72.
29. *Hansard*, 261, 22 November 1932.
30. See Bradley, 1995.
31. *The Glasgow Star*, 7 September 1935.
32. Gallagher's otherwise excellent biographical work also reflects the non-specific sub-theme of an Irish ghetto population in the west of Scotland.
33. Mr James Breen, born in 1907, a former rector of St Patrick's High School Coatbridge (1955–1973), in an interview with the author stated that he had the impression that this period was typified by many Catholics 'keeping their heads down' through fear and intimidation. In a series of interviews for the St Mary's Hamilton 150 years social history project (see reference to Devine, 1995) these impressions were also strongly in evidence, particularly in relation to Catholic difficulties in gaining meaningful employment.
34. *The Irish Post*, 19 March 1988.
35. For example, the Dumbarton AOH Hall, built in the 1930s was sold ten years later for £100 and in the 1990s was owned by the Labour Party.
36. There are also many Protestants in Scotland as well as other Scots who are critical of Orange demonstrations as well as the type of Protestantism which characterises the Orange Institution.
37. F. J. Devine, *Working Class Culture and Irish Identity: Flute Bands*, Undergraduate Dissertation, Department of Government, University of Strathclyde, 1997, p. 20.

38. For example, the St Patrick's Flute Band and the Robert Emmet Accordion Band. Interviews with Benny Kangley of Port Glasgow Hibernians, and Tommy Paton of Carfin Hibernians, 14 June 1991. Also see AOH programme for annual demonstration, Saturday, June 27th 1981.
39. Devine, p. 22.
40. Ibid.
41. Known as the RBA, later known as the Irish-Scottish Bands Association. See Bradley, 1995, p. 141.
42. For example, the Andersonstown Martyrs from Glasgow and the Crossmaglen Patriots from Wishaw. This number was probably around 10 to 12 by 1998, including AOH bands (about 30 per cent).
43. Devine, pp. 66–8.
44. See, *Lennox Herald*, 18 April 1986; *County Reporter*, 23 April 1986, also for counter demonstrations against the Orange Lodge. See, *Lennox Herald*, 15 April 1988 for Republican marches in Dumbarton, and *Sunday Mail* and the *Sunday Observer* (Scotland), for similar troubles in Edinburgh. The latter article also refers to the growing involvement of the BNP in anti Republican activities.
45. A 1990s survey found that 90 per cent of RBA members were Catholic. One third attended mass weekly (similar to the average for Catholics in Scotland), whilst 50 per cent attended sometimes and 20 per cent never. The vast majority, 84 per cent, of band activists, were found to be under 34, while again a majority (88 per cent) of the membership was male. Almost all of the RBA members were to be found in skilled or unskilled manual employments and only two were professional or technical workers. See Bradley, 1995, pp. 140–5.
46. Jimmy Wright, a leading member of the RBA, and a member of the James Connolly Flute Band from Govan in Glasgow, has been prominent in Scottish left-wing Republican circles. Wright's strong feelings, as well as connections with the Scottish Republican Socialists in the 1980s, led to him attempting to have the Scottish saltire flown alongside the Irish Tricolour, by every Irish republican band. This caused a degree of turmoil among the bands who were motivated by mainly Irish ideas, and saw themselves as having little affinity with Scotland. A compromise was reached, after some bands threatened to leave the Alliance, and which basically stated that bands could opt to fly the Scottish flag if they so wished.
47. While the writer was carrying out a survey in 1990 amongst the Jim Lynagh Republican Band in Dumbarton, an impromptu meeting was held, in which one activist encouraged the others to collect in the following days, and to forcibly prevent Poll Tax officers from entering the home of a non-paying protester. Also see Devine, pp. 31–2.
48. *Flourish* (Glasgow Catholic Newspaper), July 1987.
49. *Daily Record*, 4 May 1988 and 28 May 1991.
50. *Flourish*, May 1988.
51. *Flourish*, July 1987.
52. *Airdrie and Coatbridge Advertiser*, 1 August 1986. Also see 19 September 1986.
53. Interview with member of the Glasgow Birmingham Six committee, June 1991. See also a number of references in the SCO in early 1991; for example

22 March 1991. Previous to this *Flourish* commented on the issue on only a few occasions.

54. A Motherwell-based Lanarkshire Labour Party member informed the author that he was aware of some members attempting to have these issues debated during the 1980s and early 1990s but they were continually deflected elsewhere. In addition, a member of the Labour Party in Coatbridge, Lanarkshire, also informed the author that as soon as Ireland was introduced in Party discussions some members deliberately and quickly moved to another area for debate. The character of the Party in this area has been mainly Catholic of Irish descent.

55. Interviews with ex-member of Glasgow 'Sinn Fein', June 1991.

56. *Irish Post*, 4 March 1989.

57. See Bradley, 1995.

58. Devine, p. 56, states that the Crossmaglen Patriots from Wishaw in Lanarkshire have had almost 700 members since the band was born in 1981.

8
Bloody Sunday and its Commemoration Parades

Seamus Dunn

> Wars against Irish men or Scots
> who be of the same rudeness and wild disposition
> that ... the Britons were
> in the time of Caesar.
>
> Sir Thomas Elyot, 1531

The history of the violence in Northern Ireland, as it is resides and resonates in the public imagination, is deeply coloured by a long sequence of shocking and dramatic moments and images of brutality and horror: the Enniskillen Poppy Day bombings, the 'trick-or-treat' bar shootings in Greysteel, the sight of Michael Stone firing at a funeral crowd in Belfast, the deaths of three small boys in Ballymoney and, the last great atrocity so far, the bombing of Omagh that killed 29 people. But, perhaps for many, the most poignant and memorable images were the television pictures of an obviously shocked and terrified priest, waving a blood-stained handkerchief as a flag of truce, and leading a group of young men, carrying another dying young man, through the ranks of British army soldiers. This was Bloody Sunday, 30 January 1972: the priest was Father Edward Daly, later Bishop of Derry. These startling and chilling pictures have never lost their power to disturb, and it has been argued that they were a major factor over the years in providing the energy and stimulus needed to continue with the campaign of violence.

In January 1998, some twenty-one years later and after a long and persistent campaign, the Prime Minister of the United Kingdom, Tony Blair, announced a decision to hold a new judicial enquiry into the events of Bloody Sunday. This decision was simply the final acknowledgement of the unease and uncertainty felt about that event even at the top levels of British society. In the parliamentary debate that followed his decision was supported by most speakers from all parties, with the exception of unionists from Northern Ireland. David Trimble, leader of the Ulster Unionist Party, said that 'opening old wounds like this is likely to do more harm than good' and accused the Prime Minister of using 'mealy-mouthed language'.

The details of the background to, and events of, Bloody Sunday are well-known and fairly easily told, even though the long shadows of anger and misery cast by the events of that day have not yet eased. A parade was held in Derry Londonderry[1] to protest against recent events, the route being confined almost entirely to Catholic nationalist areas. The parade was illegal and it was predictable that, at its end, there would be the usual, almost ritualised, throwing of stones at the security forces by the young men.

Up to a point this is indeed what happened. But then, in the melée that followed, the army shot dead – sometimes in the back – thirteen young boys and men. Thirteen others were wounded by bullets, one of whom later died, making a total of twenty-six. It is now fairly generally accepted that these were all unarmed citizens,[2] most of them shot by members of the First Battalion of the British Parachute Regiment brought in specially for the event: they were watched by officers and leaders, and even, it seems, encouraged by some. (It now seems possible that men from another regiment were also shooting from the walls.) The army commander, for reasons as yet not well understood, retired early from the scene. The immediate impression of these events was described at the time as 'a sense of chaos', and that sense has prevailed in the responses and imaginations of many ever since. However, recent research and publications have gone some way towards providing a much clearer and more detailed picture of the events of the day.[3]

There is, of course, a long historical tradition of public demonstrations that have gone horribly wrong: Amritsar, Peterloo, Sharpeville, Kent State. In these events it is the fact that authority and its representatives deal out sudden and unexpected death that gives them historical power and resonance. When those who represent the state, and its great authority, break laws and disturb public order with violence and death, the magnitude of that betrayal casts a shadow that seems impossible to remove.[4] In Ireland, in particular, because the state itself is contested, and because the actions of nationalists are often treated as inherently transgressive, such events have both a symbolic emotional significance and an enormous transformative impact on the public imagination.

Looking back it is clear that Bloody Sunday marked a watershed from which there could be no return, and that it was an important catalyst in the long years of extraordinarily persistent, vicious and seemingly unstoppable violence. The iconic significance of Bloody Sunday can also be measured by the extent to which it has been recorded and reflected on by artists, writers and poets.[5]

Each year, throughout the twenty-one years between Bloody Sunday and the announcement of a new inquiry, a march to commemorate the deaths of the fourteen victims was held, over the same route as on Bloody Sunday itself. The form of this march, and the way in which it was organised and managed, along with the accompanying political nuances and adjustments, are of some interest. For example, it can be argued that the evolution of the march over time reflects a number of other processes at work within the wider society in relation to the conflict. These processes include developments such as the changing relationships between Sinn Fein and the SDLP, the Hume–Adams talks beginning in January 1988, and Sinn Fein's own evolution towards the practice of normal politics and what has become known as the 'peace process', leading right up to the Good Friday Agreement.[6]

The events of that Sunday have to be seen in the context of what had been happening over the previous year.[7] On 9 August 1971, the then Northern Ireland Prime Minister, Brian Faulkner, introduced internment, or detention without trial.[8] Early that morning British army troops went into homes throughout Northern Ireland and arrested some 342 men – all Catholics – deemed to be enemies of the state.[9] At the same time all marches and parades were banned. The nationalist community reacted with outrage and fury. Violence erupted and reached amazing new heights. The *Sunday Times* Insight Team recorded that in the four months before internment four soldiers were killed, no policemen and four civilians, but that in the four months after it, thirty soldiers, eleven members of the RUC and the Ulster Defence Regiment, and seventy three civilians were killed.[10] The Northern Ireland Civil Rights Association's (NICRA) campaign of civil disobedience and protest action[11] escalated with continuing demonstrations and illegal parades.

January 1972, therefore, marked the six-month anniversary of the introduction of internment, and there were strong and persistent rumours that a second internment camp was to be opened at Magilligan in County Derry. On 22 January, a group of anti-internment demonstrators, at a NICRA protest near Magilligan, was roughly handled by British troops – including members of the Parachute

Regiment. On 19 January 1972, Faulkner announced that the ban on marches and parades would be extended for a further twelve months – to the annoyance of loyalist organisations such as the Orange Order.[12]

It was in this context of anger, fear and uncertainty that plans were made for an anti-internment march in Derry on 30 January. The *Londonderry Sentinel* on Wednesday 26 January announced the decision by the Derry Civil Rights Association 'to march on the following Sunday to the Guildhall Square, where a rally will be addressed by Lord Brockway, the Labour peer, Mr Ivan Cooper, MP and the Rev. Terence McCaughey of Trinity College Dublin, and other speakers'. A further story in the *Derry Journal* on 28 January described 'reports of a big military build-up in the Derry area and that the British Army is determined to prevent a breach of the parade ban by even stronger methods than the demonstrators at Magilligan experienced'.

During the week leading up to Bloody Sunday, a great many meetings and consultations took place at Stormont,[13] Westminster and Downing Street: those with an eye for conspiracies can easily look back at the sequence of events on a day-to-day basis and find much to ponder on. For example, on Tuesday, 25 January, the Democratic Unionists, led by Ian Paisley, announced that they would 'hold a "religious rally" in Guildhall Square on Sunday'.[14] This was a tactic much used by this party at that time. On Saturday, 29 January, the day before Bloody Sunday, they announced the cancellation of their prayer meeting with the words 'We were approached by the Government and given assurances that the Civil Rights march will be halted – by force if necessary.'[15]

In the days immediately following the deaths of Bloody Sunday, shock, fear and confusion were everywhere. The army and the government issued a number of confused and even contradictory statements relating to what had happened, including attempts to malign the dead. Most of these statements were subsequently withdrawn or disproved.

In the Republic of Ireland the effect of the violence was traumatic, but also deeply confusing. First, there were immediate responses arising out of the emotional impact of events: the Irish Ambassador to Britain was recalled, a day of national mourning was called for the following Wednesday (2 February) and a crowd burned down the British Embassy. In an emergency debate in the Dail, the Taoiseach, Jack Lynch, strongly rejected British descriptions of events. However, this quick response was accompanied by a warning to the people of the Republic not to play into the hands of those who would 'seek to overthrow the institutions of this state'.[16]

On 2 February, three days after Bloody Sunday, a commission of enquiry was established by the British Government under Lord Widgery.[17] The commission reported quickly (on 18 April 1972) with a short forty-two page document.[18] The 'Widgery Report', if anything, made things worse. Its delphic phrasing at best implied guilt on the part of some of the dead ('there is a strong suspicion that (some) others had been firing weapons or handling bombs in the course of the after-noon and that yet others had been closely supporting them'), a view that has since been discredited. The report also appears to justify (with faint condemnation and linguistic sophistry) the actions of the army: 'At one end of the scale some soldiers showed a high degree of respon-sibility; at the other, notably in Glenfada Park, firing bordered on the reckless. These distinctions reflect differences in the character and tem-perament of the soldiers concerned.'[19]

By any standards the Report is an evasive and complacent work, full of unquestioned certainties and veiled in the niceties and subterfuges of legal language. Its lines are written in such a way that we can read between them an almost unconscious assumption that the British Army could not be the villain in such a situation.

Until Bloody Sunday much of the running in the campaign to reform Northern Ireland had been made by the Northern Ireland Civil Rights Association. Afterwards the effective non-violent Civil Rights campaign ended, and the association began a slow decline as the 'armed struggle' inexorably took its place.

Within Derry itself, two separate groups made decisions about how they intended to commemorate the first anniversary of Bloody Sunday. The Civil Rights Association, which had organised the original Bloody Sunday march, proposed to hold an 'official ceremony' and not a march: 'The Brandywell branch of the Derry Civil Rights Association yesterday said that neither they nor the Northern Ireland Civil Rights Association are holding a march to commemorate Bloody Sunday because it might lead to a confrontation with the British Army'.[20] This ceremony was held in the shadow of the Rossville Street Flats, close to the places where the victims had been gunned down: the proceedings included wreath laying, an interdenominational service and a meeting addressed by those who had been invited to speak on Bloody Sunday. This form of commemoration has been repeated each year since.

In addition to this 'official' ceremony, a public meeting was held on Friday, 1 December 1972, eleven months after the killings, 'to determine the most fitting manner by which the people of Derry could participate in public expression of their grief over the slaughter of their fellow citizens'.[21] The meeting concluded that 'the first anniversary commemoration of Bloody Sunday should take place on January 28th 1973. That it should take the form of a March and Rally, and that it should be organised by Sinn Fein.'[22] This march began in Creggan, passed through the Brandywell and Bogside and ended at Celtic Park, the endplace being chosen to try to keep the young men away from confrontation with the British Army. The crowd was estimated at 15 000 and the speakers included Lord Fenner Brockway, Ivan Cooper and Bernadette Devlin.

This pattern of two events has been repeated each year since 1972. First, a relatively small wreath-laying commemoration organised for a time by the Civil Rights Association, but eventually by the relatives of those who had been killed or wounded. This event was avowedly non-political and non-partisan and allowed all those who felt regret at what happened to attend.

The second event was an annual march, organised by Sinn Fein. Because of this it was seen by some as 'party political', with the result that it was impossible for many opposed to Sinn Fein to attend. For example, Bishop Edward Daly, whose personal feelings about Bloody Sunday and the role of the Army could not be in doubt, always expressed his worry about the Bloody Sunday marches. He felt that 'they were exploited as a platform by some people who were apologists for campaigns of violence and murder – the complete contradiction of what Bloody Sunday meant and means to me ... the dominant theme of many of these annual marches has been militant and pro-violence rather than anti-violence'.[23]

For a long time there was a clear sense that those organising the two events commemorating Bloody Sunday did not see eye-to-eye, and that there existed divided opinions within the community about the right way to commemorate and remember the dead. The *Derry Journal,* for example, in 1973, wrote that it was sad that ' ... the occasion should have been chosen by a political organisation for mounting a propagandist demonstration of its own. Such an event could only have detracted from the solemnity of commemoration and mourning that should have characterised the occasion throughout'.[24]

In the second year after Bloody Sunday, therefore, there were two marches and commemoration rallies held, one organised by Northern Ireland Civil Rights Association and the other by Provisional Sinn Fein, both over the route of the march two years previously. The Civil Rights event was announced in October 1973 and was to include the unveiling of the new monument at Rossville Flats followed by a march on Sunday, 27 January 1974.

It was later decided, however, to move the date of this commemoration from Sunday to Saturday 'Because provisional Sinn Fein in Derry have arranged a party political demonstration for the same day. ... The decision was taken to prevent any undignified insult to the memory of the dead.'[25] The Civil Rights Association march was attended by over 2000 people headed by relatives of the Bloody Sunday victims carrying wreaths, and pamphlets were distributed calling on those taking part to march in total silence, to seek no confrontation with anyone, and to give 'an orderly and dignified display of the unconquerable power of the organised people'.[26] However, a line from the newspaper report indicates that there was also present '... two men carrying a large wreath from the Official Republican Movement': this may be an indication that the two parades also reflected the split in the IRA into 'Official' and Provisional' wings. Afterwards about fifty young people stoned army checkpoints.

Similar tensions were evident in 1976. The NICRA decided not to have a march and reverted to the form used earlier, that is a wreath-laying ceremony at the monument on Saturday, 31 January, followed by an address and an inter-denominational service. They also issued a statement, which included the words 'We would ask those paramilitary organisations who will also be holding commemorations to remember those aims that the Bloody Sunday demonstration voiced. Civil rights not civil war, end internment, end repression give us democracy'.[27]

In the years that followed it became clear that the control of the Bloody Sunday parades had become a political matter within the various strands of anti-unionism. Speakers at the march each year were usually supporters or members of Sinn Fein, who often attacked the SDLP. In 1976, for example, they were referred to as a party of quislings[28] and in 1985 as a bunch of geriatrics.[29] It is perhaps not surprising, therefore, that many members of the SDLP, such as John Hume, did not attend these marches.

Despite this division, the annual parades have acted as the vehicle for the channelling as well as the exploitation of the Bloody Sunday experience. Put together, events such as Internment, Bloody Sunday and the Hunger Strikes have been powerful elements in the story of how Sinn Fein, and to a lesser extent, the IRA became acceptable to many people otherwise opposed to them and to violence.

The pattern of events in relation to the Bloody Sunday commemorations continued in a relatively uneventful way for approximately the next fourteen years, with the papers reporting attendance at the wreath-laying ceremony as small, and those on the Sinn Fein march as being about 5000. The figures involved were often disputed, and there was some sense that the numbers declined for a time. In 1978, for example, it was reported that the Northern Ireland Civil Rights Association and the Provisional Sinn Fein held separate ceremonies.[30] The former held a simple wreath-laying ceremony in the morning at their Bloody Sunday memorial plinth attended by about fifty people in the Bogside, while in the afternoon a crowd estimated at 5000 attended the Provisional Sinn Fein march from Creggan to the Bogside. It was also reported that a group of about fifty youths broke away from the main body of the crowd near the end of the meeting and stoned business premises and set fire to one.[31]

In 1980 it was reported that the crowd at the march was about 2000, and also that a shop was burned and a soldier injured by a crowd of 30–40 youths. It was also by now well established that the march would be led by people bearing wreaths and followed by fourteen youngsters carrying black flags. In front of them walked a man draped in a blanket[32] and at the head a man carrying the Irish tricolour. As a final example, in 1985, the *Derry Journal* reported that 'relatives of those who died on Bloody Sunday came early on Sunday morning last to quietly pay tribute to the memories of their loved ones. Over the years this touching ceremony has attracted smaller numbers and few of those engaged in the civil rights campaign ... now attend. It is left to the relatives to mourn their dead.'[33]

In 1985 the parade is reported as being organised by Derry Sinn Fein. However, in 1986 in response to criticisms from Bishop Edward Daly about aspects of the march, an organisation called 'The Bloody Sunday Organising Committee' explained in a public statement that 'since 1986, this march and other related events, had been organised by the Bloody Sunday Committee which is made up of trade unionists, relatives of those killed in January 1972, and local artists and photographers'. The statement also said that they were an independent organisation and that they had no affiliations to Sinn Fein.[34] Nevertheless, during speeches at the end, Sinn Fein members were involved as speakers and the SDLP was again the subject of attacks from the platform. This pattern also continued for some time, with an 'independent organising committee', Sinn Fein speakers and attacks on the SDLP. The Bloody Sunday Organising Committee was the first of a number of often confusing organisations established since 1986 in relation to Bloody Sunday. Some of these will be discussed below.

In 1990, an IRA bomb – one attributed to the IRA – exploded during the march and killed a young sixteen-year old man called Charles Love, from Strabane. The Organising Committee issued a statement severely criticising the IRA for its decision to plant the bomb along the route of the march and called it a gross error of judgement. The IRA accepted the criticism and agreed that it would endeavour to ensure that such a thing did not happen again. The statement also attacked John Hume for his comments on the event.[35] However, between 1988 and 1991, the 'Bloody Sunday Committee' appears to have evolved into the 'Bloody Sunday Initiative', and a memorial plaque to Charles Love was the responsibility of this new organisation. The aims of the Bloody Sunday Initiative were to refocus attention on Bloody Sunday, to campaign against the Widgery findings and for a new enquiry into Bloody Sunday. Its membership included, among others, relatives of those who had died.

In early 1988, John Hume, leader of the constitutional nationalist party, the SDLP, began a series of highly controversial meetings with Gerry Adams, leader of Sinn Fein, a party closely linked to the IRA. The purpose of the meetings was to try to establish a common understanding of the positions of the two parties on the central issues concerning the future of Northern Ireland. These discussions, and the debate that they generated, both reflected and helped to create changes in the approach of the various interested parties to the question of Bloody Sunday. Certainly the campaign for a new inquiry into the events of that day attracted new energy and a new momentum, and became very much more organised and skilful, with more emphasis on co-operation between all concerned and a spirit of inclusiveness – at least on the nationalist/republican side. One of the first manifestations of this approach was the agreement by Derry City Council, in January 1992, on the 20th anniversary, to write to the British government 'to call for a full international and independent inquiry into the events of Bloody Sunday, twenty years ago. The innocent had been branded guilty and the guilty had been allowed to go free'.[36] Later that year John Major's written admission to John Hume that the victims were innocent (repeated later by Tony Blair) allowed Hume to call again for a new independent enquiry into the events of Bloody Sunday.

In April 1992, on the 20th anniversary of Bloody Sunday, a group made up mainly of relatives of the victims of Bloody Sunday met and established, as a campaigning organisation, 'The Bloody Sunday Justice Campaign'. The central purpose of this organisation was to ensure that the unanswered questions and issues relating to the events of Bloody Sunday, including the Widgery Tribunal, would be made an unavoidable part of a national and an international agenda.[37] During the years that followed, this campaign succeeded, slowly and with some political skill, in its aims. By January 1997 there was enough new material to allow

John Hume to put down an early Day Motion at Westminster, calling for new independent inquiry. Later that year, in June, the Irish Government presented the new British Prime Minister, Tony Blair, with a detailed government dossier, setting out all the new information available.

It is, therefore, perhaps not surprising that the parades held in 1997 and 1998 were the largest and most successful ever, with enormous crowds marching to remember the victims. The increased numbers and enthusiasm indicated a new sense of political unity among the community and a belief that the events of Bloody Sunday would at last be properly investigated. In February 1998, Mark Durkan was the first senior representative of the SDLP to address the meeting after the parade.

The new public relations skills of the organisers can be demonstrated by the programmes of additional activities built around the marches in recent years. These have included a photographic exhibition, a play, a book launching, a commemorative lecture, music, city tours, films, lectures, workshops, along with the central events, that is the wreath-laying ceremonies and the march.

In addition, a new organisation, the 'Bloody Sunday Trust', was established in 1997. This is an educational group that collates and brings together all information relating to Bloody Sunday, liaises with the Saville inquiry on behalf of the families and collects material for a permanent centre to be built later. An overseeing group called the 'Bloody Sunday Co-ordinating Committee' also meets once a year to organise the march and the surrounding activities.

This campaign came to a climax when, on 29 January 1998, Tony Blair announced in Parliament the setting up of a full-scale judicial inquiry into Bloody Sunday under the Tribunal of Inquiry (Evidence) Act 1921. Lord Saville of Newdigate, a law lord, was appointed to chair the tribunal and two other international judges (Sir Edward Somers from New Zealand and Mr Justice William Hoyt from Canada) were also appointed to the panel. The three judges came to the Guildhall in Derry to establish the new inquiry on the 3 April 1998.

Notes

1. The city is called Derry by nationalists and Londonderry by unionists. Because this chapter is about Bloody Sunday it will be referred to throughout as Derry.
2. The Prime Minister, Tony Blair, on 29 January 1998, in Parliament repeated and agreed with the words of his predecessor John Major, written to John Hume in a letter on 29th December 1992, in which he said that 'The

Government made clear in 1974 that those who were killed on "Bloody Sunday" should be regarded as innocent of any allegation that they were shot while handling firearms or explosives.' *Hansard*, 29 January 1998. However, this wording is described by Paul Bew and Gordon Gillespie *Northern Ireland: a Chronology of the Troubles 1968–1993* (Dublin, 1993), p. 285 as 'being more definite than the 1974 statement which said that those killed. "should be regarded as having been found not guilty of the allegation"'.

3. Two books in particular have been of singular importance. The first is *First Eyewitness Bloody Sunday, the Truth*, edited by Don Mullan and published in 1997 by the Wolfhound Press. This contains a selection of statements by witnesses on the day, drawn from over 500 collected at the time. These were essentially ignored by the Widgery Tribunal. The book also contains accounts of recently released archival and other material. The second book is called *The Bloody Sunday Tribunal of Inquiry: a Resounding Defeat for Truth, Justice and the Law* written by Dermot Walsh and published in 1997. This contains analyses of statements, released recently, made by soldiers on and after Bloody Sunday. The analysis reveals substantial and material inconsistencies, discrepancies and alterations.

4. This view was also expressed by the Prime Minister in the same speech in Parliament, with the words 'Bloody Sunday was different because, where the state's own authorities are concerned, we must be as sure as we can of the truth, precisely because we pride ourselves on our democracy and respect for the law … '. *Hansard*, 29 January 1998.

5. See, for example, *The Wearing of the Black: an Anthology of Contemporary Poetry* edited by Padraic Fiacc (Blackstaff Press, 1974). The Derry playwright Brian Friel wrote a play called 'The Freedom of the City' which was a reworking of many of the moral and political issues raised by the events of Bloody Sunday. And the poet Seamus Heaney wrote:

> He was blown to bits
> Out drinking in a curfew
> Others obeyed, three nights
> After they shot dead
> The thirteen men in Derry.
> PARAS THIRTEEN, the walls said,
> BOGSIDE NIL. That Wednesday
> Everybody held
> His breath and trembled.

Seamus Heaney, from 'Casualty', *Field Work*, London, 1979, p. 22.

6. The Good Friday Agreement was signed on 10 April 1998 by all the involved political constituencies (except for two unionist parties that had refused to attend the negotiations). The signatories included the leaders of the Irish and British governments.

7. The literature on this period is very large. For a detailed examination of events in Derry during the period from the beginning of the civil rights movement in 1968 until 1972 see *From Civil Rights to Armalites* by Niall O Dochartaigh (Cork, 1997).

8. The capacity to place people under detention without trial was legal under the Special Powers Act (1922), and had been used by Northern

Ireland governments in the past to detain people thought to be members of the IRA.

9. The intelligence upon which people were chosen was later found to be out-dated and inaccurate. By the end of 1971, around 900 people, almost all nationalists, were imprisoned without trial.

10. The *Sunday Times* Insight Team, *Ulster* (London, 1972).

11. The Northern Ireland Civil Rights Association emerged as a unified move-ment after the October 1968 march in Derry.

12. The three main 'loyal orders' were the Orange Order, the Royal Black Institution and the Apprentice Boys of Derry. All of these celebrated the history and culture of Ulster Protestantism by means principally of marches. They were therefore particularly enraged at the ban on marches. See Bryan, Dominic, T.G. Fraser and Seamus Dunn, *Loyalist Parades in Portadown* (Coleraine, 1995) and Jarman, Neil and Dominic Bryan, *Parade and Protest* (Coleraine, 1996).

13. Stormont was the location of the Northern Ireland Parliament, near Belfast.

14. *Derry Journal*, 28 January 1972.

15. '*Massacre at Derry*, a pamphlet published by the Civil Rights Movement', p. 6. The document is undated but was published almost immediately after the events of Bloody Sunday.

16. Dail Eireann, *Parliamentary Debates*, Vol. 258, 1971–72, 908, 3 February 1972.

17. Archive material released by the British Public Records Office in 1995 and 1996 include a memorandum of a meeting between the Prime Minister Edward Heath, the Lord Chancellor Hailsham and Lord Chief Justice Widgery, held at Downing Street on 31 January 1972. This includes the counsel from Heath to Widgery that 'It has to be remembered that we are in Northern Ireland fighting not only a military war but a propaganda war.'

18. 'Report of the Tribunal appointed to inquire into the events on Sunday, 30th January 1972, which led to loss of life in connection with the procession in Londonderry on that day' by Lord Widgery. H.L.101, H.C.220. London: HMSO, 18 April 1972.

19. Widgery, p. 39.

20. *Derry Journal*, 26 January 1973.

21. These events are described in a letter to the *Derry Journal* on 31 January 1992 by Sean Carr.

22. Ibid.

23. *Londonderry Sentinel*, 31 January 1990. However, more recently Dr Daly has expressed his regret that for many years he would not speak to Sinn Fein.

24. *Derry Journal*, 30 January 1973.

25. *Derry Journal*, 11 January 1974.

26. Derry Journal, 29 January 1974.

27. *Derry Journal*, 27 January 1976.

28. *Derry Journal*, 3 February 1976.

29. *Londonderry Sentinel*, 30 January 1985.

30. *Derry Journal*, 31 January 1978.

31. Ibid.

32. In September 1976, republican prisoners refused to wear prison uniforms and wrapped themselves in a blanket instead. This campaign eventually escalated into the Hunger Strikes of 1981.
33. *Derry Journal*, 28 January 1985.
34. *Londonderry Sentinel*, 24 January 1986.
35. *Derry Journal*, 2 February 1990.
36. *Derry Journal*, 21 January 1992.
37. At about the same time the 'Bloody Sunday Initiative' became the Pat Finucane Centre, a human rights organisation, named after the Belfast solicitor murdered by loyalists in 1989.

9

'Miracle on the Shankill': the Peace March and Rally of 28 August 1976

Grace Fraser and Valerie Morgan

> When the two groups met at the junction of Northumberland Road and the Shankill Road, there was a tremendous gush as people came together and the march formed up. There was a great surge of people which shocked those watching. It was historic. History was being made. It was as if people were saying, 'We do not want to be divided'. It was not a march against loyalism or republicanism. It was not against any particular group. It was a cry from the heart. It was a rally for peace, for people, for their families. It was a beautiful day.
>
> Mairead Corrigan[1]

Mairead Corrigan was one of the three founders of the Peace People, the movement begun in Northern Ireland in August 1976. This was her description of the defining moment at the beginning of the march on 28 August 1976, when the two main groups of participants, Catholics and Protestants, met, merged as one, and headed up the Shankill Road in the warm afternoon sunshine into the Protestant heartland of Belfast. The marchers came from all over the city and beyond, including contingents from the Irish Republic. The majority were women, but there was a good sprinkling of men. People of all ages and circumstance took part, children in prams, youngsters holding their mothers' hands, teenage girls arms linked together, housewives in summer dresses, old age pensioners, trade unionists, Catholic nuns and priests marching alongside Protestant clergy. The security forces, the Royal Ulster Constabulary and the British Army, grouped discreetly but in sizable contingents in the little side streets off the Shankill, estimated the numbers attending to have been between 20 000 and 25 000. David McKittrick, then Northern Editor of the *Irish Times*, noted the amazed comment of an elderly woman resident that 'there must be 35 million of them'.[2] Perhaps this was indeed how it must have seemed to the onlookers as the march 'flowed' up the Shankill towards Woodvale Park, growing in size as people eagerly joined in at every street corner.

But the sheer scale of the march was not the only thing to have made a lasting, arguably indelible, impression on both onlookers and participants. Indeed, the Shankill march was not the largest of that summer's peace rallies: this took place in Dublin that same Saturday when 50 000 marched for peace. Although twenty years has erased much of the detail of the day, almost all of those interviewed could remember quite clearly how they had felt. Their abiding, undeniably wistful, memory is of a day charged with huge emotion, a day when, after seven years of savage communal conflict, Protestants and Catholics met face to face, stretched out the hand of friendship, hugged each other and wept tears of joy in the intensity of this strange encounter. Saidie Patterson, veteran trade unionist and former leader of Women Together, welcoming the marchers to her native Shankill, proudly told them, 'This day is the crowning experience of my life.' It was a euphoria born of universal relief, for, apart from one minor scuffle at the start on Northumberland Street, an interface between the Falls and the Shankill, the day had passed off peacefully. Patterson, initially opposed to the march – though not necessarily the rally – as too dangerous, had been of the opinion beforehand that it would require 'something of a miracle on the Shankill to see us through'.[3] Ciaran McKeown, also of the three original 'Peace People', had consistently argued that the march up the Shankill Road was a necessary 'blooding' of the peace movement and should go ahead despite the risk.[4] As he watched the march edge its way inexorably upwards, he, too, had begun to share a general sense of relief: 'By all that was mythologically holy, there should have been a riot, with people getting shot dead or beaten to death or worse. Yet here was one of the happiest sunlit expressions imaginable, of humanity in the mass.'[5]

It had all begun just over two weeks before, on Tuesday, 10 August 1976. That day, Terry Carlin, 'the young, hard-working secretary of the Irish Congress of Trades Unions' (ICTU) and colleagues were attending a meeting at Stormont with Merlyn Rees, the Secretary of State for Northern Ireland.[6] Carlin vividly recalled what happened when suddenly Rees was passed a message: 'He removed his glasses and bowed his head in his hands. I said, "Secretary of State, you have clearly received bad news. May I ask what it is?" He told us that reports were coming in of a shooting and car accident in West Belfast, on Finaghy

Road North, and that two children appeared to have been killed'.[7] Mairead Corrigan's sister, Anne Maguire, out walking with her young children, had been struck by a car driven by Danny Lennon, a 19-year-old IRA volunteer recently released from the Maze Prison. Lennon had been pursued and shot by soldiers after a sniping incident in the same neighbourhood. The minister's concern was not difficult to comprehend: regardless of how or where blame would ultimately be laid, these were civilian deaths as a result of interaction between the British army and republican paramilitaries.[8]

In the days immediately following, there was a widespread and continued outpouring of revulsion at the deaths of the Maguire children, Joanne (8), John (2) and Andrew (6 weeks), and the severe injuries caused their mother.[9] Given that these were not the first civilian casualties of the conflict, what were the peculiar circumstances that prompted this reaction? McKeown offers this explanation:

> There was something unmistakably different about this tragedy among all the tragedies we had lived through ... . even the most intransigent seemed to sense that there was something obscene about trying to blame either a dead youth or the soldiers who killed him, while the mother of the dead children was lying seriously injured in hospital.[10]

The killing of the Maguire children undoubtedly touched a raw nerve in the public psyche, confirming for many the futility of the communal violence and simultaneously exposing a desperate, fundamental need to find some more overt and tangible way of demonstrating opposition to it. The response came in a small way at first, in the shape of informal, partly spontaneous, gatherings, consisting mainly of women, as, for example, on the Thursday evening preceding the funeral of the Maguire children when a group of Catholic women, brought together by word of mouth, recited the Rosary at the scene of the accident. By Saturday, 14 August, the day following the funerals of the Maguire children, it had metamorphised into a mass demonstration, when around 10 000 people, mostly women, from all parts of Belfast, including Protestants who came in buses from the Shankill, gathered at Finaghy Road North before marching down the Andersonstown Road towards Milltown Cemetery. Ciaran McKeown, then a journalist reporting on Northern Ireland for the *Irish Press*, described this initial rally in Catholic west Belfast as an 'almost silent demonstration which had no particular focus, no platform, no speaking equipment and no speeches'.[11] A prominent Catholic laywoman and longtime peace activist present gave her version of events which also offers a flavour of the peace movement at this embryonic, uncertain stage:

> The fate of the Maguire children was much talked about after mass. People, particularly women, wondered what could be done to prevent this kind of tragedy repeating itself. Getting up a petition seemed one possibility, and someone in the media mentioned Betty Williams. Our parish priest had already been in contact with her and with Mairead Corrigan. An open air mass was suggested but Betty Williams wanted Protestants to be able to come too. At the meeting on 14 August, nobody knew what to do but a priest suggested we should sing hymns.[12]

For the most part, the media were not slow to praise the participants. On Monday 16 August, in an editorial headed *De Profundis*, the *Irish Times* warmly welcomed the 'grandeur of the response by the women of Belfast', warned that behind the 'hooligans' who attacked such marches stood the 'grim godfathers' of violence, republican and loyalist, 'into the shadows of whose hearts no sunlight penetrates'. But, concluded nevertheless with the hope that the 'touching unity of Catholic and Protestant women from those terrorised and stricken areas' would set an important benchmark for peace.[13]

In an astute article published on the morning of 14 August, David McKittrick, *Irish Times* Northern Editor, had defined the peace movement in ideological terms as 'beginning to fill the gap between the people and the paramilitaries', and, then, questioning the validity of traditional republican reliance on community support, he concluded, 'The existence of that gap will put to the test the dictum that the guerrilla fish cannot survive outside a sympathetic sea.'[14] The events of that afternoon had confirmed his assumption. After the rally, the 'Provos' had harassed the marchers calling them 'touts, Brit-lovers, informers and old cows'. In McKittrick's opinion, in which a number of other journalists concurred, 'the general atmosphere' had been 'anti-Provisional IRA, but not pro-British'.[15] Earlier, separate statements from Jacky Maguire, father of the dead children, Betty Williams, and then afterwards, from the Republican Clubs (associated with the Official IRA), decrying the local Provisionals, added to the chorus of demands to the IRA 'to get off our backs'.[16] All of this, plus the following well-intentioned comment from the Secretary of State, inevitably ensured the newly-launched peace movement would have a rough passage: 'The women of Andersonstown have already given a lead. It takes courage to speak out, to give information to the police, to stand up in court, to join the UDR and the RUC Reserve. More and more people are doing so.'[17]

The killing of the Maguire children provided the immediate reason for the marches that summer but it is important to understand the historical context in which the incident took place. Northern Ireland was then in its seventh year of the troubles. It has been estimated that 15 000 people 'left Northern Ireland for good' during 1975 alone. The Convention, the latest attempt to bring the warring sides together constitutionally, had ended in March with no palpable signs of agreement among the politicians. The subsequent political stalemate ensured little likelihood of respite from the daily litany of violence. 'The level of violence', *The Guardian* deplored, on August 18, 'is now higher than in any year since the troubles began, with the exception of 1972 ... every day this year there has been an average of one murder, four injured in terrorist attacks, two bombings and five shootings in a population of fewer than 1 500 000'.[18] Civilians bore the brunt as loyalist and republican paramilitaries targeted the 'other side' in pubs, social clubs, workplaces, homes and narrow city streets, at the same time maintaining their grim, relentless grip on their own communities.

The week of the Maguire killings had been particularly bad. On Sunday, 8 August, a republican rally, commemorating the fifth anniversary of the introduction of internment without trial, protesting against the government's plans to remove special category status for convicted terrorists, and fuelled by Provisional Sinn Fein vice-chairman Maire Drumm's threat to bring down Belfast 'stone by stone', had sparked off a series of disturbances in west Belfast.[19] Between 8 and 15 August, the British Army had logged 147 shooting incidents making this week the one in which 'more shots were fired at British soldiers than in any other week of the whole IRA campaign'.[20] As the first peace rally took place in Andersonstown, two high-velocity bullets, fired from a light machine gun of the type used by the British Army, had killed twelve-year-old Majella O'Hare, 'the fourth Northern Ireland child to die violently in five days', on her way to confession in south Armagh.[21] Senior army officers and the Labour government were rumoured to be in profound disagreement over what strategy should be adopted to deal with the worsening catalogue of violence.[22] At the same time, there were strong indications that the Westminster parliament's traditional bi-partisan approach to Northern Ireland might be in danger of breaking down. 'Ulster is now more spectacularly lawless than ever', the *Observer* editorial lamented on 15 August, 'if no change is made in the policy, the coming winter does not bear thinking about'.[23] Rumours that the Secretary of State, Merlyn Rees, would soon be moved from Northern Ireland in a cabinet re-shuffle added to the climate of uncertainty.[24] In the Republic, the Dail was being recalled early to sanction stiffer anti-IRA legislation as 'an adequate and appropriate response' to the assassination of Christopher Ewart-Biggs, the British Ambassador to Dublin , the previous month.[25] In times such as these, the already sorely-tried people of Northern Ireland could perhaps have been forgiven for concluding that 'nothing was sacred any more'.[26]

On 17 August, one week to the day from the Maguire incident, Mairead Corrigan, Betty Williams and Ciaran McKeown took the decision to form the organisation which became known as the Peace People. Clearly concerned over the unfocused nature of the recent 'peace' events, McKeown had concluded that 'the rally (of 14 August) had been an expression of feeling but it was not yet a "movement"'.[27] Realising that the 'emotional excitement as a factor would die down unless it was sustained', McKeown convinced Corrigan and Williams of the need to formalise their efforts within a planned programme of events, 'a time structure, including pegging in the promise of another occasion of emotional excitement between August and November'. In this way, the Peace People, it was felt, would be able to 'give voice and maximum visibility to this deeper, inexpressible feeling'.[28] At this stage, however, McKeown, though indispensable to the philosophy and planning of the Peace People, believed remaining in the background offered him unfettered freedom of operation, so that it was the images of the two women which were to so memorably catch the imagination of the public and the attention of the world's media. On 16 August, Derek Brown of *The Guardian*, in an article pessimistically entitled 'The sad history of Ulster's peace movements', pinpointed the movement's 'strength and weakness', saying of Corrigan and Williams that they 'are both formidably articulate and, in the best possible sense, utterly naive. ... Their simple, awesomely impractical demand is that all men of violence lay down their arms in response to the will of the people'.[29]

Up to this point, people had been gathering more or less spontaneously when and where the spirit had moved them, which, in the opinion of the Peace People, only served to diminish the impact of their protest. The new movement set out to bring them together *en masse*. 'A couple of big marches' would fit the bill but location would be crucial: 'obviously these should be on the Falls, the Shankill, in Derry and GB'. Ormeau Park, then straddling the divide between Protestant east Belfast and the mixed Ballynafeigh district at the top of the Ormeau Road, became the 'central, neutral ground' to which people marched, led by the Andersonstown contingent, after gathering at the BBC building in central Belfast, for the first mass rally on Saturday 21 August.[30] While the 'ownership' of this rally was claimed by the Peace People, responsibility for its organisation, considered by some to have been the largest of the peace rallies in the North of Ireland, in practice, was shared with a number of established 'peace/community' organisations which played an important part in disseminating information and mobilising groups of marchers from all over Belfast and beyond, including the Republic. The announcement, by Mairead Corrigan, of the date, but more importantly, the location, of the next big rally, Saturday, 28 August, on Belfast's Shankill, was warmly received by a huge, happy crowd. The large enthusiastic turnout seemed proof positive that mass numbers could be attracted, assembled and dispersed in an orderly and peaceful fashion, but also, more significantly, that the will was there. The Ormeau rally was a necessary preliminary for what was to follow.

Encompassing an area of roughly 200 acres in the west of Belfast and about half a mile from the city's centre, the name Shankill described not only its main artery, the Shankill Road, but included a clutch of small streets feeding off it, the whole comprising an urban village with its own shops, schools, churches and red-brick terraced houses. From its beginnings in the early part of the nineteenth century, the Shankill was to become the home of much of Belfast's Protestant working class, employed in linen mills, shipbuilding and engineering. But Belfast's rapid industrialisation continued to draw in large numbers of workers, including Catholics from the south and west, who settled mainly along the Falls Road, importantly forming 'a large irregular wedge between two extensive Protestant working-class sectors about the Shankill Road and Sandy Row'.[31] 'The Shankill has always been surrounded', commented Jackie Redpath, longtime community worker and Director of the Greater Shankill Development Agency, to an interviewer in the early 1990s.[32] The toll of two world wars and the decline of Ulster's traditional industries did little to allay Protestant paranoia. Radical urban regeneration schemes in the late 1960s on into the early 1970s dispersed many of west Belfast's Catholics and Protestants to new council housing on the margins of the city. The onset of the troubles in 1969, especially in Belfast along the fault lines of the Shankill and the Falls, where ethnic identity became contested, Stalingrad-like, street by street, forcing families into the 'safe havens' of their own kind, and thus swelling immeasurably the Catholic population of west Belfast, found a Shankill already in process of being reduced to a shadow of its former size, with a loyalist population uneasily aware of rapidly growing nationalist encroachment.[33] In Redpath's opinion, redevelopment had done more damage to the Shankill than the troubles.[34] It mattered little that both Catholic and Protestant communities were enduring not dissimilar miseries: to the Shankill, its identity was under threat from all sides, even from the former constants, Stormont and Westminster. 'If you want to destroy Ulster', said one loyalist, 'you start with the Shankill'.[35] Bereft of the old certainties, deeply suspicious of its nationalist neighbours, the Shankill turned increasingly in on itself, honing its own brand of loyalism to a fine, bleak edge as the 1970s progressed. All this provided fertile ground for the growth and spread of the loyalist paramilitary groups, the Ulster Defence Association (UDA), the Ulster Volunteer Force (UVF) and the Orange Volunteers, who, like their republican counterparts but a few streets away, vied with each other to threaten, terrorise and thereby determine the everyday existence of the very community they claimed to protect. This, then, was the complex, but historic, community where the fledgling peace movement planned to hold their rally on 28 August 1976.

Amongst the planners of the event, therefore, there were few who underestimated the symbolism of its location. If they could hold a peace rally on the Shankill, they could hold one almost anywhere in Northern Ireland. For the Peace People, and Ciaran McKeown in particular, it seemed irresistible. It was a challenge that had to be met, the movement had to be 'blooded'.[36] And while a rally in an appointed place, Woodvale Park at the top of the fiercely Protestant and loyalist Shankill Road, would be hugely significant, a march including people drawn from both communities, especially Catholics from west Belfast, travelling up that same road, as one, successfully to the place of assembly would send out a much more potent message of reconciliation. There were therefore not just one but two elements to be considered, the march and the rally. Both had been constituents of previous peace events that August. On 17 August, Protestant and Catholic women had walked together on the Catholic Andersonstown Road to rally at Milltown Cemetery but 'ugly scenes' had been caused when around a hundred republican supporters had attempted to disrupt the march; on 21 August, after travelling in groups from various parts of the city, many had marched in safety to the 'neutral' venue, the Ormeau Park.[37] On these occasions, the march was perhaps still secondary to the main event; on 28 August, however, it was to assume equal and probably greater importance, for the route taken by the marchers would be no ordinary one. And if both Catholics and Protestants could be seen to walk side by side on the 'sacred ground' of loyalism and do so with impunity, then anything was possible.[38]

Once the Shankill location had been agreed, the organisation of the event began. There are a number of sources which offer accounts of how this was done. While these apportion responsibility, credit and blame in differing degrees, the one thing on which they agree is the difficulty faced by the organisers in reaching a consensus on the issue of marching to the rally in Woodvale Park. Undoubtedly this was a consequence of there being more than one group which considered itself to be in charge of the programme. To begin with, there were the Shankill women themselves. These, including Saidie Patterson, viewed the day as an opportunity for Protestant women to return the courtesy extended them by the women of the Falls and Andersonstown two weeks before. As 'hosts', these women felt responsible for the safety of those taking part, and while some of them were keen for the march to the park to go ahead, others, particularly Patterson, thought the risk of confrontation was too great. The timing of the march was considered unfortunate, for the peace march would not be the only march that day on the Shankill. The last Saturday in August is the traditional date on which the Royal Black Preceptory also marches. The local 'Blackmen' were due to come down the Shankill Road en route to Ballynahinch in the morning and then retrace their steps in the early evening. On 24 August, a 'high ranking member' of the West Belfast Brigade of the UDA claimed that the timing of the peace march 'led by Roman Catholics' was therefore deliberately provocative and designed to 'raise tensions in the area'.[39] As self-proclaimed defenders of the Shankill, the loyalist paramilitaries would also have had their own agenda and their role in events will be examined later.

The Peace People, for their part, regarded the marching element as indispensable to the success and impact of the day. In attempts to iron out differences, the planners met at least twice, once in Betty Williams's house in Andersonstown and one in Saidie Patterson's home off the Shankill. According to McKeown, Patterson 'tried to take possession and to stop the march happening, predicting that there would be thousands dead'. 'The Shankill', he maintained, 'was her territory. It was both physical and other'.[40] Corrigan recognised that

Patterson was 'genuinely concerned' about the danger but insisted that the Peace People themselves 'did not underestimate the potential of violence'.[41] The reasons for such depths of discord are not hard to find. They lie mainly in a fundamental difference of approach. Patterson was a leading light in Women Together, a peace movement founded in 1970. David Bleakley, then leader of the Northern Ireland Labour Party and subsequently Patterson's biographer, explains its rationale: 'an organisation for working-class women, which would enable them to bring their influence to bear on the local scene, particularly in "peace-line" districts'. Characterised by an informality of approach and grounded in 'practical witness' to Christianity, it had already been 'in the front line for seven exhausting years' when suddenly in August 1976, the Peace People had erupted on the scene and 'unlike previous peace initiatives in Northern Ireland, the 1976 campaign was given committed and sustained coverage by international television and press agencies'.[42] There was perhaps, too, a clash of personalities and backgrounds: Corrigan and Williams, the two young Catholic women, compelling, increasingly eloquent, fired with the zeal of the newly committed; Patterson, the elderly Protestant, Shankill born and bred, trade unionist, her peace credentials garnered over a lifetime's work in the community; McKeown, the pipe-smoking Catholic intellectual, philosopher, journalist and civil rights veteran, who may have played no formal role in these discussions but whose influence on the decision-making process cannot be discounted. For him, the 'petition-type activities' of groups like Women Together were a 'waste of time'.[43] Although well-intentioned, he believed that they were not capturing the public imagination.[44] Overall difference of opinion was therefore not surprising. In the end, the pro-march lobby prevailed. McKeown claims that the Peace People took the decision to march, nobody else: 'Who were "they" to say it could not be done? If we had allowed ourselves to be recruited as three extras, it would not have taken place'.[45]

In Northern Ireland politics, however, nothing occurs in isolation and so it was on this occasion. The deaths of the Maguire children had taken place almost three weeks previously. In the interim, what had begun in west Belfast as a modest protest of local women against violence had become a mass movement for peace, attracting world-wide media interest and comment. The Peace People may have considered or wished to consider they were acting unilaterally but other players had already begun to show their hand, both for and against, the event. Ultimately, the interaction of a number of factors would determine what happened on the Shankill that summer afternoon.

In the first place, there were the two governments concerned. Both Dublin and London were desperate to find some means of ending the spiral of violence in Ulster. When a new peace movement, with grass-roots in the very communities which were caught up in that violence, appeared on the scene, gaining momentum by the day, it would have been surprising if there had not been some official reaction. Secretary of State Rees soon bestowed a warm welcome on the newcomer but government approval can prove a mixed blessing. The Provisional IRA lost no time in condemning the peace movement as anti-Republican and government-inspired, branding its members as a 'tribe of impecca-ble whited sepulchres' whose inconsistency led them to deliberately ignore the '500 murder victims of British and Loyalist violence', including Danny Lennon and Majella O'Hare.[46] Statements from the Official IRA, the SDLP (Social Democratic and Labour Party) and the Irish government in support of the Peace People merely served to con-vince the Provisional IRA that there was a conspiracy afoot designed to undermine their support in the nationalist community prior to some new political settlement.[47]

Back on the Shankill, anything that smacked of being anti-IRA was bound to go down well, especially with the loyalist paramilitaries. Irritated as they were by the prospect of a 'Catholic-led' march on their territory, yet conscious that the eyes of the world would be on the Shankill, they tried to tread a fine line between being seen to welcome the marchers but not to be losing face, an uncharacteristic stance sorely tried by the announcement mid-week that the ICTU (Irish Congress of Trade Unions) intended to march as a separate body to link up with the main march.[48] Loyalists had not forgotten the ICTU's attempts to break the Ulster Workers' Council Strike two years before, and indeed, as Patterson herself well knew, the prospect of union banners, emblazoned with the face of James Connolly, the leading Irish socialist executed for his part in the Easter Rising, being carried aloft up the Shankill, would be a sure-fire guarantee of trouble.[49] In the *Irish Times* on 25 August, McKittrick reflected that although the Shankill's paramilitary groups appeared to 'have no plans to cause trouble', indeed, they had publicly pledged safe passage to the peace marchers, there were still underlying rumbles of disquiet, especially amongst the UVF, whose supporters were reportedly flocking to the local RUC barracks to demand the march be banned.[50] At the same time, the leadership of the west Belfast UVF felt sufficiently con-strained by the situation to put on record that it felt 'no antagonism towards those who worked for peace' and insisted that the UVF itself had 'constantly worked and fought for peace in Ulster'.[51] The week produced two more equally strange bedfellows: running counterpoint to any hint of optimism, the Reverend Ian Paisley's *Protestant Telegraph* accused the Peace People of exploitation, insincerity and being a front for the Catholic Church. In court on anti-internment march-related charges, Maire Drumm, Provisional Sinn Fein's fiery vice-president , used the occasion to attack the peace movement as 'motivated by the British Army'.[52] The rumour mills were working overtime.

For the Peace People, it had all been a baptism of fire but there could be no more side-stepping of the issues raised by the flood of claims and counter-claims. On the evening of 25 August, Corrigan and Williams issued a personal statement in which they condemned without reservation all violence from whatever source and thereby rejected as spurious any assertion that they were prepared to accept offers of paramilitary protection.[53] Given what was at stake, perhaps they had little alternative. Corrigan recalled their determination 'not to be seen to be asking the permission of the paramilitaries to march'.[54] Their credibility was now very publicly on the line. People's expectations were high. There could be no let up either in the momentum of arrangements for the day, including the transporting of hundreds from all over Northern Ireland and beyond, to the Shankill on 28 August. The shooting of Thomas Passmore, father of the Grand Master of the County Grand Orange Lodge of Belfast, on 18 August, the attempted bombing of a furniture store on the Shankill on 23 August, and arson attacks on 27 August and in the early hours of 28 August, on both communities, one resulting in the deaths of a young couple and their baby daughter, were obvious attempts to heighten community tension.[55] On the Friday evening, the ICTU declared they would join the march not as a group but as individuals and they would not carry banners. Carlin explained that, following a meeting requested by the Peace people in his own home, he understood and appreciated that they had to 'create their own identity'. Therefore, having agreed in the first instance to support the march, the ICTU did so on these terms and not under pressure from the paramilitaries.[56] Motivation apart, the decision must have taken some of the steam out of grass-roots opposition on the Shankill.

Patterson, too, had been busy. Corrigan confirmed, 'once the decision to go ahead had been taken, she did what she could to help us'.[57] According to Bleakley, Patterson was approached by a 'deputation of peace women' as the person best placed by reputation and experience 'to encourage an orderly demonstration'. How much responsibility she ultimately bore for the undoubted success of the day is difficult to gauge, so great were the number of other influences also at work. Clearly, however, her contribution was significant. Continuing to knock on doors, looking for support, after being spat on and duly informed that there would be 'no bloody Fenian march' up the Shankill, is courageous in anyone's book.[58] Corrigan and McKeown were emphatic about their refusal, despite Patterson's wishes, to seek the permission of the loyalist paramilitaries, but it is possible that, recognising the limits of loyalist tolerance, she may have gone ahead with this on her own. Bleakley, for example, describes her efforts as having 'brought the support, or at least the neutrality, of the men of the district'.[59] Any observer of the Shankill marching scene would acknowledge the unlikelihood of such an event progressing without some kind of tacit understanding of this nature, even if, as McKeown argues, the 'hard men' appeared 'puzzled' by what was taking place on their doorstep. The *Guardian* correspondents were to report how on the day itself 'groups of men directed the parade with evident authority'.[60] Such an arrangement would also have the virtue of not having to involve the security forces, a definite plus among those community activists still paranoid about the role of the RUC in the early part of the troubles.

On Saturday, shortly before 2 pm, crowds began to assemble at the two main rallying points: Catholics at the junction of Divis Street and Northumberland Street and Protestants at the junction of the Shankill Road and Agnes Street. The plan was for them to link up where Northumberland Street joined the Shankill and then, led by representatives of the Shankill followed next by the Andersonstown contingent and so on, Protestant and Catholic groups alternating, the whole group would proceed up the Shankill Road to the Woodvale Park for the rally proper. A few hours before, the Blackmen had already marched down the same road.[61] The only unpleasantness of the afternoon occurred at this initial stage when riot troops had to step in to disperse youths attacking the marchers on the nationalist side of the divide. When the two groups finally met up amid cries of 'Welcome to the Shankill', the emotional intensity of the moment impressed even the most cynical of journalists present. Surprise too seems to have been writ large on the faces of many bystanders at the rare spectacle of Catholic clergy processing up the Shankill. 'When were you last on the Shankill, sister?' a nun was asked. 'I've never been here before in my life', was the reply.[62] One local, then a boy of nine, recalled how 'when I saw these people, I realised they must be Catholic, but now they were human beings, not bogeymen'.[63] In Woodvale Park, the vast crowd settled down in festive spirit to listen to the brief speeches from Patterson, Corrigan and Williams. The Peace People Pledge was read, the crowd joined in the saying of the Lord's Prayer, in the singing of hymns and 'When Irish Eyes are Smiling', the unofficial anthem of the peace movement. Although apparently not part of the original plan, the participants then marched back down the Shankill, 'watched, as before by little knots of UDA and UVF men standing outside their bars'.[64] More than one marcher was conscious of a sense of relief. Recalling her own memories of the day, an Andersonstown woman's comment probably reflects the feelings of most: 'There was a sense of euphoria after the strain of the fear of being attacked. But the main thing was we felt that we had done something.'[65]

But what of the long term? The organisation of large-scale rallies could not be sustained over a prolonged period and within a year support was ebbing and the movement was becoming enmeshed in controversy while violence across Northern Ireland continued unabated. Both in its immediate impact and its ultimate lack of apparent effect the Shankill march exemplifies the multi-layered complexity of Northern Ireland's 'troubles'. A strong and sincere mass antipathy to violence clearly existed and the marches were able to display this forcibly but translating the emotional response into policies which might address the underlying political issues and command similar mass support thwarted this group, as it has so many others both before and since. More specifically, analysis of a public march through the 'territory' of the 'other' community seems particularly relevant in the context of the emergence of contentious parades as one of the major issues of the late 1990s. To oversimplify, why did the Shankill march not turn into a Drumcree? Amongst the many factors perhaps the identification of the movement with women and the powerful symbolism of women and peace was especially significant. Women have figured prominently in the artistic and literary representation of Ireland and its problems for several hundred years, the abandoned old woman, the mother sacrificing her sons, the pure maiden who must be protected. The resonance of these images and the identification of women with family, children and nurture has often made it difficult for protagonists from any group to openly attack women even when they are voicing opposition to powerfully entrenched positions. The obverse of the traditional images of women in Ireland has been their virtual exclusion from actually participating in political processes and this underlines the long term problems of the Peace People. A movement identified with women had 'licence' to break the rules in the short term but could be marginalised in the longer term as the traditional power blocs reasserted their control.

Notes

The authors are grateful to those who agreed to be interviewed, especially Mairead Corrigan-Maguire and Ciaran McKeown.

1. Interview by authors with Mairead Corrigan-Maguire, 29 October 1996.
2. *Irish Times*, 30 August 1976.
3. D. Bleakley, *Saidie Patterson; Irish Peacemaker* (Belfast, 1980), p. 86.
4. Interview by authors with Ciaran McKeown, 23 October 1996.
5. C. McKeown, *The Passion of Peace* (Belfast, 1984), p. 160.
6. Ibid., p. 158.
7. Interview by authors with Terry Carlin, 26 September 1997.
8. The shooting of Lennon has been the subject of continued controversy. In his autobiography, *Before the Dawn* (1996), Gerry Adams states that the autopsy report on Lennon was suppressed, the implication being presumably that it would have proved that Lennon was already dead when the car struck the Maguire family.
9. McKeown points out in *Passion of Peace*, 138, that Anne and Mairead Corrigan had already had a young niece killed by a motorist trying to escape from a riot on Finaghy Road North in the early years of the troubles.
10. McKeown, *Passion of Peace*, p. 139.
11. Ibid., p. 142.
12. Private information from interview, 4 February 1997.
13. *Irish Times*, 16 August 1976.
14. *Irish Times*, 14 August 1976.
15. *Irish Times*, 16 August 1976. See also *The Guardian*, and the Belfast *Newsletter*.
16. August 1976 and *Irish Times*, 17 August 1976.
16. *Irish Times*, 18 August 1976.
17. *Irish Times*, 14 August 1976.
18. *The Guardian*, 18 August 1976.
19. *Irish Times*, 11 August 1976.
20. *The Sunday Times*, 15 August 1976.
21. *Irish Times*, 16 August 1976.
22. *The Sunday Times*, 15 August 1976; *The Guardian* and the Belfast *Newsletter*, 16 August 1976.
23. *The Observer*, 15 August 1976; *The Guardian*, 19 August 1976.
24. *Irish Times*, 13 August 1976; Belfast *Newsletter*, 18 August 1976. Rees was succeeded as Secretary of State for Northern Ireland by Roy Mason on 10 September 1976.
25. *The Guardian*, 11 August 1976.

26. Interview with McKeown.
27. McKeown, *Passion*, p. 143.
28. Interview with McKeown.
29. *The Guardian*, 16 August 1976.
30. Ibid., 16 August 1976.
31. A.T.Q. Stewart, *The Narrow Ground* (London, 1977), p. 144.
32. Jackie Redpath in G. Beattie, *We are the People: Journeys through the Heart of Protestant Ulster* (London, 1992), p. 160.
33. R. Wiener, *The Rape and Plunder of the Shankill in Belfast* (Belfast, 1976), p. 41.
34. Beattie, *We are the People*, p. 159.
35. Ibid.
36. Interview with McKeown.
37. *Irish Times*, 16 August 1976.
38. Bleakley, *Saidie Patterson*, p. 85.
39. *Newsletter*, 24 August 1976.
40. Interview with McKeown.
41. Interview with Corrigan-Maguire.
42. Bleakley, pp. 76–85.
43. Interview with McKeown.
44. McKeown, *Passion of Peace*, p. 155.
45. Interview with McKeown.
46. *Republican News*, 21 August 1976. See also *The Guardian*, same date.
47. *The Guardian*, 25 August 1976.
48. *Irish Times*, 25 August 1976.
49. Bleakley, *Saidie Patterson*, p. 87.
50. *Irish Times*, 25 August 1976.
51. *Newsletter*, 26 August 1976.
52. *Irish Times*, 24 August 1976.
53. Ibid., 24 August 1976.
54. Interview with Corrigan-Maguire.
55. Thomas Passmore Senior died on the evening of 25 August 1976. His son believed that he himself had been the intended target of republican gunmen.
56. Interview with Carlin.
57. Interview with Corrigan-Maguire.
58. Bleakley, *Saidie Patterson*, p. 86.
59. Ibid., p. 87.
60. *The Guardian*, 30 August 1976.
61. The Royal Black Preceptory also returned by the same route that evening without any problems.
62. *Irish Times*, 30 August 1976.
63. Interview with member of Peace People, 3 October 1996.
64. *Irish Times*, 30 August 1976.
65. Private information, interview, 4 February 1997.

10
For God and Ulster: Blood and Thunder Bands and Loyalist Political Culture

Neil Jarman

> *'Bands, bands and more bands'.*
> The organiser of the New York St Patrick's Day parade defines the essential ingredients for a good parade.

As this quotation indicates, music is a prominent feature of most public parades. In Northern Ireland the flute and drum marching bands provide much of the noise and the colour at the numerous loyal order parades. They provide the rhythm for those who are walking and much of the entertainment for those who come out to watch. A member of one loyal order was clear on the importance of the bands for a good parade: 'People come to watch the bands, they don't come to watch a group of men walking in their regalia'. He contrasted the crowds that came out for the mini-Twelfth parades and the band parades with the few people who bothered to watch church parades. These were commonly accompanied by bands playing hymn tunes in contrast to the more raucous, secular music of the main parades. Marching in the parades is also a big attraction for the men who make up the bands: 'You get a real buzz when you walk back into Belfast on the Twelfth and you see the crowds out cheering you'. One bandsman went further when he told me: 'It's better than sex'. Although his colleagues were clearly not convinced of this, belonging to one of the better bands does offer a certain status within one's community and amongst one's peers. Some of the bands attract a substantial following of teenage girls who walk alongside 'their' band throughout the duration of the parade, shouting for tunes, cheering and chanting and carrying the much-needed refreshment.

At the same time, some styles of bands and of music-making are viewed critically from within the unionist community. Older members of the loyal orders have complained that the modern bands are only concerned with making as much noise as possible and that the quality of musicianship has declined with the rise of the Blood and Thunder bands in recent years. Some lodges even prefer to walk without a band, or march to the softer sound of a solitary piper. But it is more than just the music that cause concern, since the more assertive bands are also seen as responsible for many of the problems caused by parades. Unionist politicians and parade organisers have frequently chosen to blame bandsmen if any trouble occurs, and nationalists also object to some styles of bands, accusing them of trailing paramilitary regalia and playing sectarian tunes as deliberate acts of provocation. In fact, both bodies of opinion reflect something of the ambiguous position of bands within the unionist community and within the culture of parading more generally. Bands very often do make the event into an exciting and enjoyable festive occasion, but just as easily they can help turn an otherwise peaceful social event into a sectarian riot or a violent confrontation with the police. Bands are at the heart of loyalist political culture in so far as they are an essential ingredient at the major public commemorations and celebrations. But they are also largely outside the control of the organisers of such events and they often represent contrasting political views to those of mainstream unionist opinion. They represent the 'rough' side of unionism in contrast to the more 'respectable' elements.[1] If the bands are always a central feature of loyal order parades they also represent a challenge to their order and authority. They are at the heart of loyalist culture but they bring a sometimes unwelcome, harder edge to it. This chapter will explore these complexities.

Loyal order parades are complex social occasions. They are successful because they have largely managed to avoid the schismatic factionalism of the Protestant churches and of unionist political parties. Parading is one of the few public occasions that can bring together all sections of the Protestant and unionist community, where social, political and religious differences are tentatively ignored in the interests of a unified celebration of history, culture and power. In part this can happen because of the way in which symbolic displays are used to define the collective identity.[2] The men march behind the Union Flag and the Ulster Flag, behind banners illustrating Biblical ideals, banners commemorating the Williamite wars and the Somme and other images of conflict or noble sacrifice for Faith, for the Crown and for Country, ideals which all can accept in general without the need to argue over their exact meaning. The parades at one and the same time celebrate military victories and honour religious faith; they are peaceful demonstrations and martial displays, professions of loyalty, but with the underlying threat of violent resistance. The vitality of the ritual process is built on its ambiguity. All loyal Protestants acknowledge the importance of these events even if they might question their meaning. But the parades are not the time to question meaning, they are a time for unity and celebration; of the sacred and the profane, of the secular and the spiritual, of the peaceful and the violent and of those who work within the law and those who sometimes work outside the law. Always a fragile and temporary coalition of interests, the peaceful unity of the parade sometimes fractures and erupts in violence when challenged or confronted with the excluded 'other'. In such instances a scapegoat is needed, where possible the blame is placed on the members of the 'other' community, or the camp followers and 'hangers-on'. But, increasingly, it has been the bandsmen who have been blamed for violence and confrontation at parades. In many respects they are an easy target. They are part of the parade but not part of the loyal orders. The music is often aggressive and has sectarian undertones: bandsmen are highly visible and readily identifiable in their distinctive uniforms; some bands carry paramilitary regalia; and some bandsmen do get involved in violence.

But it is also a rather simplistic view of the bands and their place in contemporary loyalist political culture. Despite their prominence in public political culture in the North, little detailed consideration has been given to the bands as institutions in themselves. *Acts of Union*, Desmond Bell's study of youth culture and loyalist bands in Derry, remains the only substantial study of the topic.[3] However Bell's study is limited by his framework, which understands the bands as a localised expression of loyalist youth sub-culture rather than something that is more fully embedded within the wider unionist culture. Such an approach tends to underplay the full importance of the bands. Youth sub-cultures are generally seen as relatively ephemeral expressions of mannered rebellion, in which the young try to make enough 'noise' to startle the authorities or their elders, but which history teaches us will swiftly be co-opted and replaced by another trend.[4] Bell sees the use of paramilitary regalia by bands as one such act of mannered bravado with no evidence of any real involvement with the world of loyalist paramilitarism. Furthermore, he regards the Blood and Thunder style as something that bandsmen will grow out of as they age and the bands evolve and mature towards musical, rather than sectarian, competition.[5] Although musical and sartorial styles change and develop, Blood and Thunder bands remain as the most prominent public expression of loyalist cultural and political identity and they make more 'noise' than they have ever done. To understand their continued prominence requires a wider contextualisation than Bell provides. This is not to deny the centrality of the young men in the bands, the significance of their economic and social marginalisation, nor the importance of bands in the construction of collective identity. But it does require recognition that band culture is more deeply embedded in the wider working-class popular culture. That it involves men (and women) of all ages, that many of the bands and bandsmen are highly politicised and that the connections with paramilitary culture are real and widespread, rather than mere wishful thinking or youthful boastfulness.

Music has been a feature of parades in Ireland since notice was first taken of such events. The earliest recorded public processions organised by the Dublin guilds in the late fifteenth century were relatively formal, if not quite regal affairs and were accompanied by the sounds of 'mynstralis' and 'trumpettors'.[6] By the eighteenth century, parading had become a more widespread and popular activity. In 1728, the bricklayers and masons of Dublin celebrated a royal anniversary by parading through the town to the accompaniment of 'drums beating and musick playing'. A few years later the local shoemakers processed through Cork to the sound of 'kettledrums, trumpets and hartboys etc'.[7] Such music was an integral part of these events, it attracted spectators to the approaching procession but it also sounded out a warning and sometimes a challenge and the rowdiness at such assemblies offered some concern to the peace. The demonstration by the Boyne Society in 1747 was described as a 'warlike parade' and the authorities were only too aware that such symbolic displays often led to real violence.[8] Later in the century the Oakboys raised similar concerns as they marched the roads of rural Armagh accompanied and announced by a cacophony of 'drums, horns, fidlers, and bagpipes' in protest at increases in the local tithes.[9] By the end of the century this varied range of instrumentation had been reduced to the rather more simple and standardised consort of fifes and drums that Lord Gosford noted at the first Orange Order parade at Markethill in July 1796.[10] Many of the early Orange parades relied on the musical skills and instruments of the local militia or military units to mark out a regular martial rhythm and the fife and drum formed the basic musical accompaniment at parades for much of the century. Although they have now been largely replaced by more extensive marching bands, simple Lambeg drum and fife combinations, sometimes a 'drumming party' can still be seen at Orange parades in rural areas today.

It was not until the turn of the century that more formalised bands became a dominant feature of parades, although the drumming parties remained a prominent form of popular marching music and retained their place at the main parades. It was at this time that the contemporary polarised identities of British unionism and Irish nationalism began to be elaborated and consolidated, and parades served as a means of defining, publicising and marking cultural and social boundaries. As a part of this process it became common practice for bands and drumming parties to parade around their own areas throughout the summer months. This seems to have been more widespread at times of political tension and was a common practice during the period of debate over home rule. Such band parades were minor public events but they easily stirred up sectarian tensions and provoked antagonism and an aggressive response from the other community, largely in response to the playing of party tunes in mixed areas. The recurrent violence on these occasions caused some concern for the authorities. In June 1900, a motion was put to the Belfast Council Police Committee to impose a ban on all band parades in the city. However, no decision was formally taken on the matter and the proposal was quietly dropped.[11]

These types of public performance have to be seen principally within the context of the sectarian and political divide in the north of Ireland, but there is also a resonance with the much wider customs of playing 'rough music' (or *charivari*), which had been widespread across Europe. Rough music was used to shame, taunt and intimidate neighbours and the marginalised, and although it was largely a symbolic expression of disapproval it could lead to real violence.[12] These practices have largely been considered as a means by which a section of the community would draw attention to the unacceptable morals or behaviour of individuals within it and to mobilise and focus public opinion against them. The aim of the rough music was not to entertain or to make music as such but to make noise. The discordant sound symbolised the abberant behaviour of the victim, and thereby attracted attention to the deviant and thence to their public punishment and humiliation. In extreme cases the victims were forced to flee their homes.

The performance of rough music aimed to re-establish and re-confirm the moral boundaries of the community and in a similar fashion the performance of sectarian music in the north of Ireland focused on the discordance between the two moral communities. During the home rule debate musicians often marched to the boundaries of the two communities or played outside houses belonging to members of the other community. The sound of the drums and the party tunes readily mobilised both supporters of the musicians and members of the opposing community. Sometimes confrontation occurred, sometimes people were intimidated from their homes, and sometimes the police maintained an uneasy calm. Both communities produced 'rough' marching ensembles but it is perhaps significant that the descriptive name of 'Kick the Pope' band was already being used in the press by 1900. This was a time when the Protestant community was most strident about defining their identity as Protestant and British and distinct from the Catholic Irish other.[13] Around the turn of the century such small band parades were part of the wider repertoire of popular culture which were used to mark out and define the sectarian boundaries between Protestant and Catholic in the north of Ireland. These kinds of practices help to illustrate something of the dual nature of music-making in public, which persists to this day. Though the marching bands are used to keep the marchers in step and to entertain the public, at the same time the beating out of party anthems serves to raise sectarian feelings and can be used to deliberately antagonise the 'other', and thus define the boundary of the community.

A century later, the issue of musical provocation remains a factor at parades. It is often reported that bands sometimes deliberately play loudly at sensitive locations, for example, when passing Roman Catholic churches and nationalist residential areas. The playing of party and paramilitary tunes is regularly cited by nationalists as one of the factors that they object to when the loyal orders parade and this has been acknowledged to some extent by the imposition of restraints on music by parade organisers. But the music remains popular and for many the louder the better. When the calls go up for the playing of 'The Sash' and other loyalist anthems then the drums are beaten out more loudly and in turn are greeted by loud cheers. On one level this is clearly done for the enjoyment of their supporters but it can also be designed to raise the atmosphere. Such playing can readily provoke violence at times of tension.

In 1995, trouble flared at the Apprentice Boys parade in Derry as the procession moved through the centre of the city. The playing of party tunes provoked a violent response from nationalists and after the police moved in to clear spectators the town erupted into rioting. The bass drummers from two Blood and Thunder bands were later convicted of playing their drum 'excessively hard'. The magistrate stated that he felt that the playing of 'The Sash' close to opposing groups was an inappropriate gesture.[14] Party tunes are not only played to provoke nationalists, they are also used to stir loyalist supporters and to antagonise the police. When the RUC re-routed a band parade in Downpatrick in September 1995 each of the dozen or more bands marched to the barriers and played 'The Sash' at the police officers before continuing on their route. As the bands beat out their tunes the police were pelted with a variety of missiles and fireworks by 'spectators'. This continued throughout the two hours that the band parade lasted. In both of these cases the loud percussive and aggressive music helped to provoke violence; in the first example it was the opponents of the parade that reacted; in the second it was the supporters of the bands. These brief examples serve to illustrate how easily music can be used to raise the temperature at parades and provoke violent reactions. They also suggest that in Northern Ireland the playing of 'rough music' has remained a prominent feature in maintaining social difference and the sectarian divide and that it is a 'traditional' feature of the broader culture of parading. But this view also tends to understate the changes that have occurred within popular street music and fails to explain why it is still a vital element of loyalist political culture.

During the twentieth century the range and variety of bands has increased. As well as the widely established flute and drum bands, accordion bands, concertina bands, bugle bands, bagpipe bands, brass and silver bands, have all been seen at Orange parades. Styles and instrumentation have waxed and waned as fashions come and go. Concertina bands, which drew on sea-faring traditions, were popular in the 1930s but rarely feature in Ulster parades, though they remain a part of Orange parades in England. Similarly bugle bands are no longer heard at parades. Bagpipe or kilty bands are largely confined to rural parades where their slower pace can be more readily accommodated within the marching rhythm, as are brass and silver bands, which have always been a minority of the public bands. Flute bands continue to be the most popular style across the North and when many people talk of bands they mean the raucous Blood and Thunder single-keyed flute and drum bands that visually and aurally dominate the parades. But such bands are largely a product of the Troubles. In the inter-war and post-war years it was the accordion bands that were most popular in the working-class areas and which had a reputation as provocative and troublesome. They were the Blood and Thunder bands of their day, played by young males in an aggressive manner. But as a sign of how fashions change, today the accordion bands are seen as the 'respectable' and melodic end of loyalist music and the urban accordion is regarded as a woman's instrument.[15] The flute bands are now the most attractive style for young males while the accordion is left to girls, women and elderly men. Some youths will join an accordion band in order to learn to play side drums but they are often seen as little more than a stepping stone to a Blood and Thunder band. As a result of these perceptions, the accordion bands are a declining force in urban areas although they still remain a popular ensemble in rural areas.

Until the 1970s, the majority of loyalist bands were connected to an Orange lodge. They accompanied their own lodge on the main parades and walked with local Black Preceptories and Apprentice Boys clubs at their events. Band culture was encompassed within the broader realm of Orangeism. In this way the musical practices of the Ulster Protestants could be seen as similar to working-class musical customs in Britain, which were maintained by factory brass bands and colliery bands. The development and survival of such bands was to a great extent dependent on the broader structure that nurtured them and the decline of heavy industry and mining has witnessed a parallel decline in the social culture they supported. One of the important developments within Protestant parading culture during the troubles has been the disappearance of the lodge band. Most loyalist bands now have no formal connections with the loyal orders, but are self-organising, self-financing independent bodies. A number of reasons are put forward to explain these changes. One factor has been a general disenchantment with the Orange Order itself among working-class Protestants. Although the exact membership of the organisation is uncertain due to the decentralised nature of the Order, its numbers have dropped considerably over the past thirty years, from a maximum of 100 000 to probably just over 40 000 today. It seems clear that it is the younger working-class males who have abandoned the organisation, the very people who now parade as members of bands. Many bandsmen often express a dislike for the staid conservatism of the order and its emphasis on religious matters. For many loyalists, being a Protestant is an expression of their cultural and political identity, not a matter of religious faith. Others regard the loyal orders as representing the political and economic interests of the middle-class and question what the order can do for them. They see it as less relevant to their daily lives than it was when personal contacts and patronage were important in securing employment and housing. The violence of the Troubles has been another factor, some bandsmen talk of the failure of respectable bodies like the Orange Order to defend the interests of the loyalist community and this has led many loyalists to look to paramilitary groups for leadership. It is the apparently widespread support given to loyalist paramilitary groups by bands that causes much of the unease with Protestant parades.

Many of the bands do appear to have a close relationship with one or other of the loyalist paramilitary organisations, the Ulster Volunteer Force (UVF), Red Hand Commando (RHC), and the Ulster Defence Association (UDA). This is most obviously displayed in symbolic form on band uniforms and regalia. Some bands appear in replica military uniforms and a few adopt more explicitly paramilitary styled combat fatigues. Most bands also march behind a colour party that carry a range of flags and bannerettes and often these include symbols and emblems of a paramilitary group. Although the loyal orders do not formally permit carrying flags or banners supporting paramilitary organisations, they have rarely attempted to prevent them being carried by bands. In recent years symbolic displays of paramilitary regalia at major loyal order parades have attracted media attention and have provoked hostile reactions from members of the nationalist community. From the loyalist perspective, the parades are inclusive events which represent the broad sweep of unionist opinion and it was argued that displays of support for the UVF and UDA were perfectly legitimate. Most UVF band regalia include reference to the historical organisation formed in 1912 to oppose home rule and a list of battles fought by the 36th (Ulster) Division during the First World War. Bandsmen state that such regalia honour those who were killed at the Somme rather than the contemporary UVF.[16] Although the UDA has no such line of historical legitimacy, it remained a legal organisation until 1992, and while Ulster Freedom Fighters were proscribed their flags and symbols are much scarcer at Orange parades. Nevertheless, for members of the nationalist community such displays are perceived as a reference to contemporary paramilitary groups and their appearance at Orange parades suggested at best a general tolerance of illegal organisations and at worst a public display of support for them. Displays of support for paramilitary groups have been one factor in the protests against parades that became widespread after 1995.

Teasing out the exact nature of these relationships is obviously difficult and band members are naturally reluctant to admit any more than 'sympathy' or 'support' for the more militant defenders of the Union. However, a number of recent events indicate that in some cases the connection is more than symbolic. During a trial for UVF activities in 1995, it was revealed that the accused was also a member of a band in Craigavon. Several band members in South Belfast, who were also members of the Red Hand Commando, were convicted of the murder of Margaret Wright in 1995. In February 1998, members of another band formed a guard of honour at the funeral of fellow member and UDA man Bobby Dougan who was killed by the IRA.[17] These examples indicate that some bands do have members who have, or have had, paramilitary connections, or rather, that some men with paramilitary connections were also members of loyalist bands. However, one should be cautious of making a more general assumption about the links between the bands themselves and the paramilitary groups; many have no formal paramilitary or political connections. Nevertheless, one should not be surprised that some bands do express sympathy for the paramilitary groups since they draw on the same sections of the community for membership. The Blood and Thunder style flute bands emerged from the same working-class communities that provide the paramilitary groups with support and membership. Both developed around the same time, in the late 1960s and early 1970s, in response to feelings that their community and culture was under threat. The paramilitary groups took up the gun to defend working-class areas against the perceived threat of republican attacks and to resist any moves towards a united Ireland. The Blood and Thunder bands took up the flute and drum and emerged as more militant proponents of loyalist public culture by introducing a more strident edge to Orange parades. As part of this process the more radical types of bands used the parades to demonstrate their support for the more militant activists. As a result of their displays of UVF and UDA regalia at public events, the Blood and Thunder bands have, for many, come to be seen as the public face of loyalist paramilitarism.

Many members of loyalist bands have abandoned the loyal orders themselves, but they have not abandoned the larger Orange culture of parading, rather they have redefined their position within it. They have formally separated themselves from the structures of the orders, but they have retained their place within the wider unionist family and they remain committed to the custom of parading. In fact, much of the vibrancy of loyalist public political culture derives from the energy and enthusiasm of the bands. In spite of distancing themselves from the loyal orders themselves, the bands still retain strong links with the ethos of the brotherhood that underpins much of Protestant popular culture. They are largely male organisations, they are non-hierarchical and democratically run by committee; roles such as treasurer, secretary and band leader or band captain are elected annually, and all members are consulted over important decisions whether this be to take part in certain parades or to buy new uniforms. Band members usually come from a restricted geographical area such as a village, small town or a housing estate. Joining a particular band, therefore, often seems a natural step and it is not a question of choosing the best one.

Many of the bandsmen follow friends or relatives into their local band and some bands will include two or even three generations of a family within their ranks. Most bandsmen would be within the 18–35 age range, but many bands have older members and sons and neighbouring children are often encouraged to join at a young age. Bands, therefore, function as extended social networks and members have strong social bonds and loyalty to one another, as neighbours, friends or relatives. Although all bands have a number of fringe members, most also rely on a core of committed and long-standing members who sustain the band on a day-to-day basis. Such members leave only when they retire from band life, if they move away from the area, or perhaps as a result of family pressures, but would rarely leave to join another band. For many men the band is their main social institution outside their immediate family. Some bands have a relatively short life span, but once they get established a band often develops a presence beyond the present generation of members. Although most Blood and Thunder bands have been formed in the past twenty-five years, some marching bands can trace a history going back a hundred years or more.

Belonging to a band involves more than simply parading the streets on a regular basis, it also demands a commitment to an organisation, which often struggles to survive, but perhaps most importantly it demands a commitment to learning a musical instrument (although levels of musicianship vary considerably) and practising a repertoire of anything between 40 and 80 tunes that are regularly played on parades. Bands usually meet once a week for practice, to learn new tunes and to teach new members the most important tunes to get them started.[18] However, without the regular routine of parades, interest in belonging to a band declines. In the winter months and outside the marching season many bands barely tick over. The core members maintain the weekly practice sessions, but they are barely more than social gatherings and interest only picks up as the first of the new season of parades approaches. Many members of the loyal orders may take part in no more than three or four parades each year. They will walk on the Twelfth, on a mini-Twelfth parade and a church parade or two but rarely more. The more committed who belong to two or more orders may well take part in considerably more parades but few will parade as often as a bandsman does. The better bands will parade at each of the major loyal order parades and at many smaller local events, but they will also take part in many of the band parades that are held each weekend across the north. In the course of a marching season they may parade on fifty or sixty occasions. Band parades were recorded at the end of the last century but the contemporary form of these parades as competitions, as social gatherings, and as fund raising events is a relatively recent phenomenon.

As independent bodies, bands need to raise significant amounts of money to maintain themselves and to be able to present a smart appearance on the streets. Many bands have between thirty and forty members and with each member needing a full uniform and an instrument the costs can be considerable. Flutes cost around £60 each, side drums up to £400, bass drums around £250, and a new bannerette costs between £300 and £400. The uniform is the biggest expense, however, and with a basic uniform costing from around £300 per head a new set can cost a band between £12 000 and £17 000. Furthermore, because fashions change and there is competition amongst bands to appear well turned out, the top bands change their uniform every few years. Although some money may be recouped by selling the old uniform to another band, fundraising is a regular concern for bands. Money is raised in a number of ways. Most bands require members to pay weekly or monthly dues, but this raises only a small proportion of the required amount and a small amount also comes from fees from Orange lodges for walking on the Twelfth or other major parades. Many bands also run ballots, organise sponsored walks or similar events. Some even have their own band halls or run social clubs and these can be used to hold dances, discos and other events which can raise considerable amounts of money. All these are collective efforts; being part of a band involves far more commitment and effort than simply turning out on parades. Nevertheless, the core of a band's activities is parading, and hosting an annual band parade is another way of raising money and, perhaps more importantly, raising the profile of the band in their home area.

On most Fridays and Saturdays from the end of April through to September, band parades are held across Northern Ireland.[19] These parades have no commemorative purpose but rather are organised as competitions; they generally attract a lot of interest with thirty or more bands attending the larger parades. Each band competes for a range of trophies donated by a host band and which are awarded for individual and collective musicianship, for marching skills and for visual style. But while the trophies are an attraction, the visiting bands also know that to be able to attract bands to their own parade they need to turn up and support other band parades. These events are, therefore, also significant social occasions at which bandsmen renew acquaintances, receive invitations to other parades and have a night out. For many small towns and villages the annual band parade is also a big attraction. Large numbers of people spend the evening drinking and socialising as they watch the bands march through the streets, with many parades only ending well after dark. Off-licenses, bars, shopkeepers and fast-food sellers all do a good trade at band parades.

Most band parades are social events and although there are trophies to be won they generally do not have any more serious intent. But just as the band parades have been a significant extension of the Protestant culture of parading, so some bands have also begun to establish their own commemorative parades which further illustrate their support for the wider political culture of loyalism. The linkage between bands and the paramilitary groups was vividly displayed on the first anniversary of the Combined Loyalist Military Command cease-fire in October 1995 when dozens of bands from across Northern Ireland paraded through the centre of Belfast. Although there has not been any attempt to mobilise on subsequent anniversaries, the UVF in particular has begun to extend the culture of parading and mobilise the support they have within the bands to establish their own commemorative events. Many small parades are held each November on Remembrance Sunday, with local supporters of the UVF marching with a band to a local memorial site, sometimes a mural painting, sometimes a grave, where wreaths are laid and a short service is held. More prominent commemorative parades are now held each year on the anniversary of the death of UVF men Trevor King (in July) and Brian Robinson (in September). Each of these anniversaries attracts thirty or more bands which parade through the Shankill and Woodvale areas before laying wreaths on the large murals that have been painted in these two volunteers' memory. These commemorative parades are held in the heart of the loyalist areas of Belfast and have received little publicity but they mark the beginnings of a new development in loyalist commemorations and illustrate the continued importance of parading among the Protestant community.

The marching bands are one of the most prominent elements within the loyalist culture of parading, but they are also rather ambiguously situated within it. While band members would support the rights of the loyal orders to parade their 'traditional' routes each year, they do not feel so bound to the strictures of the past. The bands have introduced a range of new sounds, styles of dress and forms of display into the body of the parade. The public presence of the bands serves to bolster the loyal orders and at the same time to undermine them. Their presence helps to maintain the interest of the younger generation in the culture of parading and Orangeism, in its most general sense, and it encourages members of the wider Protestant community to come out and watch what would otherwise be rather dull processions of middle-aged men in their Sunday best. Bandsmen have also been vocal at opposing the re-routing of parades and their music is often used to mobilise supporters to defend 'traditional' rights, even though few band parades have been considered contentious. But the violent percussive sound of the drum ignores the spatial boundaries of interface barriers, army screens and police lines and the beat of the drum carries the claims of the Protestant community to all parts of the province.[20] The parade may be invisible but its presence is heard, and even felt, far and wide thanks to the bands. The bands have introduced numerous innovations, which help maintain the parades as significant events, but in so doing they threaten to undermine the claims for tradition, with its emphasis on continuity and lack of change. Of course, parades have always been contemporary practices and are therefore both reflective of and a consti-tutive factor in the wider political context, the bands merely help to bring this more clearly into focus. Their presence, as independent bodies, illustrates the decline in power and importance of the Orange Order within the Protestant community, while their visual displays indicates where some of that allegiance has gone. The growing number of band parades shows that there is still a popular interest in parading but this also indicates that there is a demand for innovation and change within Protestant popular culture. In recent years much of that dynamism has been provided by loyalist marching bands.

Notes

1. See A.D. Buckley and M. Kenney, *Negotiating Identity: Rhetoric, Metaphor and Social Drama in Northern Ireland* (Washington, 1995) Ch. 4.
2. N. Jarman, *Material Conflicts: Parades and Visual Displays in Northern Ireland* (Oxford, 1997).
3. D. Bell, *Acts of Union: Youth Culture and Sectarianism in Northern Ireland.* (Macmillan, 1990). However, Buckley and Kenney (1995) and Jarman (1997) also deal with some aspects of band culture as does C. De Rosa, 'Playing Nationalism' in A.D. Buckley (ed.), *Symbols in Northern Ireland* (Belfast, 1998). Also of relevance is Lorelei Harris' RTE radio documentary *No Surrender* (1997), on the York Road No Surrender Flute Band, and Kate Radford's film *The Last Accordion Band* (1998) for An Crann/The Tree which follows the Prince William Accordion Band from the Shankill Road.

4. S. Hall and T. Jefferson, *Resistance through Rituals: Youth Subcultures in Post-war Britain* (London, 1976). D. Hebdige, *Subculture: the Meaning of Style* (London, 1979).

5. Bell, *Acts of Union*, pp. 115–16.

6. J. Webb, *The Guilds of Dublin* (Dublin, 1929).

7. *Dickson's Dublin Intelligence*, 3 August 1728, *Faulkner's Dublin Journal* 5/8 August 1732.

8. *Dublin Courant*, 4 July 1747.

9. Cited in J. Donnelly, 'Hearts of Oak, Hearts of Steel'. *Studia Hibernica*, no. 21, 1981.

10. W.H. Crawford and D. Trainor (eds), *Aspects of Irish Social History* (Belfast, 1969).

11. N. Jarman and D. Bryan, *From Riots to Rights: Nationalist Parades in the North of Ireland* (Coleraine, 1998). *Irish News*, 1 June 1900; 2 June 1900.

12. E.P. Thompson has a full discussion of the historical use of rough music in *Customs in Common* (London, 1991).

13. For discussions on the role of music in the construction of ethnic identity see the varied essays in M. Stokes (ed.), *Ethnicity, Identity and Music: the Musical Construction of Place* (Oxford, 1994).

14. *Irish News*, 2 July 1996.

15. Radford (1998) focuses on the role of women in Protestant music-making.

16. N. Jarman, 'Commemorating 1916, Celebrating Difference: Parading and Painting in Belfast' in A. Forty and S. Kuechler (eds), *The Art of Forgetting* (Oxford, 1999).

17. *News Letter*, 30 November 1995; 13 July 1995; *Sunday Life*, 3 March 1996; *Irish News* 14 February 1998.

18. Radford (1998).

19. N. Jarman and D. Bryan, *Parade and Protest: a Discussion of Parading Disputes in Northern Ireland* (Coleraine, 1996).

20. Stokes, *Ethnicity, Identity and Music*, p. 9.

11

The Apprentice Boys and the Relief of Derry Parades

T.G. Fraser

It is one of the paradoxes of modern Irish history that the collapse of unionist authority in Northern Ireland was ushered in by the event held to commemorate the most historic event in its tradition, the annual parade held by the Apprentice Boys of Derry to celebrate the city's relief from its historic siege in 1689. On the afternoon of 12 August 1969, as the final Apprentice Boys' clubs were passing through the city's Waterloo Place, missiles were thrown at the police and the marchers by nationalist youths from the nearby Bogside. This triggered rioting of such dimensions that two days later British troops had to be deployed in the streets of Londonderry and Belfast, fatally undermining the authority of the unionist-dominated Stormont parliament which had ruled Northern Ireland since 1921. These events were themselves unfolding in the context of a winter of demonstration and counter-demonstration which followed the banning of a proposed civil rights march from the predominantly Protestant Waterside area of Derry on 5 October 1968. By 1972, such was the subsequent pace of events as the Provisional Irish Republican Army mounted a campaign of growing intensity against the state, that the Stormont parliament itself was suspended by a British government desperate to find a way forward. Here, too, what happened in Derry was crucial to the turn of events, since the fall of Stormont followed only weeks after the tragedy of 'Bloody Sunday' in the city. Northern Ireland's second city was forcing the pace, or at least its nationalist residents were. In a sense, the Relief of Derry parade of 1969 was an unexceptional affair; such celebrations had been taking place since at least the late eighteenth century, their nature changing and adapting over time, but with the same essential purpose, namely the preservation of the memory of the siege of 1688–89, when the Protestants of Ulster had defended themselves against the forces of King James II. But in the circumstances of 1969, the parade brought to the surface all the simmering tensions of Ulster society.[1] In 1995, when Northern Ireland was embarked on a search for a peaceful constitutional settlement, the Relief of Derry parade once again proved to be the focus of deep-seated tension both within the city and beyond.

There is no doubt that the man chiefly responsible for keeping alive the traditions of the siege was Colonel John Mitchelburne, who had succeeded Major Henry Baker as Governor. From records which are no longer extant, it is possible that in 1714 Mitchelburne formed a club of Apprentice Boys. What subsequently happened in the eighteenth century is not clear, but since a parade was held in 1759 to commemorate the Battle of the Boyne it is likely that the siege was also publicly marked. The first clear indication of a siege commemoration, in the *Londonderry Journal* of 5 August 1772, confirms that this was not a new event.[2] There are extensive accounts of the centenary events of 1788 and 1789, when public processions were held in the city, which was still largely Protestant in character. Such was the spirit of the times that these were joined by the Catholic bishop, Dr McDevitt and his clergy, but this was not a tradition fated to last. By the early nineteenth century, the events of 1798, the Acts of Union and the campaign for Catholic Emancipation had brought a new tone to Irish politics which had little place for the politics of accommodation. The hitherto Protestant city of Londonderry was also changing very rapidly, as Catholic workers from Donegal came into the city to take advantage of its growing industries. By the 1851 census, Derry had a Catholic majority, for whom the traditions of the siege meant nothing, or if they did it was as the prelude to the period of the Penal Laws and the Protestant Ascendancy. In these circumstances the Protestant community increasingly turned to the traditions of the siege for inspiration and a sense of identity, symbolised by the completion of the Walker Pillar, or Testimonial as it was called, on the city's walls in 1828. The Pillar overlooked the growing suburb of the Bogside, home to the large numbers of Catholics who were flocking into the city at that time. As a symbol of Londonderry's Protestant traditions it could not have been bettered. From its plinth, reached by a narrow winding staircase, the statue of Governor George Walker beckoned northwards towards the relieving fleet on Lough Foyle.

Apprentice Boys' clubs flickered into existence, called after the heroes of the siege. In 1814, the first Apprentice Boys of Derry Club was formed, at a time of some tension in the city when the authority of the Catholic bishop, Dr Charles O'Donnell, was being vigorously challenged by Father Cornelius O'Mullan. What O'Mullan represented was a new spirit in the Catholic community, associated with the campaign for Emancipation. The next few years saw turbulence increasing, with the siege commemorations as their focus. In 1824, the army forbade the Yeomanry to take part, and in 1832 the celebrations were banned for five years. During these years, a number of clubs were formed, none of which had a sustained existence. In 1824, the ban on the Yeomanry prompted the formation of the No Surrender Club. There was also a Death and Glory Club. Both these clubs lapsed, as did the original Apprentice Boys of Derry Club. Williamite and True Blue Clubs also came and went in the course of the nineteenth century.

It was not until the reconstitution of the Apprentice Boys of Derry Club in 1835 that the modern Apprentice Boys movement really began. Other clubs followed: the Walker Club in 1844, the Murray Club in 1847, the Mitchelburne Club in 1854, the No Surrender Club in 1865, and the Browning Club in 1876. Two other clubs which had lapsed were reformed in the twentieth century, the Baker Club in 1927, and the Campsie Club in 1950. In 1859, the clubs were given an overall structure with the formation of a General Committee, soon followed by the office of Governor. The stated aim of the association was 'the purpose of Celebrating the Anniversaries of the Shutting of the Gates and the Relief of Derry, and thus handing down to posterity the memorable events of the years 1688 and 1689 connected with this City'.[3] Such was the emotive legacy of the siege that such sentiments were not confined to Londonderry's Protestant community. By the 1870s there were requests for the formation of branch clubs outside the city. Although at first opposed by the General Committee, the No Surrender Club opened branches in Belfast in 1877 and Glasgow in 1903, while the Walker Club granted charters to clubs in Armagh and Dungannon in 1891, Belfast in 1904 and Kilrea in 1907.[4] This modest development of clubs outside the city heralded the dramatic expansion of the Association after the Second World War, and particularly from the 1970s, which changed the scale and nature of the commemoration parades in the city.

By the 1960s, the two annual commemorations seemed to have fallen into a regular, and seductively predictable, pattern. For the main parade in August, members of the Association formed up on the Mall Wall, marched to the Diamond for a wreath-laying ceremony, before attending a service in St Columb's Cathedral at midday. The Cathedral service was regarded as the central, and most important, part of the day's celebrations, St Columb's flying the Crimson Flag which had symbolised the city's defiance during the siege.[5] The larger procession in the afternoon, which included the branch clubs, took a different route each alternate year. One route went from the Diamond across Craigavon Bridge, and then, after parading the main streets of the Waterside, re-crossed the river to march up Abercorn Road and Bishop Street before disbanding. The 'cityside' route went up Great James Street and down Clarendon Street. By the 1960s, as numbers expanded, this route had to be extended to come down Rock Road before marching along Strand Road and through Waterloo Place to the city centre. These routes are important, since, while neither of them went through nationalist areas, such was the tight geography of the city that each held the potential for tension and possible confrontation. The corner of Abercorn Road and Bishop Street had long been a classic interface between the unionists of the Fountain and the nationalists of the Long Tower; in 1920 it had been the scene of a major gun-battle between them. The cityside route took in a part of the city which down to the late 1960s was still predominantly Protestant but at Waterloo Place the junction with William Street passed a main entrance into the Catholic Bogside. Mall Wall, where the parade assembled, overlooked the Bogside, particularly Naylor's Row, and the banners and music could be seen and heard by the area's inhabitants. It was not a spectacle they welcomed, and led to the tradition whereby Bogside residents set their chimneys on fire to incommode the marchers, relying on the prevailing wind to carry the smoke towards the parade on the walls.[6] The potential for tension was, therefore, present on both routes. When it finally erupted it triggered events beside which chimney-burning seemed the very age of innocence.

Even so, the 1960s were a period of self-confidence in the unionist community. The IRA's border campaign which began in 1956 was abandoned in 1962, the Nationalist Party under Eddie McAteer accepted the role of official opposition at Stormont, and under the able guidance of Brian Faulkner new industries were being set up. This sense of stability was reflected in the Apprentice Boys' parades. As we have already seen, the Association was expanding, not just in Northern Ireland. In the late 1950s, a few enthusiastic members in Scotland decided to expand from the small number of clubs in Glasgow. Branches of the Walker Club were started in Caldercruix and Irvine, so successfully that by the early 1960s the Scottish branches were sufficiently flourishing to hold their own annual parade. Some of those involved saw the Apprentice Boys as an alternative to the Orange

Order.[7] By the late 1990s, the Scottish Amalgamated Committee presided over a network of forty clubs, from Maybole in the south to Aberdeen in the north. Like the Orange Order in Scotland, the strength of the Apprentice Boys lay in west-central Scotland, with the Walker Club in particular having a vibrant string of clubs along the Ayrshire coast.[8]

The other British centre of loyalist sentiment, Merseyside, saw a more modest growth in the Association, though one which was to have a direct impact on events in the city of Derry and beyond. A branch of the Walker Club had existed in Birkenhead in the late 1930s but went out of existence. By 1964, the Murray Club had re-established a presence in Liverpool, its members crossing for initiation within the Walls on the first Saturday in October to take advantage of the cheap excursion fares. Led by the Bootle Imperial Drum and Fife Band or the Garston True Blues Flute Band, these Liverpool members paraded on that particular Saturday afternoon back to the Waterside railway station after the initiation ceremony.[9] It was their intended presence on 5 October 1968, coinciding as it would have done with the planned Civil Rights march from Duke Street in the Waterside, which helped trigger the historic events of that day. The view recorded by the Cameron Commission into the Northern Ireland disturbances of the winter of 1968–69 that their proposed procession was not a genuine annual event is incorrect.[10] By the late 1990s, the English Amalgamated Committee accounted for fourteen clubs but stretched between Barrow in the north and Solent and South Downs in the south they were a marginal presence compared with their brethren in Scotland. With five clubs, Merseyside was the main centre, but two clubs in London and one in Essex enabled the Association to make an annual statement in the capital.[11] In the 1960s, the growing presence in the August parade of Scottish and English members was noted approvingly, as were members of the Toronto Murray Club and the Philadelphia Apprentice Boys of Derry Club, even though the latter did not survive the remorseless attrition of 'Orange' sentiment in the United States.

Prominent members of the Unionist Party also regularly paraded in the city. Perhaps the Association's most prestigious recruit was the new Prime Minister, Captain Terence O'Neill, who joined in December 1963 in time for the 275th anniversary of the relief the following year. In August 1964, the press indicated that he would be at the head of the procession, though subsequent press reports do not record his presence.[12] Two years later, the Governor of the Association, Dr Russell Abernethy, confirmed in advance of the parade that the Prime Minister would not be attending. This was almost certainly the consequence of the growing strains within unionism which dated back to O'Neill's meeting with the Republic's premier Sean Lemass in Belfast in January 1965. O'Neill's most public critic was the Reverend Ian Paisley, but the real danger to his position lay within the Unionist Party. Significantly, the minister who was to lead the campaign against him, William Craig, was initiated into the Larne Baker Club on the occasion of the 1966 Relief parade.[13]

These signals that all was not well within unionism matched a deeper malaise in the city, whose nationalist majority had never rested willingly within Northern Ireland. Their discontent was powerfully reinforced by the nature of the ward boundaries within Londonderry Corporation, whereby in 1967 8781 Protestant voters, concentrated in the North and Waterside wards, elected twelve unionists, whereas 14 429 Catholic voters, largely in the South ward, elected eight non-unionists. Housing conditions in many working-class areas were poor and overcrowded. While the Corporation did make efforts at council house building, these were felt to be both inadequate and concentrated in the South ward to keep Catholic voters from spreading into the North ward where they might threaten the precarious unionist majority. Feelings of in-built discrimination were further strengthened by the Benson Report on transport which scrapped much of the city's rail links, and, above all, by the recommendation in 1965 of the Lockwood Committee which identified Coleraine as the site of Northern Ireland's second university. These feelings of frustration found their focus in September 1968 when the Northern Ireland Civil Rights Association (NICRA) announced its intention of holding a march from Waterside station to the Diamond on Saturday, 5 October. When the Apprentice Boys served notice that their members from Liverpool would be parading on the same route at the same time, the Minister of Home Affairs, William Craig, prohibited all processions in the Waterside and within the walled city. The subsequent events in Duke Street on 5 October, when the civil rights march assembled in defiance of the ban, are too well known to require repetition but are universally accepted as marking the start of the 'Ulster troubles'.[14]

Events quickly gathered momentum. On 16 November 1968, the newly-formed Derry Citizens' Action Committee organised a march estimated at some 15 000 in defiance of a further ban; in view of events at parades discussed elsewhere in this book it is important to note that the police took the pragmatic view that they did not have the strength to enforce the ban. Such was the pace of events that six days later

Londonderry Corporation was abolished, signalling the demise of unionist control of the city's affairs. The following months saw substantial change on other fronts. On 28 April 1969, after a Stormont election had failed to give him the backing he felt he needed, O'Neill resigned. His successor, Major James Chichester-Clark, only just beat Brian Faulkner, whom many believed to be unionism's ablest figure. By the time Chichester-Clark's government had to confront the issue of the Relief of Derry parade, the situation throughout Northern Ireland, but especially in the city, had further deteriorated. Central to any understanding of feelings amongst nationalists were the events of 19 April 1969 when police followed rioters into the Bogside, entering the home of Samuel Devenney who was batoned along with members of his family. He died on 17 July and his funeral to the City Cemetery two days later was attended by a crowd as large as any of the earlier civil rights demonstrations, possibly as many as 30 000. Although an investigation into the affair was held by police brought over from England, it was felt that this was unsatisfactory.[15] Samuel Devenney's funeral was a dismal prelude to the events of August.

There were other clear signs of gathering tension. The return of the City of Derry Grand Orange Lodge from its rally in Limavady on the evening of 12 July triggered serious rioting which lasted for two days. Certain aspects of these events were danger signals for what was to follow. The trouble flared as the lodges returned to the Mall Wall overlooking the Bogside. At one point a party of RUC had to fire warning shots when they felt themselves cut off by a nationalist crowd. As the rioting developed, Catholic and Protestant crowds confronted each other at the long-established interface in Bishop Street, an ominous enough development in a city not recently noted for overt sectarian violence. Symptomatic of the growing unease was the redeployment of the Prince of Wales Own Regiment from Ballykinlar in Co. Down to nearby Magilligan.[16] Nor should events in Derry be divorced from fast-growing tensions in Belfast and other parts of Northern Ireland. In particular, 2–5 August saw widespread rioting in Protestant areas of west and north Belfast. Here, too, parades were at the heart of events, for the occasion was provided by attacks on two Belfast Junior Orange Districts at Unity Flats at the foot of the Shankill Road and near Carlisle Circus. The resulting riots in the Shankill and Crumlin Roads which left the police badly overstretched undoubtedly affected the decisions taken over the forthcoming Apprentice Boys parade. They were an ominous symptom of the mood of the Protestant community.[17]

In these unpromising circumstances efforts to avert trouble at the Relief parade went on at several levels. Initiative within the nationalist community now lay with a new body, the Derry Citizens Defence Association (DCDA). Its avowed purpose was to prepare for a possible invasion of the Bogside by police and loyalists on 12 August; republicans in its ranks were also aware of the possibility of challenging the state itself. In fact, on 10 August, there was a meeting between leaders of the DCDA and Apprentice Boys at which attempts were made to prevent sectarian clashes. As a result of this meeting the Apprentice Boys agreed to several minor changes to their route, which in 1969 was to be on the cityside, to take the marchers further away from the Bogside.[18] At the official level, power to ban the march lay with the Minister of Home Affairs. The government was sufficiently alarmed about the situation for it to convey its anxieties to the Apprentice Boys but the organisation was not prepared to cancel the parade. No specific request for a cancellation of the Relief celebrations was apparently received and in its absence the Association saw no need for any unilateral action. The Minister was not convinced of the wisdom or necessity of a ban, believing that the stewarding arrangements proposed by the both the Apprentice Boys and the DCDA would see the day pass without major incident. Equally, the police were conscious of the possible strength of the Protestant reaction in the event of a ban and of how difficult it had been to contain the riots in Belfast the previous week. The great imponderable was the temper of sections in the DCDA, and, of course, the strength of feeling in the Bogside in the aftermath of Samuel Devenney's death.[19]

The day of the Relief parade started promisingly enough with DCDA stewards controlling nationalist tensions over the traditional Protestant celebrations in the Fountain. The morning parades, too, passed without incident. At lunchtime the main procession of Apprentice Boys clubs from throughout Northern Ireland and beyond began. By then, nationalist feelings had been raised by two incidents. The first was the tossing of coins by some Apprentice Boys from the walls to groups of people in Naylor's Row on the edge of the Bogside. The second was the behaviour of two loyalist women who disported themselves in Waterloo Place, singing 'The Sash'. In others respects the procession was well marshalled; in the words of Lord Scarman's official enquiry: ' ... the procession was disciplined and orderly: its members under the efficient control of their marshals gave no provocation. In happier times the procession might well have been a cheerful and harmless celebration. But not in 1969'. The temper of the nationalist crowd which had assembled at Waterloo Place lasted until about 2.30 in the afternoon when the first nails were thrown at the police barriers. At first, missiles were entirely directed at the RUC but by the time the Murray Clubs at the end of the procession were crossing Waterloo Place around 3.00 they, too, were the target of stones.[20] As the Apprentice Boys clubs left the city, the 'Battle of the Bogside' between the RUC and nationalists began. It only ended on 14 August with the deployment of the Prince of Wales Own Regiment, by which time substantial areas of Belfast as well as other towns had been engulfed in the violence which had broken out. These events, for which the Relief parade had provided the catalyst, changed forever the political face of Northern Ireland.

These changes also saw the collapse of unionist power in the city. When the elections for the new city council were held in 1973, the United Loyalists could win only nine of the twenty-seven seats. By then, the city had hit the world's headlines as a result of the armed campaigns of the Official and Provisional IRA. Above all, the shooting of fourteen unarmed men by soldiers of the Parachute Regiment on 30 January 1972, 'Bloody Sunday' as it came to be known, and the shortcomings of the subsequent Widgery Enquiry, cut a scar on the nationalist community. It was a situation in which the Protestant population of the West Bank felt isolated and under threat, a process which had begun with the death of William King, a Protestant from the Fountain, in September 1969.

In these rather unpromising circumstances, the Apprentice Boys struggled to keep their Relief celebrations alive. In 1970, with a ban on parades throughout Northern Ireland, members of the Association held an open-air rally in St Columb's Park in the Waterside. The following year saw the commemoration touch its nadir. The introduction of internment by Brian Faulkner's government on 9 August 1971 triggered widespread violence in nationalist areas, including those in Derry where thirty-one barricades were erected in and around the Bogside. Although the parade had been banned from most of the walled city, the General Committee decided to postpone all the Relief celebrations apart from the service in St Columb's Cathedral. In the event, only seventy-four people turned up, including the clergy and choir, though in the circumstances it would clearly have been irresponsible to encourage a larger attendance.[21] 1972 was a crisis year for Ulster loyalism. The suspension of the Stormont parliament by Edward Heath's government on 30 March left the unionist community both angry and fearful. On 31 July, the new Secretary of State for Northern

Ireland, William Whitelaw, moved against the so-called 'No Go' areas of Belfast and Derry. Although 'Operation Motorman' caused fewer casualties in Derry than anticipated, three car bombs in nearby Claudy killed eight people. With emotions still running high, Whitelaw banned any parade on the city's west bank. The General Committee announced the celebrations would be confined to the service in St Columb's, and the initiation of new members. But faced with the third ban on parades in successive years, a special committee of Apprentice Boys, including some General Committee members, announced that they would march on the Waterside. Some forty clubs and bands responded to their call. The parade ended with a rally in Duke Street, addressed by the leader of the newly-formed Democratic Unionist Party (DUP), the Reverend Ian Paisley, who had taken a prominent part in the procession.[22]

It was not until 1973 that the city again witnessed something approaching the traditional Relief parade when some ninety clubs and bands paraded through the Waterside, the only presence on the west bank being a parade of the Parent Clubs from the Memorial Hall to cross the bridge.[23] Only two weeks later, however, a bomb destroyed one of the major symbols relating to the siege and its commemorations, the Walker Pillar on the city walls. Nationalists had regarded it as a particularly offensive symbol of Protestant domination, particularly so since the effigy of Lundy was suspended from it and burned every December. To the Apprentice Boys it was the loss of a treasured symbol, made more bitter by the failure of the army posts on the walls to guard the monument, despite assurances that they would do so.[24] The following year an even larger procession followed the same pattern, but on this occasion a significant number of politicians made the journey to the city. The Ulster Unionist Party (UUP) was represented by its leader, Harry West, and other leading personalities, while DUP figures like John McQuade and the Reverend William Beattie were also amongst the marchers. In the aftermath of the overthrow of the Sunningdale Agreement, it was a symptom of the siege's continuing resonance and importance to the two main unionist parties.

The attack on the Walker Pillar was part of a more general campaign waged by the Provisional IRA which had as a prime target Protestant businesses and property in the city centre. As Protestants in the city perceived the IRA campaign to be directed against them, a steady exodus began from the west bank. Although precise figures are not known, it seems that over 7000 Protestants moved either to the Waterside or out of the city altogether. By the 1980s, virtually all that remained of the west bank's Protestant population lived in the small Fountain estate, itself a particularly poor example of 1970s redevelopment. Such profound changes could not but have an effect on the Apprentice Boys and their parades. On one level the Association mirrored the divisions within the Protestant community once unionism began to fragment as a political force. Ian Paisley's role in the 1972 parade has already been noted. A widespread view in the city's Protestant population that when put to the test the Unionist Party had failed them led to a surge in support for the DUP and was reflected in the Association's decision to end its affiliation with the Ulster Unionist Council.[25] Although leading UUP figures remained members, Londonderry DUP activists like Gregory Campbell and William Hay were to emerge as articulate advocates for the Association. Tensions also emerged over other issues, notably the response to the decision of the city council's decision to change its name to Derry City Council. In 1990, there were serious divisions over an application to the International Fund for Ireland to help finance a heritage centre.

More positive from the standpoint of the Apprentice Boys was a steady expansion in the number of clubs from the mid-1970s. At one level this reflected a feeling amongst many Protestants that they should show solidarity with their embattled co-religionists in the city, but it also showed the abiding appeal of the siege at a time when loyalists felt vulnerable to the joint pressures of the republican campaign and unsympathetic governments in London. The slogan painted in the Fountain estate – 'West Bank Loyalists. Still Under Siege' – perfectly captured the latter sentiment. Expansion was not without its critics.[26] Others felt that the parade was losing dignity as the nature of the bands changed, something not unique to Apprentice Boys' parades. Down to the 1960s, it was felt, high quality military or pipe bands had accompanied many clubs, whereas from the 1970s more aggressive 'Blood and Thunder' flute bands predominated. Even so, the August parade seemed to become less problematic. In an editorial in July 1974 entitled 'Live and let live', the *Derry Journal* argued that the days were over when the parade took a route that could be regarded as coat trailing and that as result there was no reason to take offence.[27] The following year the main parade returned to the west bank for the first time since 1969. Two main areas of tension had gone. The demographic changes in the city meant that the cityside route taking in Northland Road, Strand Road and Waterloo Place, which had sparked the rioting in 1969, was no longer a viable option. While the Association never formally abandoned it as a possibility, there was a tacit acceptance that it had gone for good.[28] Equally, the security situation resulted in the closing of the walls. The fact that the morning parade of the Parent Clubs no longer marched along the section of the walls overlooking the Bogside meant the absence of another potential flashpoint.

Although tensions remained, the result was overall easing of the parading situation in the city. In 1989, the Tercentenary of the Relief, the Association was able to celebrate in some style. The commemorations took on a new dimension with a re-enactment of the Relief and a historical pageant. In December 1992, the Apprentice Boys were able to replace something of what they had lost in 1973 when the restored plinth of the Walker Pillar was re-dedicated and a memorial garden, with the governor's statue as its feature, was opened. The following year, the Association launched a well-produced magazine, *The Crimson Banner*, for the benefit of its expanding membership. The 1994 Relief parade saw another significant move when the general easing of the security situation allowed the RUC to permit members of the Parent Clubs to parade a section of the walls prior to the service in the cathedral, the General Committee having unsuccessfully applied for such permission every year since 1969. Although some republicans protested at the police decision, there was no major trouble. Interviews conducted in the spring of 1995, in the context of the republican and loyalist cease-fires, reflected a feeling amongst many Apprentice Boys that their parades were no longer contentious and, indeed, should be marketed by the City Council as part of the city's tourist attractions.[29] Such optimism was to be short-lived, however.

When in 1995 the General Committee renewed their application to the RUC for the Parent Clubs to parade the walls in the morning of the Relief, two things had changed which conspired to bring certain tensions to a head. The first was that the cease-fires had enabled the security forces to open the entire circuit of the walls to public access. Allowing the parade would see the Parent Clubs and their bands pass along the stretch of wall overlooking the Bogside. The second was the major crisis which had developed over the Drumcree church parade in Portadown in July. The 'Siege of Drumcree' had raised passions on both sides, with loyalists convinced that there was a threat to their parading rights and nationalists incensed that the parade had been permitted. With its clear nationalist majority, overwhelmingly so on the west bank, Derry was the reverse image of Portadown, something never far from people's thoughts in the subsequent crises. When news of the General Committee's application broke, nationalist leaders were quick to voice their opposition. Councillor Gerry O hEara, National Chairperson of

Sinn Fein, accused the Apprentice Boys of trying to turn the clock back to 1969, something the city's nationalists would not allow.[30]

Since it was clear that an RUC decision on the application would only be made at the last minute, tension inevitably grew, fuelled by a newspaper report that the County Down Amalgamated Committee of the Apprentice Boys might suggest a blockade of Catholic churches if loyalist parades were re-routed, something which the Governor was quick to distance the General Committee from.[31] Nationalist concerns found their focus at a public meeting held in Pilot's Row Community Centre in the Bogside on Thursday, 10 August. The spokesman for the as-yet-unnamed group, Donncha Mac Niallais, while not objecting to parading on other parts of the walls, said they were not prepared to allow a 'triumphalist' march along the sections overlooking the Bogside.[32] On the afternoon of Friday 11 August, a group of about fifty protesters occupied part of the wall around Butcher Gate. By the following morning this had grown to over two hundred.

The situation in Derry on Saturday, 12 August, was tense in the continuing absence of a police decision. With thousands of Apprentice Boys and their accompanying bandsmen due to converge on the Waterside in the course of the morning, some action was needed. Given the numbers involved, the situation was potentially more difficult than Portadown.[33] At 9.30 am the RUC began an operation to remove the protesters from the walls. Only non violent resistance was offered by the protesters who were then hemmed in to Magazine Street by the police. At 10.00 am the members of the General Committee, the eight Parent Clubs and four bands, two local, one from Glasgow and one from Portadown, were allowed on to the walls. The parade proceeded quietly along the stretch of the walls overlooking the Bogside, before the four bands in turn struck up. The demonstrators in Magazine Street turned their backs in silent protest. The major crisis of the day had passed.[34]

The tensions were not yet over. As the main parade crossed Craigavon bridge at 12.30 pm, police were involved in removing loyalists from the walls overlooking the Bogside. Towards the end of the parade, which took three and three-quarter hours to pass a given point, trouble broke out at the Diamond, long a potential trouble spot given its proximity to Butcher Gate and the Bogside. One band reacted against the sight of some Glasgow Celtic scarves by confronting nationalists and playing 'The Sash'. Despite attempts by Apprentice Boys marshals and the police to move the band on, disturbances developed. As the RUC attempted to press people back along Butcher Street and down Shipquay Street, rioting developed which lasted for some five hours.[35] Street violence had returned to the city on a major scale, with consequences which would work themselves out in succeeding years. While SDLP chairman Mark Durkan castigated RUC behaviour as 'disgraceful', a report by the Pat Finucane Centre, published on 28 August, was even more hostile to police actions. It recommended that in future the Apprentice Boys should not be allowed to parade on the controversial section of the walls except with the agreement of Bogside residents, and in the city centre subject to satisfactory stewarding.[36] The Monday after the parade, the Bogside Residents' Group, as it was now called, convened a meeting to discuss the implications of what had happened and questioned the future of loyalist parades on the west bank.[37] The Apprentice Boys had walked the walls after an absence of twenty-seven years, but the future of their parades was now at the top of the city's agenda and some members of the Association feared the possible implications of what had happened. In the next few weeks parades through the city centre by the Ancient Order of Hibernians and the Royal Black Institution passed without incident, but the presence in the centre of the city in December of a band carrying a paramilitary bannerette served to fuel nationalist resentments.[38]

The tensions of 1995 proved but the prelude to even greater difficulties the following year when the situation in Northern Ireland and in the city had deteriorated to an alarming degree. The sense of optimism generated by the ceasefires had been punctured by the IRA's resumption of violence in February. Parading tensions in the Lower Ormeau and Portadown had not been resolved. The second Drumcree crisis of 1996 was worse than the year before. Faced with widespread violence in loyalist areas, the RUC reversed an original decision to ban the Garvaghy Road march. As a result, three nights of serious rioting broke out in Derry, in the course of which one man, Dermot McShane, was killed by an army vehicle. Sinn Fein's Martin McGuinness led a 'black flag' demonstration estimated at 10 000 in protest at McShane's death. At the rally speakers drove home the message to the Apprentice Boys that they could only parade on the west bank with the permission of its residents. Tensions were further generated by demands from nationalists that the recently appointed Ulster Unionist mayor should be dismissed over his public support for the Portadown Orangemen.[39] In addition, 9 August, the day before the Relief commemoration, was the twenty-fifth anniversary of the introduction of internment, an anniversary of great significance to nationalists. Omens for the August parade could not have been bleaker.

As the Drumcree crisis unfolded, a meeting was held at which the Bogside Residents', Group, the Lower Ormeau Concerned Community and the Garvaghy Road Residents' Coalition pledged mutual support and set out six principles which they felt should govern parades. Central to these principles was that while people had the right to march, this was not unconditional. Residents of areas of proposed parades had the right to withhold their consent. Traditional routes should take into account demographic changes. Finally, parade organisers should ensure the good behaviour of marchers. Donncha Mac Niallais made clear that underpinning the Bogside Residents' Group's stance was 'parity of esteem' and that he did not believe the nationalist people of Lower Ormeau or Garvaghy Road should be abandoned.[40] These principles set the nationalist agenda as the Apprentice Boys' Governor, Alistair Simpson, confirmed that his Association would once again be seeking permission to parade around the walls. To the *Londonderry Sentinel*, Protestants in the city would no longer accept a diminution of their heritage.[41] There was no obvious common ground.

Even so, unlike other areas of Northern Ireland, a series of direct meetings between Alistair Simpson and William Moore of the Apprentice Boys and Donncha Mac Niallais and other Bogside Residents' Group representatives was convened by local MP, John Hume. The essence of the Apprentice Boys' case was reportedly that they wanted their two hundred and fifty local members to walk the circuit of the walls led by a reduced number of bands which would not play on the stretch between Bishop Gate and Butcher Gate. They also suggested that screens be put up along the sections of the wall overlooking the Bogside and that the walls be closed off after the morning parade to prevent any recurrence of the previous year's problems. For its part, the Bogside Residents' Group offered to facilitate a parade around the walls by thirteen Apprentice Boys and a full parade through the city centre, but argued that this would have to be based on the principle of consent and conditional on agreements on loyalist marches elsewhere.[42] It did not prove possible to reconcile these two positions; on Tuesday 6 August, negotiations ended amongst mutual recrimination. The Bogside Residents' Group announced plans for a series of internment commemoration parades to converge on the Diamond on the evening of Friday 9 August.

Faced with this dangerous stalemate, the Secretary of State for Northern Ireland, Sir Patrick Mayhew, moved to take control of the situation. At six o'clock in the evening of 7 August, large numbers of troops with heavy lifting gear erected substantial barricades along the disputed section of the walls, sealing them off from public access. A ban was put on parading the area for the rest of the month. With Protestant opinion in Derry incensed by the government's move, the city was awash with rumours over the likely outcome of Saturday's parade, though tension was eased when the Bogside Residents' Group announced that their Friday evening parade would disperse at Free Derry Corner in the Bogside rather than the Diamond.

On the morning of Saturday 10 August, the city centre was deserted, save that is for a substantial security force and international media presence. At 10 o'clock, led by Glasgow's Black Skull Flute Band and three other bands, the Parent Clubs marched to the Diamond which they circled in silence to a single drum beat. After observing their traditional commemoration at the war memorial, the procession marched straight to St Columb's Cathedral. The tension in an uneasy city centre was only relieved by a mounted peace rider from Cork. At 12.30 pm, Alistair Simpson mounted the walls outside the Apprentice Boys Memorial Hall to announce that they would walk the walls 'at a time of their own choosing'. His statement, cheered by the crowd, immediately defused the tension.[43] The main parade then got under way. The remainder of the day passed largely without incident. Rioting did break out that night, though it was nowhere near the scale of July's disturbances. There was an almost universal sense that the city had been lucky to pass through a major crisis, though less unanimity as to why.[44]

On Saturday 19 October 1996, Alistair Simpson's pledge to his followers was redeemed. No negotiations took place between the two groups, though John Hume publicly endorsed the right of the Apprentice Boys to parade the walls. On the morning of the 19th, some two hundred protesters assembled at Butcher Gate, while the two leaders of the Bogside Residents Group were permitted to stand on the walls with a placard asking '1969–1996 Has Anything Changed?' At 9.35 pm the Parent Clubs were allowed on to the walls led by the local William King Memorial Flute Band. As they advanced towards Butcher Gate to the sound of a drumbeat, the two protesters were removed by the police. On passing Butcher Gate, the band struck up and the protesting crowd jeered in response. After completing their circuit, the Apprentice Boys dispersed after singing 'God save the Queen', while Donncha Mac Niallais made a speech denouncing the parade as sectarian and offensive.[45]

By October 1996, then, parading had once more exposed the fault line in the city. While the August negotiations were portrayed as showing a more hopeful climate than existed over parades elsewhere in Northern Ireland, it is clear that there had been no real meeting of minds. The Apprentice Boys rested their case on their right to celebrate an event which lay at the heart of their history and culture. They pointed to the central meaning of the walls for the members of their Association, both in the city and elsewhere, and to the important symbolism of the war memorial and the cathedral within the walled city. They saw their right to parade as the test of the continuing acceptability of the minority Protestant population in the city, especially on the west bank. While willing to accept that the walled city had that particular significance for members of the organisation, and for Protestants more generally, the Bogside Residents' Group continued to assert the principle of consent as basic to the concept of 'parity of esteem' within Northern Ireland. For them, too, there was a wider dimension; namely, that of loyalist parades in nationalist areas like the Garvaghy Road and the Lower Ormeau. The question of how the Relief parades were to be held proved to be a touchstone of how the two communities regarded each other's rights and heritage.

Notes

I owe a deep debt of gratitude to all who either consented to be interviewed or who provided material on which some of the above discussion is based. I wish to respect their confidentiality. My thanks are also due to Neil Jarman who conducted a number of interviews in 1995 at the start of this research.

1. See Niall O Dochartaigh, *From Civil Rights to Armalites. Derry and the Birth of the Irish Troubles* (Cork, 1997).
2. See T.G. Fraser, 'The Siege: its History and Legacy, 1688–1889', in G. O'Brien, ed., *Derry and Londonderry. History and Society* (Dublin, 1999), pp. 379–403; I. McBride, *The Siege of Derry in Ulster Protestant Mythology* (Dublin, 1997).
3. Fraser, 'The Siege'.
4. C.D. Milligan, *The Walker Club Centenary* (Londonderry, 1944), pp. 28–30; *Official Brochure of the Tercentenary Celebrations of the Apprentice Boys of Derry Association* (Londonderry, 1989).
5. Interview.
6. Interviews.
7. Correspondence; personal observation.
8. Interview.
9. *Londonderry Sentinel*, 10 October 1973.
10. *Disturbances in Northern Ireland. Report of the Commission appointed by the Governor of Northern Ireland* (CMD. 532, Belfast, 1969), p. 26.

11. Interview.
12. *Londonderry Sentinel*, 12 and 19 August 1964.
13. *Londonderry Sentinel*, 10 and 17 August 1966.
14. See O Dochartaigh, *From Civil Rights to Armalites*.
15. Interviews.
16. *Report of Tribunal of Inquiry into Violence and Civil Disturbances in Northern Ireland, 1969* (CMD. 566, Belfast, 1972), pp. 31–40.
17. CMD. 566, pp. 48–62.
18. O Dochartaigh, *From Civil Rights to Armalites*, pp. 112–19.
19. CMD. 566, 66–7.
20. CMD. 566, p. 69; interview.
21. *Londonderry Sentinel*, 11 and 18 August 1971.
22. *Londonderry Sentinel*, 16 August 1972.
23. *Londonderry Sentinel*, 15 August 1973.
24. *Londonderry Sentinel*, 29 August 1973.
25. Interview.
26. Interview.
27. *Derry Journal*, 30 July 1974.
28. Interview.
29. *Crimson Banner*, no. 4, winter 1994–1995; interviews.
30. *Derry Journal*, 8 August 1995; *News Letter*, 9 August 1995.
31. *Irish News*, 9 August 1995; *Belfast Telegraph*, 9 August 1995.
32. *Derry Journal*, 11 August 1995; *Irish News*, 11 August 1995.
33. Interviews; *Derry Journal*, 15 August 1995.
34. Notes by Neil Jarman.
35. *Derry Journal*, 15 August 1995; *Londonderry Sentinel*, 17 August 1995.
36. *One Day in August* (Derry, 1995).
37. *Derry Journal*, 15 August 1995.
38. *Londonderry Sentinel*, 21 December 1995.
39. *Derry Journal*, 16 July 1996.
40. *Derry Journal*, 26 July 1996.
41. *Londonderry Sentinel*, 24 July 1996.
42. *Derry Journal*, 2 August 1996.
43. Observation.
44. *Derry Journal*, 13 August 1996.
45. Observation; *Derry Journal*, 22 October 1996; *Londonderry Sentinel*, 23 October 1996.

12

Drumcree and 'The Right to March': Orangeism, Ritual and Politics in Northern Ireland

Dominic Bryan

> If we cannot go to our place of worship and we cannot walk back from that place of worship then all that the Reformation brought to us and all that the martyrs died for and all that our forefathers gave their lives for is lost to us forever. So there can be no turning back.
>
> Reverend Ian Paisley – speech outside Drumcree Church,
> 9 July 1995

In characterisitic style the Reverend Ian Paisley, leader of the Democratic Unionist Party (DUP), suggested that the future of Northern Ireland lay in the right of members of the Orange Order to parade back from their annual Boyne commemoration church service along the Garvaghy Road, a predominantly Catholic, nationalist area of Portadown in County Armagh. Members of the Garvaghy Road Residents' Group were holding a protest in the road against the parade. The service had been held during the middle of the previous day, a Sunday, and when the Royal Ulster Constabulary (RUC) blocked their return route, the members of the Portadown District Lodge decided that they would remain on the road until they were allowed down. So began what became known as the Siege of Drumcree. There were violent clashes between the RUC and loyalists. Eventually, after mediation, an agreement, the nature of which is still contested, was arrived at to allow the parade along the road and back into Portadown. When the marchers reached Portadown, Ian Paisley and David Trimble, the local Ulster Unionist MP, joined the parade and held their arms aloft in celebration. Their message was that they had won a victory.

These events raised the profile of David Trimble to such an extent that before the end of the year he become the new leader of the Ulster

Unionist Party (UUP). These events worsened already poor community relations in Portadown and by the time of the Drumcree parade on 7 July 1996 the conflict over the parade seemed even more intractable. Again the RUC stopped the return parade but this time there seemed little chance of a resolution. Members of the Orange Order organised parades and road blocks all over Northern Ireland; the resources of the RUC were fully stretched as violent confrontations developed in Belfast; and in Lurgan a Catholic taxi driver was shot dead by loyalists. On the morning of 11 July, Hugh Annesley, the Chief Constable of the RUC, reversed his initial decision and the RUC removed protesters from the Garvaghy Road to allow the parade to proceed. In 1997, despite efforts to mediate by Mo Mowlam, Secretary of State for Northern Ireland, from the newly elected Labour government, the security forces conducted a massive operation early on the Sunday morning, 6 July, which involved the violent removal of protesters from the Garvaghy Road to allow the return parade to take place, on time, around twelve hours later.

Since 1995 there has been a significant increase in the number of disputes over parades in Northern Ireland. There are a large number of parades held every year, up to 3500, of which the large majority are defined by the RUC as 'loyalist'. But the dynamics of the dispute at Drumcree have made it the focus of the debate over the right to march. This chapter will examine some of the relationships which have made this parade so important. The folk understanding of what takes place is based upon the notion of 'tradition', that the parades, particularly that at Drumcree, are important because they express a sense of community amongst Protestants. While nationalists view the parade through a clearly Catholic area as an expression of triumphalism over their community, or 'croppies lie down', attempts to stop the parade are perceived by many unionists as an attack on the Protestant community. Yet viewing these events as a simplistic opposition between Orange and Green does not explain why the disputes arise at certain points in time; it fails to explore complex political relations within the communities; and, importantly, it makes assumptions about the unchanging nature of the parades over time. By exploring the political dynamics of the events themselves – defined here as rituals – and examining the relations between those events and the state, as well as relations within the nationalist community, the importance of the Drumcree parade can best be understood.

Defining a ritual event has been a matter of great debate amongst social anthropologists.[1] Nevertheless, certain features can help to distinguish ritual as a particular category of action. Rituals tend to be routinised and formalised actions with established ways in which those involved must conduct themselves and with strong sanctions for those that do not conform. Ritual also has the tendency to be repetitive, giving it the appearance of continuity through time, providing the ritual community with legitimation by claiming 'tradition'.[2] Ritual is an action in which participants need not share meanings and in which it is possible that participation is more important than meaning. Yet for many or all of the participants a ritual also has meaning. Rituals are occasions *par excellence* when a community makes its symbolic displays, symbols which themselves can have a range of meanings and can be understood differently by different individuals involved. Crucially, a community can participate and adhere to a ritual – common rituals and symbols give diverse communities a sense of consciousness – yet those rituals and symbols may be understood in diverse even contradictory ways within that community. Common participation does not require common understanding.

As rituals provide both the possibility of historical legitimacy, but are also adaptable and changeable, they remain an important part of political processes.[3] Rituals can appear unchanging yet be utilised or appropriated by different *loci* of power at different points in time. Bell has argued that up to four perspectives can be utilised in understanding ritual: how 'ritualisation empowers those more or less in control of the rite;' 'how their power is also limited and constrained'; 'how ritualisation dominates those involved as participants'; and 'how this domination involves a negotiated participation and resistance that also empowers'.[4]

Individuals take part in Orange parades for diverse but intersecting political, religious and social reasons. For some, they may be a public, 'respectable', expression of the Protestant reformed churches, for others they are a bulwark against Catholicism, Irish nationalism and republicanism, while for others still they are a time to meet friends or dress up and drink heavily. Such understandings overlap and reinforce each other, and allow the events to maintain popular appeal, yet when the conduct of the events is disputed such diverse understandings can result in fragmented reactions. Organisation of the parades also provides for political differences and contradictions. The Orange Order is organised into local private lodges, grouped into Districts and Counties, with the Grand Lodge of Ireland acting as the ruling body. However, local lodges and Districts are highly autonomous and vary in background. Some are based geographically, others on particular churches, others may have formed out of a work place. Political, class, religious and denominational differences can be apparent at local lodge level. On parade, Orange lodges usually hire musical bands that may be close to the lodge but are nevertheless independent of the Orange Order. Also associated with the musical bands is an army of young followers that walk alongside the parade. In addition to this diversity within the apparent unity of an Orange parade, the variety of unionist politicians who participate in, and make speeches at, the parades reflect less-than-unified unionist politics and particularly the competing interests of the UUP and DUP.[5] As such, Orange parades exist within a complex network of social relations within the Protestant community providing unity only so long as the issues and interpretations surrounding the events remain general. As soon as the nature of the parades is questioned, or the nature of Ulster unionism is expressed in detail, then unity breaks down.

Each Orange parade takes place within relations of power. Relations of power change over time. To understand Orange parades in general and to explore the Drumcree parade in particular we need to abandon the idea that because the symbols of Orange and Green appear to show continuity over time nothing has changed, and, rather, analyse the changes in relations of power that might help explain specific parade disputes. We need to look at how local political elites have utilised the events, how communities have utilised the events, and we need to examine the effect the events have had on communal politics. But we also need to look at the role of the state in both utilising and limiting the parades and the effect this has on inter-communal and intra-communal relations.

Portadown is the nearest large town to the village of Loughgall outside which the Battle of the Diamond took place in 1795 between Protestant Peep O'Day Boys and Catholic Defenders after which the Orange Institution was formed. It has been persuasively argued that local economic and social conditions specific to Armagh provide us with the reasons for the early development of the Orange Institution.[6] Many of the oldest Orange lodges are found in what is now Portadown No.1 District, and a number of the longest standing parades in the north of Ireland take place in the Portadown area. The Drumcree parade itself seems to date from 1807 and could be older. Early Orange parades were small scale and, although they often involved some local land owners, Orangeism developed as part of popular culture as well as through Protestant churches. Weapons were often carried and the ability to hold parades was very much dependent on population sizes. Clashes with Catholic Ribbonmen were frequent. Frank Wright has characterised organisations such as the Orange Order and Ribbonmen as forms of communal deterrence in an environment in which representative violence is present.[7] Public demonstrations, particularly at the end of the eighteenth century and in the first half of the nineteenth century, were, in part, an expression of a community's strength. The founding of these organisations, their symbolic repertoire, and their physical displays were all aspects of communal deterrence.

The control of public space through symbolic displays was, to a certain extent, determined on relative population sizes. The size of the Catholic population in Portadown has meant that the Catholic community has always found it difficult to make any public displays of its presence and, until recently, also found it impossible to oppose Orange parades. The only predominantly Catholic part of Portadown was centred around Obins Street near the railway station in an area still known as the Tunnel. In the 1860s and 1870s, there were regular efforts by Protestant drumming parties to assert themselves by marching through the Tunnel and around the Catholic church. Attempts by Catholics to commemorate St Patrick's Day (17 March) or Lady's Day (15 August) were often met by violent opposition from within the Protestant community. On Lady's Day in 1872, nationalists were attacked on their return from a parade and in 1880 riots broke out in the Tunnel area as attempts were made to stop a Green Arch being raised. On St Patrick's Day 1885 a band was prevented from leaving the area to go to a parade.[8]

It appears that in historical periods when Irish nationalism was organised and prepared to assert itself, disputes, over parades were liable to become more frequent. In 1931, after the IRA had threatened loyal order parades in County Cavan, there was rioting in a number of towns including Portadown. Similarly, after the 1932 International Eucharistic Congress in Dublin brought widespread symbolic displays in Catholic areas in Northern Ireland, Portadown was one of the areas where returning pilgrims were attacked. During the 1950s and early 1960s there were relatively few disputes with nationalism offering little threat. Any threat that was offered was adequately dealt with by the state.[9] However, the civil rights movement completely changed the situation.[10] Civil rights marches were perceived by many Protestants as a reassertion of Irish nationalism, with elements of the Protestant community and institutions of the state reacting accordingly. In 1968 and 1969, civil rights parades were restricted and attacked so that by the early 1970s working-class Catholic communities took a more defensive and violent posture withdrawing into more clearly defined 'No Go' areas. Inevitably, with the state struggling to deal with – and becoming involved in – communal violence, Orange parades that went near or through Catholic areas became more problematic.

Communal violence and parades became even more important in defining territory and the control of public space. Orange parades became more assertive and confrontational and attempts to stop them were seen by unionists as part of the challenge to British sovereignty. Any possibility that parades might develop into more apparently benign ritual occasions, as might have seemed possible in the 1950s, quickly receded. The right to parade was one of the political arenas in which communal confrontations were to be played out.

The relation of the state to Orange parades and Orangeism in general has been complex. From their formation there were those who saw Orange lodges as a useful resource to counter Catholic insurrection, and they were mobilised to oppose the United Irishmen in 1798 and the Young Ireland Movement in 1848. But concern remained about the potential for such an organisation to mobilise against the interests of the state and also over the frequent disturbances caused by parades. In the 1820s and 1830s a number of measures were introduced to restrict Orangeism and from 1832 to 1844 and from 1850 to 1872 Party Processions Acts prohibited parades. Enforcement of public order, while often conducted by Protestant magistrates and sometimes by a Protestant dominated police force, was nevertheless frequently a function of communal strengths in a particular area. While in Portadown the Catholic population was unlikely to be able give public expression to their religious or political identity, in Derry, up until partition, both communities were given access to public political expression.[11]

Under Stormont, the closeness of the relationship between the Orange Order and the UUP saw Orange parades effectively become rituals of state. Senior unionist politicians were nearly always Orangemen and used the speeches made on the Twelfth of July to deliver their message. Similarly, the relationship between the RUC, particularly the B Specials, and the Orange Order, was close, with many police officers being members of the loyal orders. While it was not unknown for restrictions to be placed on Orange parades, incidents were rare.[12] These relatively unproblematic relationships started to change from the mid 1960s onwards. Divisions within unionism, for and against the meagre reforms suggested by Prime Minister Terence O'Neill, left a number of government ministers unwilling to attend the Twelfth. The violent reaction of the RUC to the civil rights movement in part led to the rapid development of the IRA – at first largely defending Catholic areas – and the introduction of British troops. Parades and demonstration were often the focus of disturbances so that the security forces were soon less willing to facilitate Orange parades in all circumstances and on 13 August 1969 and again on 23 July 1970 the Stormont Government introduced periods when all parades were banned. The Orange Order also felt it necessary to re-route a number of its parades and reduce the number of small lodge parades prior to the Twelfth of July.

For many in the Protestant community, the security forces appeared to be increasingly impotent and apparently no longer always acting in their interests. Local community defence organisations formed into the Ulster Defence Association (UDA), working as a paramilitary group alongside the Ulster Volunteer Force (UVF). Loyal order parades began to reflect these communal defence groups as the number of marching flute bands that took names such as 'Defenders' 'Volunteers' and 'Conquerors' and began to display paramilitary symbols increased. Orange parades became more assertive. In 1972 the communal situation was so serious that doubts were being expressed as to whether the Drumcree parade that went through the Tunnel area and returned along the Garvaghy Road could go ahead. Eventually, after bulldozers had removed various blockades in Obins Street, 50 UDA men advanced to the Tunnel to offer the Orangemen protection if required.[13] Clearly, some within the Protestant community felt dissatisfied by the role now being played by the security forces in protecting their 'right to parade'.

The introduction of direct rule in 1972 significantly reduced the political influence of the Orange Order. Around this time there also appears to have been a drop in membership. In working-class Protestant areas disenchantment with leading Orangemen and unionist leaders grew, while amongst the middle classes the Orange Order became less important as an institution of economic and political patronage. In significant ways the Orange Order was moving from being closely tied to the institutions of the state to being an interest group struggling to maintain a position of respectability and power. This involved major contradictions as the state to which Orangemen professed loyalty appeared to many of them no longer to be acting in their interests. The Twelfth of July, once a ritual of state, now became an occasion at which Orangemen voiced their grievances with British governments perceived as soft on IRA terrorism and open to influence from Dublin. At the same time unease with the assertive nature of Orange and loyalist band parades developed within the RUC to the extent that new Force Orders were issued in 1984 to deal with 'an upsurge in the number of bands whose members are predisposed to overt and unruly displays of sectarian bitterness'.[14] In the early 1980s, disputes over parades developed in three County Down towns: Castlewellan, Ballynahinch and Downpatrick. The relationship between Orange parades and the forces of the state was changing.

The suspicions held by many Unionists as to the role of British governments appeared justified when negotiations between the British and Irish governments through 1985 resulted in the Anglo-Irish Agreement, signed in November of that year, while at the same time, in Portadown, 'traditional' parades through the Tunnel were re-routed. The Drumcree Parade on 7 July 1985 was eventually allowed to proceed on its traditional route through the Tunnel and along Obins Street, returning via the Garvaghy Road, but on the Twelfth, eight lodges that normally proceeded from Cocrain Orange Hall, along Obins Street, through the Tunnel, to the centre of town before catching buses to the Twelfth venue in County Armagh, had their route blocked by the RUC. This led to major disturbances.[15] Similarly, the blocking of preceptories of the Royal Black Institution the following day also resulted in riots and there were serious disturbances after a band parade on 16 August. On 16 September, a group of loyalists was only just stopped from conducting an early morning parade right through the Tunnel. There were other disputes over parades around Northern Ireland but none approached the intensity of those in Portadown.

In 1986, following the signing of the Anglo-Irish Agreement, the disputes in Portadown were more explicitly linked with 'Dublin interference'. Easter Monday 1986 witnessed some of the worst clashes between loyalists and the RUC that had ever taken place as the Apprentice Boys of Derry attempted to hold a parade in the town. The RUC had banned the parade the night before, but within hours up to 3000 loyalists conducted an early morning march down the Garvaghy Road. The next morning police attempts to stop loyalists reaching the town led to clashes. During the afternoon, a young man became the first Protestant to be killed by a police baton round. Tension in Portadown remained high leading up to the Drumcree church, parade which again ended in confrontation when police attempted to remove 'non-local' Orangemen from the parade as it entered the Tunnel area. Clashes took place between residents and marchers in Obins Street and there were more clashes with police at Drumcree church. Ian Paisley argued that the 'issue in Portadown is far more than an Orange parade and its route ... it is the issue of obedience and submission to Dublin',[16] an argument he was to repeat nine years later over the same parade.

On the Twelfth, the Orange lodges that usually went down Obins Street were re-routed along the Garvaghy Road, but there were disturbances later on in the day near the Tunnel area and a further confrontation the following day as members of the Royal Black Institution protested at the Tunnel end of Obins Street. Effectively the Tunnel and Obins Street were no longer open to the loyal orders; instead, the police had suggested the Twelfth parade should proceed along the return route of the Drumcree parade down the Garvaghy Road. From 1986 onwards significant opposition developed in the Garvaghy Road area to these parades.

The confrontations in Portadown may also have encouraged the British government to introduce the 1987 Public Order (NI) Order. Much of its content was similar to legal developments in Britain as a whole, a product both of the various reports by Lord Scarman and of disturbances surrounding the miners' strike. The new Order in Northern Ireland introduced a seven days' notification period and, crucially, no longer recognised 'the desirability of not interfering with a public procession customarily held along a particular route' – there was no longer a category for traditional parades.[17] In effect, legal protection of particular rights for loyal order parades had been withdrawn. The RUC were becoming less likely to protect Orange parades and part of the legal apparatus that gave the loyal orders 'historic' control over public space had been removed.

The changes in the relations between the Protestant community and the state in the control of public space have important repercussions within unionism, particularly affecting the role played by Orangeism in local politics. Since the 1960s there appears to have been a collapse in the numbers attending Orange lodges. Although figures for membership are not made public, there is little argument that middle-class membership has declined, particularly in urban areas, but it is probably also true to say that there has been a falling away in working-class areas. The reasons for this can only be speculated on. Most obviously the decline in locally based heavy industry, such as the shipyards, in which Orangeism played its part as economic patron, would seem important. Also the lack of a local assembly meant that its role in providing political patronage also declined. The UUP and, by inference, the Orange Order, were seen by many Protestants as failing them in the early 1970s. Since Orange parades led to civil disturbances and then clashes with the RUC, some within the order became disillusioned with its role. On the other hand, there were also loyalists attracted both to the DUP and to the paramilitaries that viewed the

Orange Institution as not taking a hard enough role in defending the Protestant community. As unionist politics fractured with the development of the DUP, Alliance and UDA, so the Orange Order's relationship with the UUP became strained. For many young men in working-class communities, joining a loyalist band held many more attractions than joining an Orange lodge.[18]

The Portadown Orangemen decided to oppose any attempt by the RUC to re-route their return parade from Drumcree Church; they were articulating the views of many Orangemen and unionists. Yet in spite of Trimble and Paisley parading through Portadown hand in hand, in a sense they were competing for Orangeism. Similar competition had been evident in 1986 when senior figures in the UDA and Ulster Clubs were involved in the disputes in Portadown and Grand Master and Ulster Unionist MP Martin Smyth had been forced to remind Orangemen that Paisley was not an Orangeman: 'he's appealing to non-Orangemen, I'm dealing on behalf of the Orange Order'.[19] The reality was that many in the Orange Order placed more faith in Paisley than in the Grand Orange Lodge of Ireland.

Martin Smyth came under considerable criticism after the Siege of Drumcree in 1995 for his apparent lack of involvement in Portadown and on the basis of this a ginger group developed within the Orange Institution known as The Spirit of Drumcree Group. The various aims of the group included the replacing of the Grand Master, making the Grand Lodge of Ireland more democratically accountable, and forcing the Orange Order to take a hard line in the increasing number of disputes over parades. The first major meeting on 14 November filled the Ulster Hall in Belfast. While there was clearly widespread support for changes in the Orange Order, those in the Ulster Hall stressed different problems and particularly after Martin Smyth decided not to stand in the Autumn of 1996 the Spirit of Drumcree group failed to mobilise large numbers.

As July 1996 approached, the Grand Lodge became far more active in organising a response to any attempt by the RUC to block the parade. In 1995, confrontations over Drumcree had become violent and fears that this might happen again led the Orange Order to employ different tactics. Rather than calling for Orangemen to arrive at Portadown, parades were arranged all over Northern Ireland. Applications were put in for parades in advance of the Drumcree parade to ensure legality. In the days and evenings that followed the stand-off that started on 7 July, the RUC and Army were stretched to the limit. Orangemen and their supporters set up road blocks and almost inevitable confrontations developed with the security forces. The Orange Order had successfully mobilised to put the forces of the state under extreme pressure but in doing so had created a situation which brought Northern Ireland to a standstill, creating an environment which appeared to threaten the fabric of the state to which they expressed loyalty. Just as Orange parades have acted to give the appearance of unity to a diverse community, so Drumcree provided a moment of common action. The problem was that despite claims to be representing the 'Protestant people', the Orange Order were bound to be alienating significant numbers in 'their community'. On 11 July, with violence increasing and the Twelfth of July imminent, Chief Constable Hugh Annesley reversed his decision, removed protesters on the Garvaghy Road, and allowed the parade to proceed.

Drumcree in 1996 provided a rallying point for the Orange Institution, particularly allowing the UUP and DUP to find common political purpose at a time when divisions were developing over their involvement in the peace process. But a reassertion of the Orange Order's ability to mobilise had costs within and without the community. The Orange Institution was able to conduct a campaign capable of forcing the RUC to reverse a decision, but they had, in effect, relied on tactics which they were unable to control. This left the Institution open to widespread criticism, not least from within Protestant churches. Since 1995 many within the Church of Ireland, Presbyterian and Methodist churches, with congregations north and south of the border, have given new and critical consideration to the links between the loyal orders and their churches. There had also been huge financial cost to the community: the figure of £50 million was suggested. While many in both the churches and business may have been sympathetic to the argument that the Orangemen had a right to march, the social and financial costs appeared enormous.

As in 1985 and 1986, events surrounding the Drumcree church parade in 1995 and 1996 seemed to provide the Orange Institution with a unifying political event, allowing it to reassert its position as defender of the Protestant community. However, such unity tends to be short lived as competing political groups attempt to gain political capital from what has taken place and there is considerable evidence to suggest that the political position of the Orange Order had been weakened. The contradictions presented when members of the Institution confronted the forces of the state, particularly when the effectiveness of such confrontations seemed to be based on maximising problems for the RUC resulting in widespread civil disturbances, proved problematic for the Orange Order, raising questions over its religious pretensions and respectability. While such confrontation might have endeared the organisation to sections of the loyalist community, there is evidence that its relations with many others in the Protestant community were becoming strained. This was perhaps most evident during the campaign over the 1998 Good Friday Agreement where most – though not all – Orange District and Counties, as well as the Grand Lodge, came out against the Agreement while most – though not all – UUP constituency associations supported David Trimble in calling for support for the Agreement.

The nature of the campaign for the Drumcree parade to take place was bound to raise questions over the respectability of the Orange Institution and damage what support the UUP had in Parliament. After the 1996 crisis, Secretary of State for Northern Ireland, Sir Patrick Mayhew, almost immediately announced a review of the current legal provisions surrounding decisions made on public processions. The Independent Review of Parades and Marches was published on 30 January 1997.[20] It recommended changes in public order legislation with the setting up of a Parades Commission which could make decisions over parades and demonstrations not only under criteria of public order but also taking into account broader community relations. The Public Processions (Northern Ireland) Act 1998 was opposed by unionists and the Orange Order, even though it again contained a clause expressing 'the desirability of allowing a procession customarily held along a particular route'.

There was no new legislation in time for Drumcree 1997, but there was a new administration with Labour Prime Minister, Tony Blair, appointing Mo Mowlam as Secretary of State for Northern Ireland. She took a more hands-on approach to the parading problem, eventually putting in place 'proximity talks' to search for solutions over the Drumcree parade. These proved unsuccessful and her style alienated many of the residents on the Garvaghy Road who had put faith in her more personal approaches. The Chief Constable, Ronnie Flanagan, decided not to risk a stand-off and the RUC violently cleared protesters from the Garvaghy Road in the early hours of Sunday 6 July. But enormous pressure was placed on the Orange Order and eventually, much to the anger of those in the Spirit of Drumcree Group, four parades in key areas – Ormeau Road (south Belfast), Derry, Newry and Armagh – due to take place on the Twelfth, were voluntarily rerouted. The Orange Order's decision almost certainly averted a major crisis.

The Orange Order, in supporting the hard-line stance taken by Portadown No. 1 District, has undoubtedly had to pay costs elsewhere. Nationalists have been galvanised to mount effective campaigns over Orange parades, in the case of Derry explicitly in support of Catholic communities in other areas. Indeed, the parades disputes provided the republican movement with a useful form of community mobilisation and two leading members of the residents' group on the Garvaghy Road were elected as independent councillors in 1987. Political pressures and the attention from the world press have also been focused on the RUC. In a period when the RUC were looking to improve their relations with the Catholic community the parades disputes – particularly high profile events on the Garvaghy and Ormeau roads – provided material to those calling for reform of the force, despite an increasing number of Orange parades being blocked and re-routed.

Prior to the Drumcree parade of 1998, pressure from hard-liners within the Orange Order became intense. Results in referendum and Assembly elections, brought about by the Good Friday Agreement, had not allowed anti-Agreement unionists to stop the process. While some Orangemen saw Drumcree as an issue over the right to parade, significant numbers saw it as the next step in the campaign to undermine the position of pro-Agreement unionists. Days before the parade David Trimble was voted first Minister. The Parades Commission, which the Orange Order refused to recognise, re-routed the parade and yet another stand-off developed. The RUC and Army made ready to enforce the decision and there never looked to be any likelihood that the decision would be reversed. Road blocks and demonstrations held around Northern Ireland were more effectively dealt with by the RUC than in 1996, while in the field at Drumcree confrontations between the security forces and protestors developed. As had happened in the past, the Orange Order was ineffective at controlling what was taking place. The stand-off started on Sunday 5 July; by Thursday 9 July, petrol bombs and blast bombs were thrown nightly. Protest parades were generally peaceful but attacks on police and petrol bombings of Catholic-owned houses often followed later in the night.

Although a number of observers noted that support for the Orange Order at the Drumcree field had started to wane on the Thursday, when the violence reached significant levels, the key event occurred on Saturday night when a petrol bomb thrown into a house in Ballymoney, County Antrim, killed the three sons of the Catholic woman who lived there. The political fissures and tensions within the Orange Order immediately began to open. Deputy Grand Chaplain

William Bingham had his sermon at the Presbyterian Church in Pomeroy televised in which he said: 'a fifteen minute walk down the Garvaghy Road by the Orange Order would be a very hollow victory because it would be in the shadow of three coffins of little boys who wouldn't even know what the Orange Order is'.[21] Other voices within the Orange Order, particularly those of clergymen, began to speak out against the Drumcree protests. At the field speeches during the Twelfth commemorations at Pomeroy, Spirit of Drumcree spokesperson Joel Patton denounced William Bingham, who was on the platform, and scuffles broke out in front of the television cameras. Senior individuals within the Church of Ireland also became more vocal in expressing concern over the use of church property for the conducting of the protest. After the police cleared one of the fields owned by the church, padlocks appeared on the gates. The diverse constituent parts of Orangeism and unionism were yet again becoming evident; the apparent unity of Orange parades shattered by contradictory interests and understandings of the events held by groups and individuals taking part. For some there could be no turning back, while for others the Garvaghy Road was simply not worth a life.

Orange parades are commonly understood as unchanging 'traditional' events and characterised as being largely representative of the Protestant community in Northern Ireland. By looking at parades in Portadown, this chapter has argued that the politics of Orange parades are far more complex: that they provide a point of articulation for relations of power in the community. For a number of reasons the parades in Portadown have proved particularly effective in mobilising a political community. Orangeism is perhaps stronger in that area of Armagh than anywhere else in the country and the Drumcree parade would appear to be one of the longer standing parades on record. If Orangeism has a symbolic home, it is Portadown. Portadown No. 1 District carries symbolic power which the Grand Lodge of Ireland would find it difficult to oppose. Defending the parading tradition in Portadown has been seen as important for Orangemen outside the area and for senior unionist politicians. That the Drumcree parade is a church parade has also been important, allowing those who view Orangeism as largely religious rather than political to join those with more overt political motivations. It can be argued that Portadown, a town twenty five miles from Belfast with an industrial base, provides a point of intersection for both the rural and urban unionist constituencies. The Drumcree parade has, therefore, provided a ritual event offering an empowering sense of unity to diverse sections of unionism and

Orangeism. For a few hours, respectable Orangeism could stand next to diverse unionist and loyalist groups holding a more ambiguous relationship with the state. Nearly all senior unionist politicians have utilised the event. The Drumcree parade had emotional resonance right through the unionist community.

Yet such unity could never be sustained. The limits to apparent unity were found when the forces of the state physically opposed the parade. For a time 'respectable' Orangeism could explain the violence being prosecuted on police officers and the Catholic community as being isolated – something they disapproved of, and which they were making an effort to control – after all, a unified unionist position was at stake. But such a position could not be maintained for any significant period of time. Just as happened during the dispute over the Tunnel in 1985 and 1986, the violence that resulted from confronting the police was going to produce fissures within the community that had formed around the Drumcree parade. Also, there were clearly those in the loyalist paramilitaries, particularly in Belfast, who have been suspicious of Orangeism since the 1970s and felt that the parades issue was not one worthy of drawing their members out on the street.

Political relations have changed. Orangeism, powerful from the 1870s through to the 1970s, its members prominent in key institutions of the local state – the judiciary, the police, business, local and national parliaments, and sections of the media – defined 'respectability' and controlled public space. Orange parades marked status, defined a community and were signifiers of power. But this relied upon particular economic and political conditions which from the 1960s onwards started to change. The interests of the British state were no longer so closely allied with those of a local UUP elite and the ability of that elite, utilising the Orange Order, to maintain a unified Protestant, unionist community was waning. Drumcree provided a moment of apparent unity. It provided the circumstance to help propel a Unionist politician, David Trimble, to the leadership of the UUP with the possibility that he might provide long-term unity. But three years on from his triumphant march with Ian Paisley through the centre of Portadown, David Trimble became first Minister Designate of Northern Ireland under the Good Friday Agreement and did not even appear at Drumcree. Neither did he speak at any Twelfth fields. Instead, the rituals he felt bound to participate in, were the appearances in front of the press along with Seamus Mallon, the nationalist Deputy First Minister.

The public rituals associated with Orangeism have the appearance of continuity over time. They are legitimised as being 'traditional'. Yet to understand what is taking place it is important to understand both the constituent parts of the events and the contemporary political and economic conditions in which they take place. By examining the relations between Protestant and Catholic communities and the British state through public events such as parades, and by looking closely at the way local politicians negotiate their involvement, we can better understand changes in local relations of power. The disputes in Portadown provide important evidence of changing politics in Northern Ireland.

Notes

1. See, for instance, Jack Goody, 'Against "Ritual": Loosely Structured Thoughts on a Loosely Defined Topic', in *Secular Ritual* Sally Moore and Barbara G. Myerhoff (eds). (Assen, 1977); Maurice Bloch, *From Blessing To Violence* (Cambridge, 1986); C. Bell, *Ritual Theory, Ritual Practice* (Oxford, 1992); C. Humphrey and J. Laidlaw, *The Archetypal Actions of Ritual: a Theory of Ritual illustrated by the Jain Rite of Worship* (Oxford, 1994).
2. Elizabeth Tonkin and Dominic Bryan, 'Political Ritual: Temporality and Tradition.' in *Political Ritual*, Asa Boholm (ed.) (Gothenburg, 1977).
3. Pierre Bourdieu, *Language and Symbolic Power* (Cambridge, 1991); D. Kertzer, *Ritual, Politics, and Power* (London, 1988).
4. C. Bell, *Ritual Theory, Ritual Practice*, pp. 211.
5. Dominic Bryan, 'Ritual, Tradition and Control: the Politics of Orange Parades in Northern Ireland' (Unpublished PhD Thesis, University of Ulster: Coleraine, 1996).
6. Peter Gibbon, *The Origins of Ulster Unionism* (Manchester, 1975).
7. Frank Wright, *Northern Ireland: a Comparative Analysis* (Dublin, 1987) and *Two Lands One Soil* (Dublin, 1996).
8. Neil Jarman and Dominic Bryan, *From Riots to Rights: Nationalist Parades in the North of Ireland* (Coleraine, 1998: pp. 21–2); Neil Jarman, *Material Conflicts: Parades and Visual Displays in Northern Ireland* (Oxford, 1997).
9. Dominic Bryan, T.G. Fraser, and Seamus Dunn, *Political Rituals: Loyalist Parades in Portadown* (Coleraine, 1995); Neil Jarman and Dominic Bryan, *Parade and Protest: a Discussion of Parading Disputes in Northern Ireland* (Coleraine, 1996).
10. Eamon McCann, *War and an Irish Town* (London 1974); Michael Farrell, *Northern Ireland: the Orange State* (London, 1980); B. Purdie, *Politics in the Streets: the Origins of the Civil Rights Movement in Northern Ireland* (Belfast, 1990); Niall O Dochartaigh, *From Civil Rights to Armalites: Derry and the Birth of the Irish Troubles* (Cork, 1997).
11. Jarman and Bryan, *From Riots to Rights*, pp. 23–4.
12. See Henry Patterson, 'RUC and Orange Order frequently at odds', *Irish Times*, 11 July 1997; and Jarman and Bryan in Ch. 6 above.
13. Bryan, Fraser and Dunn *Political Rituals*, pp. 19–20.
14. Quoted in the *Belfast Telegraph*, 4 September 1986.

15. See Bryan, Fraser and Dunn *Political Rituals;* and Anthony Buckley and Mary Kenney, *Negotiating Identity: Rhetoric, Metaphore and Social Drama in Northern Ireland* (Washington, 1995).
16. Quoted in the *News Letter,* 10 July 1986.
17. Tom Hadden, and Anne Donnelly, *The Legal Control of Marches in Northern Ireland* (Belfast, 1997).
18. Desmond Bell, *Acts of Union* (London, 1990).
19. Quoted in the *Irish News,* 9 July 1986.
20. Peter North, Oliver Crilly and John Dunlop, *Independent Review of Parades and Marches* (Belfast, 1997).
21. Quoted in the *Irish Times,* 18 July 1998.

Index